4-25-84

Economic Development in the Long Run

by A. J. Youngson

Britain's Economic Growth

Economic Development in the Long Run

EDITED BY
A. J. YOUNGSON
Professor of Political Economy
University of Edinburgh

ST. MARTIN'S PRESS   NEW YORK

AFFILIATED PUBLISHERS: Macmillan and Company,
Limited, London – also at Bombay, Calcutta, Madras
and Melbourne – The Macmillan Company of Canada,
Limited, Toronto

Contents

1799859

Contents

1

Introduction

A. J. YOUNGSON
University of Edinburgh

Economic development is something that has happened. The study of this experience should provide an understanding of the processes of development that could be applied in some way to the problems of poor countries today.

This was the idea lying behind a small conference which took place in Edinburgh in September 1971. The number of speakers, and of participants, was limited in order to preserve an informal atmosphere in which discussion could take place freely. The disadvantage of this arrangement was that many topics and many questions of undoubted importance could not appear on the agenda. The history of economic development is a vast subject; the nine papers given in September, and now printed in this volume, can illuminate only a few aspects of that subject. Other experiences and further problems could have been discussed if time and numbers had allowed. For example, a paper on Latin America, such as was to have been read by the late Professor Joslin, would have been a very desirable item; but this was made impossible by Professor Joslin's untimely death, a sad blow to historical study. Nevertheless, it can perhaps be claimed that the papers now printed all deal with sectors or aspects of development where at any rate significant insights are to be had. It may be too much to hope that a better understanding of the past will directly help us to solve the problems of poor countries today; but at least it may help us not to misconceive them.

Nothing is done by taking thought alone. Without the support and encouragement of Mr Alan Peters, and through him of Shell International, this conference could not have been arranged and assembled; and thanks are due to Mr Peters and to his colleagues for their help and co-operation.

It may be objected that to review historical experience – still more to review selected parts of it – with the intention of arriving at some operable conclusions is an illegitimate exercise. History is a record of particular cases; to try to deduce general rules from these cases – still more from a few of them – is notoriously dangerous and probably foolish. The idea of the 'lessons of history' is apt to send shivers down every upright historical spine. And yet, as one speaker put it, history is all we have. Knowing that we cannot deduce a great deal, can it be right therefore to deduce nothing? Surely something useful can be learned from history, provided we do not draw conclusions which are too brief, too simple, too general, too inflexible. This proviso arises evidently from the historical demonstration of the variety of human experience. History tends to show that there is no such thing as 'the development problem' because problems of development are constantly being restated in different forms, in different decades, and in different societies. There has been some temptation among economists in recent years to try to find 'the solution' to the problem of economic development. But the variety of history strongly suggests that there is no 'solution' – there is no formula. It is even useless, as Crouzet suggests, 'to look for some dominating factor of backwardness, in order to build a model around it'. The prerequisites of growth appear in different combinations in different cases: what is a disadvantage in one instance, even, may be – or may be turned into – an advantage in another. It is partly for this reason that the way forward is almost always difficult, although retrospectively it may look easy. Even for the United States, for example, the economic prospects looked rather bleak in the 1780s, as they did for France in the 1820s, and for Sweden in the 1850s; yet these today are rich countries, having found the way to riches at different rates, and along decidedly dissimilar paths.

Moreover, these three countries – and they are named only as examples – are different societies. They differ in religion, ethnic origin, rate of population growth, and in a hundred other ways. In the long run – meaning here at least in the life of a generation or two – these non-economic factors are important. The longer the time considered, or the greater the changes in contemplation, the wider must be the scope of economic or historical explanation. It was Mill who spoke of 'the question how a nation is made wealthy' as though it was the most obvious question with which political economy could concern itself; and it was Mill who stressed 'the universal consensus of social phenomena, whereby nothing which takes place in any part of the operations of society is without its share of influence on every other part', or, in another passage, 'the paramount ascendancy which the general state of civilisation and social progress in any given society must exercise over all the partial and subordinate

10

phenomena'. Economists have made familiar the idea of the inter-dependence of economic variables; the study of different societies in the long run shows that interdependence between the economic and other aspects of life is also important. Hence we may have to take a less mechanical view of economic development than theory some-times seems to suggest: or in other words, to widen our categories of thought.

Discussion at the Conference ranged over many topics. To record all the points which various speakers made would require much space, and the result would be rather amorphous and excessively inconclusive. But it was noticeable that certain topics recurred, that the Conference returned several times, by different routes, to a fairly limited number of problems. And perhaps it is worth recording these, even at the risk of giving undue prominence to one individual's impression of the balance of what was said; and at the same time to mingle a few comments with some signposts to the papers themselves, which are, after all, what really matters.

Faced with a vast array of different cases, the historian is bound to notice that, besides social organisation, the supply of natural re-sources varies, and to ask himself whether or how far this is part of the explanation of differences in performance. In England, for example, good supplies of coal and iron were found in close proximity to one another, whereas in France the distribution of coal resources, as Crouzet remarks, was much less convenient. Opinions at the Conference differed as to the importance of natural resources. Good progress has sometimes been made with scanty resources – the classic case is that of Holland in the seventeenth century. And perhaps it is worth remarking that most eighteenth-century writers on economic development thought that a poor natural endowment was a positive advantage; where a country is naturally rich, says Hume, there is removed 'in part, that necessity, which is the great spur to industry and invention'. This paradoxical view, that nothing suc-ceeds in the end like initial poverty, was not supported. It is, of course, one of the functions of economic development to uncover resources (after 180 years of development Australia is still engaged in this task, with striking results) and to convert mere possessions into resources. To this extent, even natural resources are not 'given', and it may be correct that what matters more is the social framework and the economic response. Yet the balance of opinion was probably to the effect that suitable resources, in alliance with an established or readily developable technology, can be an important factor at least in getting growth started.

It need hardly be said that technology was itself a topic to which the Conference frequently returned. Men come to consume more because they come to produce more; and the use of an improved technology is obviously a central factor in their increased capacity to produce. But how is this new technology obtained? This is a fundamental question. And it suggests to Parker a novel way of looking at the whole process of economic development; is its course dependent on the adjustment of population growth and saving 'to the relationship between technology and resources on the one hand and demand on the other'? And he raises another searching question: is there an internal logic in the way the human mind has approached nature? – for technology does not seem to be simply demand-determined. These questions may seem remote from the problems of poor countries today. But they may help to explain, for example, the relatively late development of agricultural technology, especially with reference to the tropics. In the industrial sector, as Saul points out, a technology has often been built up from small beginnings in one industry, from which it has spread into other, possibly more important parts of the economy. The development of textile machinery, and of agricultural machinery, were important lines of engineering development in nineteenth-century England; agricultural machinery and the servicing of transport equipment were important 'nurseries' of engineering skill in Denmark and Sweden. And it may be significant that in Europe in general, as one speaker observed, technology has for centuries been a subject of peculiar intellectual fascination. But what is more important for the developing countries today is the transfer of technology: not only the transfer of new techniques, but the spread of general technological utilisation and 'success. Often this seems to be a very personal matter; an individual combines the knowledge, skill, and enterprise required, and a new technology is imported; other individuals follow suit, and an industrial transformation is begun. It is difficult, for example, to account for industrial development in India without mentioning the extraordinary achievements of Tata; or to explain modern Denmark without reference to Tietgen. There is, perhaps, a stage in development when 'heroic' activities may alter the course of the economy. Yet sometimes, in apparently favourable circumstances, the unique individual has not appeared, and little has happened. Perhaps this is only to say that no innovation is more delicate or difficult than technological innovation, that enterprise is needed for innovation, and that individuals are the carriers of enterprise. On the other hand, Rosovsky emphasises the role of institutions in Japan in borrowing and adapting technology – as indeed he emphasises the collective constructive attitudes towards their economy of which the Japanese have been capable. This sounds very un-British, although perhaps not so very un-French; in any case it brings us back to those national differences, those idiosyncracies of national, even of regional behaviour which history demonstrates; and also to the importance, underlined by Supple, of understanding not only what institutions are called and how they are organised, but what they actually do.

Of all the institutions which were discussed at the Conference, that of land ownership was the most frequently mentioned. The predominant importance of the agricultural sector is one of the best-known characteristics of poor countries. Yet economists often spend rather little time in discussing the problems of agriculture, especially the institutional and organisational problems. Good theory does not ignore institutions – but it may underestimate the difficulty of changing them. Perhaps too fascinated by what is modern and measurable, many economists in recent years have chosen to concentrate their attention on industry and capital accumulation. But for the historian it is impossible to side-step the agricultural question, which is to a large extent a question of land and land ownership. In a poor society, land is almost sure to be the most important form of property. Moreover, it is not to be understood simply as a scarce resource. In nineteenth-century Ireland, as in much of twentieth-century Africa, economic activity is seen to be extensively affected by the tenacious retention of land. Peasant and tribal attitudes to land ownership and utilisation are peculiar. These affect the possibilities of reorganising agriculture, as well as the mobility of population and the availability of labour for other purposes. The modernisation of agriculture is thus a fundamental problem in economic development.

And even when the attitudes of the ancient established users of land (that is to say, the majority of the population) have been changed and the problems of agriculture have become, in a sense, 'modern', the importance of attending to them is not reduced. It is now well-known that in Japan, as in eighteenth-century England, agriculture was an important source of capital for non-agricultural development. Also, it seems often to be true that a retarded agricultural development is a severe handicap for industry on the demand side. Macpherson observes that the slow rate of agricultural growth in India limited the growth of other sectors; and Crouzet likewise notes 'the fragmentation and inadequacy of the Continental markets', arising in part from a poor agriculture, as a factor delaying general development. Yet the reverse argument is also possible, and was put forward at the Conference as it has often been put forward before: transport changes and the growth of cities (which imply manufacturing *inter alia*) provide a market for the product and consequently there is agricultural development. It is clear that industrial and agricultural development are both desirable, and they mutually support one another. Difficulties arise where the local linkages are few, and in such a case the development may have to be contrived. One speaker suggested that the Nkrumah experiment could be viewed as an attempt to lift a successful agricultural economy onto a new basis, using the profits from cocoa to build up an industrial infrastructure.

References to transport were less frequent than to primitive agriculture, but were frequent enough to deserve mention. It is a familiar observation that one of Britain's early advantages was the proximity of all regions to water. Conversely, it was pointed out that in Africa almost all the advantages of a seaboard environment are absent, and communities tend to live isolated, surviving in a harsh environment. The result is that markets are small, and economies of scale, so readily available *via* modern technology, are unattainable. In France similarly, although to a far lesser degree, communications problems contributed to the difficulties before the 1850s; yet Crouzet questions whether high transport costs can properly be treated as a 'primary' difficulty, being themselves rather than the consequence of some other defects.

Finally, there is the problem of human attitudes and behaviour. After all, no economy functions automatically. It goes on either because people continue to act as before (and much effort may be required just to keep things going), or because some act as before while others innovate. If we are to find a 'primary' difficulty, this must be reluctance to innovate. But why should people be more reluctant in some circumstances than in others? One obvious answer is that the size of the risk involved in innovation varies. In conditions of severe poverty the risks may be enormous. Where crop failure is possible and is the ultimate disaster, innovation is to be feared; or, as Frankel put it, very poor people are stickers, not innovators. But where there is scope for manoeuvre, responses still differ. It is sometimes suggested that socio-religious-institutional obstacles are the explanation. No doubt these can be a difficulty, and no doubt cases differ. There are cultural environments which in diverse and complicated ways are favourable to economic development – Rosovsky's conception of late Tokugawa and early Meiji Japan as a 'progressive, advancing traditional society' is in this connection of the greatest interest. But in more hostile cultural environments – as probably in India – one finds a powerful interaction taking place. Social practices, under the influence of economic motive, are, as Macpherson puts it,

14

'bendable'; and if bent sufficiently often they begin to give way completely. Likewise, Crouzet inclines to the view that market opportunities and the available factor-mix are a better basis for explaining French development than 'social values' or 'national attitudes'. If the 'social values' argument is pressed by economists, either they should hand over the study of economic development to applied sociologists or (if such exist) applied social anthropologists; or they should consider that the argument seems to lead to the view that some people are not capable of economic development. This may be true; but it is, of course, an untestable hypothesis. Those who understand poor societies best are usually the least prone to regard them as unchanging, and unchangeable. 'The African can quickly become a modern man.... The Bantu are a fine, flexible people, they can absorb capital.' No doubt similar statements could be made of most poor people.

These five topics – the supply of natural resources, technology, land ownership and utilisation, transport, and human attitudes and behaviour – appeared, at least to one listener, to be those which participants at the Conference regarded as the most interesting, possibly as the most important. Protection was mentioned occasionally, but there was apparently little inclination to regard it as a significant aid to development. The interaction of economics and politics was more often discussed, and might almost be added to the five topics already listed. It appeared, of course, in Nove's paper on Russia, and was indeed prominent in that case. Nationalism and peasant proprietorship (more shades of Mill!) appeared in connection with Ireland; and it may be that useful research work could be done on the role of nationalism in economic development. Politics also figured in Rosovsky's analysis of Japanese development, principally in the form of the general political (or perhaps one should say social) attitude (involving once more a self-conscious nationalism) and of certain public institutions. And of course again, in the form of imperialism, politics appeared in connection with India. The vagaries of politics, the whims of politicians, corruption in public administration – these matters excited little attention. Perhaps this was justified, and those were right who thought that the chief task of politicians was to provide a legal system which would facilitate the mobility of resources, and production for exchange.

Some other matters, often treated as important, were scarcely discussed at all: capital accumulation (as distinct from technology), population growth, education. The last of these was perhaps a surprising omission, for it is often mentioned, for example, in comparisons between Britain and the United States in the nineteenth century. In the long run, education is surely a powerful influence on social attitudes and behaviour, helping (or hindering) mobility and adaptability. Precisely how it does so is a very difficult question, to which the answers must differ in different cases; and it is also not easy to know exactly what is to be understood by education, whether it is to teach skills, or, in the longer run, to change attitudes. Precisely for these reasons, historical study of the role of education in economic development could be useful. As regards population growth, perhaps less is to be said. As everyone knows, there is no precedent for the population explosion of the twentieth century. In the nineteenth century, in certain places and at certain times, there was severe pressure of population; but there was the escape valve of emigration, international or intercontinental. Our present situation is different, and the chief service of history must be to underline its unique character, in which national objectives as well as means may require to be altered.

Economic development has been going on for a long time. From the point of view of technology, it has been virtually continuous, taking one of its greatest steps forward with the start of the Iron Age, and another with the early development of Western science in the seventeenth century. Nor is there anything new in the division of the world into two different kinds of society: 'From soon after 10,000 B.C. to the Christian era, we are confronted in the Old World by the antithesis which in classical antiquity was recognised as that between the civilised and the barbarian peoples of the then known world; a distinction which was also broadly between literate and non-literate societies.'[1] Between these two groups there was little to choose technologically; the differences lay in intellectual and moral attitudes. But in the modern world the gap is technological as well as moral and intellectual. It is for this reason that the idea of accelerating development may be inadequate, for what is needed is to some extent a change in the nature of development as well as in its pace.

No one doubts that it is going to be very difficult to raise living standards in many parts of the world; difficult, indeed, to prevent them from falling. Fifteen or twenty years ago, many people entertained far too sanguine hopes of raising living standards in poor countries. Now there is a reaction. But there are grounds for hope, provided that population growth is not too rapid. Historical experience is unfavourable to the idea of very fast development (not only because it has rarely happened), but equally it is unfavourable

[1] Stuart Piggott, *Ancient Europe* (1965), p. 16.

to the idea of near-stagnation. The aim must be to raise living standards, not to transform them in the space of a generation into those of Western Europe or the U.S.A. Even Japan, after a hundred years of remarkable economic development (albeit interrupted by a disastrous war), is a long way short of the living standards enjoyed in Britain or France. Modest growth is an attainable objective, in which a society can take pride.

History, said Marshall, is prediction written backwards. The conclusions of historians are not unanimous, and their expectations for the future must differ no less. But if history supplies no answer to the question, what happens next? at least its study may produce a few suggestions, and keep open a variety of avenues of thought.

2

Thinking About Economic Development

BARRY SUPPLE
University of Sussex

Like most vague titles, the title of this chapter masks (or, for con-
noisseurs of such things, exposes) an unspecific purpose. Its object is
to examine, in a fairly discursive way, a few of the general problems
which economic historians encounter when dealing with economic
development in the long run. And it is concerned less with what we
know (indeed, we probably know relatively little about economic
growth *in general*), than with what we may learn, at a somewhat
high level of generality, from our attempts to know. How do economic historians set about visualising 'the' process of development?
How do they break it down in order to study it? What success can
they hope for in their efforts to build up generalisations about it?
These are some of the questions which need to be raised in any general
discussion about long-run growth. My title is sufficient indication
that this paper will not succeed in answering them.

When economic historians think about long-run economic development they presumably have, or should have, a fairly specific concept
or set of concepts in mind. In a lazy, or a statistical, mood they might
agree to define it straightforwardly as a sustained increase in the *per
capita* output of goods and services. There is obviously nothing wrong
with such a definition, even though it raises certain quite practical
problems – notably, the well-known conceptual pitfalls involved in
compiling an index of this sort, and the lack of specificity about what
we mean by 'sustained increase' in such a context. (Thus the growth
rate of the British economy in the period conventionally seen as that
of the Industrial Revolution seems to have been fairly low, and could
well have been preceded by growth rates almost as high.) Basic ag-
gregative statistical work is certainly a useful, and presumably a
necessary, means of identifying periods and types of growth. Moreover, in some instances such an approach transcends 'mere' measurement and provides the immediate basis for and content of fruitful

and significant analysis of a varied range of problems. At the same time, however, what we actually think of as economic development is not solely its outcome in terms of increasing quantities of income and wealth, but also (and perhaps primarily) a set of large-scale changes in economic and social processes and attitudes. These are changes – in population and its distribution, technology, industrial structure and business organisation, patterns of consumption and investment, and so forth – which we envisage as being more or less distinctively associated with changes in the level of aggregate economic activity, even when we are unable to specify the nature of that association very precisely. Moreover, although we are all interested in the nature and significance of pre-industrial economic trends, 'economic development' tends to be envisaged as a fairly recent phenomenon, characterised by the emergence of technologies, economic patterns and institutions analogous to those of the advanced nations of the twentieth century. In other words, when we think about or attempt to explain economic development in the long run, we tend to think about or attempt to explain the emergence of the sort of modern industrial society with which we are familiar.

All this is fairly trite. But it is perhaps worth saying partly in order to remind ourselves that other cultures and other times have known economic development, but also to emphasise two important methodological points. First, a concept (in this instance, 'economic development') which in principle might be given a very sweeping meaning and application, is usually made more manageable by attributing to it a more limited content ('modern industrialisation'). This is to some extent a function of the tendency for social scientists to choose subjective orientations: we all have a 'modern' view of economic development – and legitimately so. In addition, however, it derives from the need to temper our ambition according to our ability to comprehend and analyse: the broader our generalisations are, the more abstracted they become, and the constant need to strike a balance between the scope and the useful insight of generalisations restricts the range of phenomena with which we are (or should be) prepared to deal. Further, since the concept with which we deal is derived from a limited range of particular temporal examples, there is an obvious risk that our generalisations will have a very partial validity: future industrial societies may evolve in fundamentally different ways from existing industrial societies.

This raises the second point: our definition of economic development, as necessarily happens with any fairly restricted conceptual definition, embodies at least the elements of an explanatory theory.

For, just as our explanation of a phenomenon depends in part on how we see it, so how we see it reflects certain presuppositions about its nature (and, therefore, explanation). In other words, when we define economic development we implicitly define what we think is important not only *in* but *to* economic development. And in this respect, the difference between the approaches of economists and historians is clearly not the presence of analytical concepts but the explicitness or implicitness of such concepts. As a result, historical writings on economic development tend to give rise to fairly serious specification problems, with the functional interrelationships between defined and undefined variables largely implicit in the form and style of argument. This remains a severe problem even when historians (as they often but not invariably do) restrict the scope of their generalisations on grounds of analytical modesty. For although many historians rightly pride themselves upon their avoidance of sweeping and absolute generalisations, the explanations they actually offer when they undertake chronologically or spatially limited case studies are often extremely far-ranging in terms of the number and type of variables involved. This can obviously get them into hot water with social scientists, for the view that theories must be seen as relative to time and place, and to this extent restricted in scope, is rarely tempered by a realistic sense of the inadequacies of theory when dealing with complex situations. But with the exercise of a little charity, it is possible to interpret this apparent contradiction as a commendable willingness to sacrifice precision and scope of generalisation in order to deal more roughly with 'real' phenomena involving a multiplicity of factors in a fairly narrow compass. Put another way, the two principal avenues in the modern exploration of economic development have been 'economic-type' studies, which attempt to reach a general level of explanation by concentrating on a limited number of variables and limited aspects of the phenomenon; and 'historical-type' studies which concentrate on one or two examples or on a critical moment in time.

Now just as much of what we think of as modern social science originated in the need to understand the workings and evolution of modern economic and social systems (the need, in John Stuart Mill's words, 'to find the laws according to which any state of society produces the state which succeeds it and takes its place'[1]), so a fundamental objective of modern economics was to explain the performance of modern economic systems ('the explanation of the diversities of riches and poverty in the present and past, and the ground of whatever

---

[1]John Stuart Mill, *System of Logic* (1865 edition), II, 506. Quoted in Bert F. Hoselitz (ed.), *Theories of Economic Growth* (1960), p. 119.

increase in wealth is reserved for the future'[2]). One way and another, therefore, economists have been concerned with long-run economic development for at least two centuries, Nevertheless, the approaches of the past two or three decades provide various significant contrasts to those which went before.

In earlier times, and particularly in the case of classical and neo-classical economists, economic development was approached at two related levels. On the one hand, economists were concerned with the working-out, on an almost purely deductive basis, of a few relatively simple variables. And economic development was seen as the outcome, in a particular institutional setting, of interactions between such factors as capital accumulation, population movements, changes in agricultural output, wages, rents and profits. On the other hand, the nature of their logic, in conjunction with their assumptions, gave an olympian character to the theories of classical and other economists: they were led into a concern with the very long-run evolution of the industrial system. The orthodox classical view of a declining profit rate and an ultimate stationary state, Marx's apocalyptic vision of the collapse of capitalism and its supersession by a new form of society, Schumpeter's prediction of negative feedback in the evolution of entrepreneurial institutions and outlooks under capitalism – all exemplify this tendency to large, searching generalisation, although in each case the generalisation is based upon a fairly specific body of concepts and the deployment of rigorous logical tools. Even the historical school of economists, having rejected, at least to its own satisfaction, the use of deductive logic, was led, through its concern with the relativity of economic laws, to a characteristic preoccupation with the centuries-long sequence of stages of economic evolution.

Considered in this light, therefore, the approach of modern economists is superficially much less ambitious than that of their precursors. Compared with the contemplative work of classical economists, contemporary social scientists have been far more 'problem-' and 'policy-oriented'. And the traditional emphasis placed on generalised analyses of the long-run development of whole societies is now increasingly supplemented by empirical investigations of restricted aspects of economic expansion – the nature of investment decisions for example, or the role of the state, or the importance of demand, or demographic factors. By the same token, growth theory has become much less insular: a good deal of work has been motivated, and largely influenced, by an awareness of the problems and expectations of non-Western underdeveloped economies. This shift in attention,

[2]John Stuart Mill, *Principles of Political Economy* (1921 edition), p. 21. Quoted in Hoselitz (ed.), *Theories of Economic Growth*, p. 117.

22

particularly at a time of relatively satisfactory performance by Western economies, may help explain the absence of any dominating concern with the long-run future of capitalism. And in measure as a preoccupation with modern pre-industrial societies has replaced an observation of growth in advanced economies as the central concern of growth theory, so the study of development has increasingly become an interdisciplinary, or at least a multi-disciplinary, affair. Economic variables no longer dominate the stage. At the same time, and for the same reason, the 'long-run' is no longer taken to mean a period generations and perhaps centuries long, but one in which substantial economic change can happen: a matter of a generation or two. And a lot of effort is therefore devoted not merely to the total pattern and path of development, but also to an analysis of the characteristics of the presumed 'take-off' – to the point of transition from a pre-industrial economic performance to the hopefully decisive beginning of modern industrialisation.

All this can be phrased in terms of the interests and approaches of economists and other social scientists concerned with contemporary problems. But it is equally true of historians (and in many respects the nature of the problem with which we deal blurs the professional distinction between historians and other social scientists). Hence this way of characterising the approach to economic development raises two themes which can serve as the basis for much of the rest of this paper: first, the attempt to incorporate non-economic variables in the explanation of development; second, the continuing concern with general hypotheses about growth, some, but not all, of which involve a concentration on the idea of a single, discontinuous 'take-off'.

(i) *Non-economic variables*

A fairly simple-minded view of one difference between the approaches of history and of theoretical economics to economic development would be that while the former tries to take into account the role of so-called 'non-economic' factors, the latter tends to ignore them. In fact, of course, this is a highly vulgarised interpretation of economic theory – which, when it abstracts from social and institutional changes, does so not in order to minimise their significance but to sharpen understanding of underlying economic processes. Hence, although the classical economists (for example) apparently took for granted the presence of institutions and habits of mind in industrialising Britain which we have come to consider as critical variables in the general process of growth, they were clearly aware of the significance of the absence of circumstances favourable to growth at other times or in other places, They were perfunctory in their discussion of this fact solely because it was not their immediate task. Thus, Ricardo noted that 'ignorance, indolence and barbarism' in fertile countries made for poverty and famine, and that 'the evil proceeds from bad government, from the insecurity of property, and from a want of education in all ranks of the people'.[3] Even more cogently, John Stuart Mill felt that in Asia and what he called 'the less civilised and industrious parts of Europe', economic growth depended not only on greater security of property, more moderate taxes, and the import of foreign technology and capital, but on fundamental, and possibly fairly remote, psychological changes: 'the decay of usages or superstitions which interfere with the effective employment of industry; and the growth of mental activity, making people alive to new subjects of desire'.[4]

Indeed, economists have always been well aware of what they have been doing in making explicit or implicit assumptions about non-economic factors: they have been concentrating their attention on understanding the problems of growth in advanced societies – that is, societies which already have fairly 'modern' institutional frameworks. (That this has occasionally led to shoddiness in the application of theory to other sorts of societies, is merely evidence of human frailty, rather than the particular fallibility of economists.) The real difficulties clearly arise when the problem ceases to be the elaboration of our understanding of expansion in an industrial society, or the incremental improvement of inherited growth theory, and revolves around an appraisal on the one hand of why underdeveloped economies do not grow, and on the other of how growth actually starts. For it is these rather general and empirical questions which appear to demand global and complex answers.

Of course, conventional growth theory has been deficient in the ability to provide such answers. But this is only to say that the methodology of economics is ill-equipped to handle problems involving the interaction of a multiplicity of variables of different types. Yet this obstacle to comprehension is not specific to economics: it applies generally to the social sciences, and it is not at all clear that historians are any better equipped than economists to proffer a *systematic* analysis of the interrelationship of 'economic' and 'non-economic' factors in growth. This seems to be the case even at the level of national case-studies. For example, attempts to generalise about

[3]David Ricardo, *The Principles of Political Economy and Taxation*, Ch. V ('On Wages').
[4]*Principles*, pp. 189–9, quoted in Hoselitz (ed.), *Theories of Economic Growth*, pp. 123–4.

the importance of non-economic variables in the British Industrial Revolution very rarely attain a very much higher level of operational usefulness – although they are frequently more extensive in scope and detail, and sometimes more subtle in approach – than Adam Smith's comment about private frugality and materialistic ambition in England: 'It is this effort, protected by law and allowed by liberty to exert itself in the manner that is most advantageous, which has maintained the progress of England towards opulence and improvement in all former times, and which, it is to be hoped, will do so in all future times.'[5]

Of course, it must be admitted that the detailed treatment of British industrialisation by economic and social historians has marked a considerable advance in our understanding of various aspects of the Industrial Revolution. We now know far more than we used to about demographic factors, the nature of enterprise, the roots of innovation, the influence of nonconformity, and so forth. At the same time, however, it is not yet possible to integrate this sort of work into general analyses of the problem of development. Moreover, even if we confine our attention to single variables then, compared with the work which has been done on, for example, capital accumulation or agricultural productivity or the labour supply, there is still a long way to go for research into the determinants of entrepreneurship and its functional role in growth or into the impact of particular social institutions and attitudes or the economic consequences of particular social structures. Admittedly, in these respects our generalised knowledge of Britain in the throes of industrialisation has certainly been enormously increased over the last twenty-five years; yet in the last resort, from the viewpoint of 'explaining' economic development, the resulting generalisations remain at a fairly high level of abstraction. Having said this, however, it is worth emphasising two points in mitigation and explanation.

First, as regards Britain, the very fact that there seem to have been few 'obstacles' to the first Industrial Revolution makes it conceptually difficult to deal with non-economic factors – which are characteristically more tangible when they are assumed to act unfavourably to expansion, or when they contrast radically with the situation in examples of Western-style, market-based, 'open' economic development. This is perhaps the reason why historians seem to have had more to say about the economic implications of (for example) conservatism in France or traditionalism in Japan – although even in these respects they have very properly tended to shun generalisations about 'the' process of development in favour of hypotheses

[5] *The Wealth of Nations*, Bk II, Ch. III, 'Of the Accumulation of Capital'.

about particular cases. Indeed, it is probably significant that two of the more elaborate attempts to take account of psychological attitudes in long-run economic processes are the work not of historians, but of a psychologist (David McClelland) and an economist (Everett Hagen).[6] Moreover, their efforts have been greeted by historians with a certain amount of scepticism – based, it would seem, not merely on a wounded sense of professional *amour-propre*, but also on an unwillingness to approach historical explanation with quite such a single-minded concentration on the quantitative appraisal of the significance of a single variable such as 'the achievement motive', or on the rather elastic concept of a 'withdrawal of status respect'.

This raises a second, and more general, point – namely whether it *can* be the function of historians to formulate social theories in the sense in which economists formulate economic theories. For, while sociological and psychological theory are still only able to provide imprecise analytical tools (however great the variety of their interesting ideas) for use in the study of development, historians cannot really be expected to build a body of testable theory to explain the processes of socio-economic change. Indeed, it is presumably premature to base the study of economic development on any definite and articulated body of generalizations concerning 'the' interrelationship between 'social' and 'economic' variables. Hence, whatever our illusions, when we think about long-run development, we are still thinking about socio-economic changes too complicated to be adequately explored 'in the round' with the aid of existing theory. And at this level, therefore, it is perhaps more efficient to envisage a series of partial and isolated problems, each of which might be tackled with a limited conceptual tool kit, rather than a single generic problem which can be resolved by the formulation of a large-scale, multi-disciplinary model. Of course, history has to be both realistic and ambitious – although the two qualities are not always consistent. Its 'realism' presents it with interrelated rather than conceptually isolated problems, in which it is difficult to make apparently arbitrary decisions to accept variables as parameters. And its 'ambition' drives it in the direction of attempted explanations of 'total' phenomena – i.e. actual case-studies of growth as a socio-economic process. The inevitable result is a looseness of approach and a scientifically unsatisfactory set of conclusions. Hence, when all is said, if not done, as long as we are concerned with the complexity of tangible episodes in long-run economic development, the lack of any feasible alternative drives us back to the historical and diffuse approach, which must

[6]David C. McClelland, *The Achieving Society* (1961); Everett E. Hagen, *On the Theory of Social Change* (1962).

live in an uneasy relationship with fairly narrow research into a strictly limited range of phenomena.

Having said all this, however, it may well be that the original way of presenting the problem – the assumption that 'non-economic' factors have to receive the same sort of scientific treatment as 'purely' economic factors – is somewhat misleading. In fact the problems of 'non-economic' explanations of development may not really be analogous to the problems of articulating more precise economic theories. For when we try to explain the occurrence and patterns of growth, such phenomena as social institutions, relations and attitudes are important not for their own sakes but in terms of their functional role with respect to economic variables – savings, investment, innovation, factor mobility, and the like. Hence it is probably unnecessary for growth theory to concern itself very directly with the dynamics of social processes except in the sense of incorporating explanations of the proximate economic impact of social change. And it is extremely unlikely that general theories of development could incorporate hard-and-fast references to particular institutions or particular institutional changes or to the internal dynamics of such institutions. Rather, they need to specify the sorts of *functions* that such institutions or changes fulfil. The importance of such an approach derives from the obvious fact that the economic consequences of particular institutions and attitudes are not predictable solely in terms of such phenomena themselves. Any given institutional arrangement can in fact serve quite different economic functions, depending on circumstances. To take a relatively simple example, serfdom can either retard agricultural innovation or facilitate capital accumulation; its abolition can therefore either liberate the agricultural sector and increase production and demand, or impose restrictions on growth through the excessive fragmentation of peasant tenure. Even the traditionalism which Rostow saw as characterising and stultifying pre-industrial societies can be turned to good account, in some of its manifestations, through its effects on the recruitment of labour, work habits and entrepreneurial motivation. Of course, none of this means that it is in any sense easy to incorporate non-economic factors in the analysis of development. But it does provide a specific context for and limit to what might otherwise be an excessively formidable task. For our interpretation of the nature of institutions will vary (and legitimately so) depending on the relationship which we envisage between such institutions and the process of economic change; correspondingly, we have a means of focusing on limited aspects of the diffusiveness of social change.

This is, presumably, one sense in which we can interpret Professor

Gerschenkron's fruitful contribution of the idea of substitutability to the discussion of the prerequisites of industrialisation. For if we define prerequisites in functional rather than institutional forms (capital accumulation rather than private enterprise, mobility of factors of production rather than the reform of tenurial systems and social relations, the expansion of demand and the diversion of primary products rather than the transformation of the agricultural sector), then we are much nearer to an understanding of the uniformity in variety which must characterise any comparative view of the initiation of economic development. Along these lines, therefore, the concept of a single set of prerequisites – certainly the concept of uniform *institutional* prerequisites – for all economic development is no longer easily accepted. And if, following Professor Gerschenkron, we see the British case as a classic or bench-mark instance, then, although the absence in other countries of what were 'preconditions' of growth in Britain differentiates them from Britain (and from each other), they also derived from their own situations fairly effective substitutes for the 'missing prerequisites'.[7] It is partly for this sort of reason that one must agree to reject simplistic appraisals of the retarding role of social attitudes. For on the one hand the importance of, say, social approval or disapproval to successful entrepreneurship is by no means clear; and on the other, the really important effect of value systems on economic development may have far more to do with its structure and timing than with whether it takes place or not. While 'an adverse social attitude towards entrepreneurs may . . . indeed delay the beginning of rapid industrialisation . . . viewed over a somewhat longer period, more important than the mere fact of delay is the fact that the character of the industrialisation process is affected by those attitudes.'[8]

It seems to me fairly clear that this sort of approach – that is, an attempt to specify fairly precisely the functional role of particular institutional patterns and then to investigate them in that light – is a far more useful way of tackling the 'problem' of the role of non-economic factors in development than attempts to generalise about particular institutional forms themselves. Moreover, it implies that what can be called the historical approach (by which I mean, in this instance, faily detailed case-study) is still important to an understanding of growth in the long run.

[7]See Alexander Gerschenkron, *Economic Backwardness in Historical Perspective* (1962), especially Ch. II, 'Reflections on the Concept of "Prerequisites" of Modern Industrialisation'.

[8]Gerschenkron, *Economic Bachwardren*, Ch. II, 'Social Attitudes, Entrepreneurship, and Economic Developments', p. 62.

(ii) *General hypotheses*

Whatever may be said about the attractiveness or desirability of general historical models of economic development, it is probably worth emphasising that the most useful contributions to the historical study of long-term economic development have tended to come from fairly concentrated work on particular aspects of the process of growth: measurements of capital formation, for example, or of changing industrial structures; examinations of the role of entrepreneurship in particular settings, or of the problems of labour supply or the capital market; and so on. At the same time it is possible, albeit rare, to combine the detailed measurement of salient features of economic development with quite far-ranging generalisation about critical aspects of that process – as exemplified quite notably in the work of Professor Kuznets. In general, however, the painstaking measurement or analysis of individual variables, although the most practical and methodologically most defensible line of enquiry, cannot really satisfy our ambitions to generalise about the overall process of economic development and its complex interactions. Broadly speaking such generalisations take place at two levels: the elaboration (or implicit use) of historical models of development, and the discussion of the growth of particular national economies at particular points in time.

The obvious difficulties involved in constructing, let alone defending, large-scale models of economic development mean that such systematised attempts to explain the main contours of growth are no longer particularly fashionable among economic historians. One can only think of two which have had any very general currency in the last ten years or so. On the other hand, all of us presumably think about development in general terms, and therefore must make implicit use of models, no matter how crude – while in any case we frequently need to make explicit use of general models, if only as points of criticism and departure.

In this respect perhaps the most widely known – certainly the most widely publicised – generalisation about economic development in the long run is Walt Rostow's *Stages of Economic Growth*. In the eleven years since its publication it has come under some pretty severe and sustained criticism, and I suppose that few economists or economic historians would now deny that, as an attempt to identify an empirically useful and general framework for the study of growth – or even, in Rostow's words, as 'an arbitrary and limited way of looking at the sequence of modern history'[9] – it has been a failure. Indeed, its main failings have been generally recognised from the outset. As a

[9] W. W. Rostow, *The Stages of Economic Growth* (1960), p. 1.

result the Rostovian version of a sequence of developmental stages, together with its analytical trappings, survives in the academic world largely as a straw man for teachers of economics and economic history – with the ironical if predictable result that it enjoys persistent toleration in the subterranean world of undergraduate essays. Admittedly, as far as the profession at large is concerned, Rostow popularised various conceptual terms – 'the take-off', 'the drive to maturity', 'the age of high mass consumption', etc. – which have achieved a sort of linguistic orthodoxy. But in his formulation these concepts have been found to lack any very fruitful empirical content. And the most successful of them, the 'take-off', has been particularly severely criticised in terms of its conceptual specification and its methodological utility.

Having said all this, however, I must hasten to add that in introducing Rostow's theories in this context it is no part of my intention to mount yet another assault on *The Stages of Economic Growth*. Rather, since the *idea* of stages is a common one, it may be useful to discuss whether the problems which are so manifestly associated with Rostow's sweeping efforts are inherent in this *type* of approach, or are primarily characteristic of *his* particular mode of execution.

First there is the methodological drawback which Rostow's approach apparently shares with many other attempts to encompass long-run and varied economic evolution in general stages. This is the tendency to concentrate on a descriptive taxonomy with a negligible, or at least an imperfect, regard for the twin need to stipulate the separate and distinctive features of different stages, and to specify how the system gets from one stage to another. Of course, as I emphasised at the outset of this paper, it is not always possible to distinguish between description and analysis, if only because description involves selection and selection implies analytical priorities. On the other hand, although in Rostow's case he hardly acknowledged the existence of this problem and allowed his intellectual ambitions to draw him into far-flung and weakly based generalisations, the fact remains that any detailed attempt to specify and perhaps even discover important distinguishing characteristics of phases of expansion is useful[10] – even if we cannot always explain how one set of characteristics gives way to another. Leaving aside for the moment the problems of stages which purport to have general applicability to all or most economies, the detection of regularities is surely one of the

[10]However, it is obviously misleading to talk of 'the' important distinguishing characteristics of 'the' phases of expansion. Our concepts of importance and of what the phases are in any particular instance derive from analytical presuppositions and conclusions which can have only a relative and subjective 'truth'.

prime tasks of the historian of economic growth. And there is certainly no *a priori* reason why long-run economic development should not be encompassed and described in a series of stages, even if the series is primarily a heuristic device. Indeed the very idea of 'economic development' inescapably implies the presupposition that regularities of *some* sort exist.

A second general argument implied in the debate about Rostow's work concerns the path of economic development – and particularly its discontinuous or continuous character. Whether or in what sense all major historical processes move discontinuously is a deep philosophical question which need not concern us here. Moreover, looking at the long-run course of economic development, it seems very unlikely that there are persuasive empirical or theoretical grounds for expecting the process to be uniformly or systematically discontinuous – although, of course, the conceptual device of stages of growth does not logically depend upon the existence of such discontinuity. On the other hand, however, Rostow's popularisation of stage analysis, by emphasising the idea of the take-off, dramatised an extremely widespread concept as to the discontinuous *origins* of modern economic growth. Obviously enough, this goes right back to the very idea of an Industrial Revolution. And there is no doubt that the view that growth begins with a more or less abrupt spurt is deeply embedded in the way we think about development. Yet the evidence that this is what happened – that the modern economic history of advanced societies began with a sharp and decisive increase in the growth rate of *per capita* income – is ambiguous to say the least. And, indeed, it seems on reflection unlikely that the necessary massive changes in factor inputs or productivity would occur in enough sectors and in a sufficiently short period of time to make a large and sudden difference to the growth rates of whole economies. A more realistic possibility (implicit in a distinction which was not made sufficiently clear in Rostow's work) is that the beginnings of modernisation in *manufacturing industry* may be characterised by a 'big push', even though the sector may be so small that it has relatively little effect upon aggregate output. (This, of course, is the basis of Professor Gerschenkron's view of the nature of growth in backward economies in the nineteenth century.)

A third and more serious criticism of models based upon more or less universally applicable stages of economic growth derives from the uniformity which they often attribute to the sequences of long-run economic development wherever it occurs. As Professor Gerschenkron points out, in the long run and taking a very broad view it *is* possible to see all instances of industrial expansion as part of a single, repetitive sequence but only at the possible cost of also accepting a fairly innocuous and trite set of generalizations.[11] There seems to me little doubt that, useful and suggestive as it may be to organise historical data in terms of stages, Professor Gerschenkron is essentially correct on this point: our natural temptation is to seek a single model of growth, but we must resist that temptation if it implies that we view long-run economic development as falling into a simple, repetitive pattern. Even so, of course, this does not mean that we shall end up with as many models as there have been examples of developing economies. For, quite apart from the ultimate need to see world economic development (including the uneven distribution of growth) as a single phenomenon, we have strong grounds for anticipating that the varying experiences of different economies can be accommodated into patterns – which provide systematic links for obvious differences. The most stimulating attempt to produce such a framework has been Professor Gerschenkron's work on a model designed to incorporate important deviations within a general system: 'a pattern . . . arranged along a scale of gradations of backwardness'.[12] What are the implications of this particular attempt to propound a general historical model at a time when historians are reluctant to commit themselves to a precise schematic view of long-run economic development?

The most important point to make in this respect is that Professor Gerschenkron's theory does not relate to the long-run course of development but to the characteristics of the early phase of industrialisation – with the degree of the pre-existing backwardness of various countries playing a critical part in determining the speed, organisation, technology, financing, entrepreneurial institutions and ideological virulence of the 'great acceleration in their industrial growth'.[13] Moreover, he claims no more coverage for this model than is to be derived from his case studies of actual industrial spurts in Europe before 1914. He certainly does not offer it as adequate explanation of industrialisation in other places or at other times than the nineteenth century – and, indeed he is obviously sceptical about the possibility of universally applicable models, arguing that the economic historian should not forget 'that in constructing his approaches and in his very attempts to improve them, he also pushes towards

[11]Alexander Gerschenkron, 'The Early Phases of Industrialization in Russia: Afterthoughts and Counterthoughts', in W. W. Rostow (ed.), *The Economics of Take-off into Sustained Growth* (1963), p. 166.

[12]Gerschenkron, 'The Early Phases', p. 166.

[13]See the summary in Alexander Gerschenkron, *Europe in the Russian Mirror* (1970) pp. 98–9.

the limits of their applicability, to the point that is, at which the approach has fulfilled its exploratory function and must recede before a different method of looking at the process of economic change'.[14]

This is by no means to diminish the importance of Professor Gerschenkron's contribution to our understanding of the process of industrialisation. But it does incidentally highlight the limitations which our knowledge imposes on our hypotheses – although it is doubtful if this is a very serious limitation, since most economic historians think of the historical experience of economic development in a context and in terms largely derived from the European experience between the late eighteenth and the early twentieth centuries. The importance of a systematic understanding of this series of events is, therefore, derived from the fact that it is the key turning point of modern economic history. From this viewpoint Professor Gerschenkron's model has an enormous amount to offer, even though it sheds little light on the British Industrial Revolution, and is open to the criticism that it cannot provide us with a precise enough indication of the degree of backwardness and the circumstances which would generate an industrial spurt, as against the degree of backwardness which would impose decisive obstacles rather than offer opportunity to expansion.[15] But what is important from the present viewpoint is not the intrinsic utility of the set of hypotheses, but the reasons for the existence of limits to their application. Here I come back to the earlier point: for the great (and still growing) variety of the experience of economic development, together with the multiplicity of viewpoints from which it can be studied, seem to me to invalidate the search for a single very useful *historical* model of expansion – or even industrialisation. This is not the same as claiming that all historical events are unique or that generalisation about growth is impossible. But whatever they have in common in terms of concepts, it may well be that the model most useful for understanding the growth experience of, say, the United States will differ markedly from that appropriate to Western Europe. Correspondingly, therefore, we should be extremely cautious in allowing ourselves to think of economic development in general within a context derived from one set of episodes.

If we accept this line of argument it therefore becomes not only

[14]Gerschenkron, 'The Early Phases', p. 169.

[15]In a summary of his own view Professor Gerschenkron confessed to having 'increasingly felt that after (spending) some time and thought in exploring the growing advantages of backwardness, it may be in order to devote attention to such difficulties and obstacles to economic development as accumulate with the increase in the degree of economic backwardness.' ('The Early Phases', p. 169.)

permissible but necessary to envisage different sorts of explanatory frameworks for different 'types' of economic development – with the choice or formulation of such frameworks shaped not by the supposed uniqueness of national experiences but by the affinities within different groups of experience. Yet even if the historical understanding of long-run economic development necessitates the use of a *set* of apparently different hypotheses, it will remain the function of social science to explore the conceptual interrelationships between them. For there is an important sense in which development remains the same sort of pheno-menon, and its explanation demands the same sort of methodology, wherever and whenever it occurs. Hence, as with other sorts of prob-lems in the social sciences, the appropriate conceptual apparatus will vary very much less than the models to which, in relation to dif-ferent circumstances, it gives rise. Here it is important to acknowledge another important point about Professor Gerschenkron's approach – and the approach of all economic historians trained in the tradition of economic analysis. This is that, quite apart from the particular hypothesis which he formulates, his model is in fact derived from the fairly rigorous examination of a few key concepts (prerequisites, 'obstacles' to growth, the mobilisation of capital and its relation to enterprise and technology, etc.).

Now, there is a sense in which the derivatives of these concepts, in the form of the institutional structures which have shaped obstacles to and opportunities for development, are culture-bound. But the concepts themselves, whatever the temporal circumstances with which we are concerned, are part of the language in which we tend to think of economic development – and, it is surely right to do so insofar as they reflect general functional relationships (factor mobility, capital accumulation, the maximisation of social returns, etc.) which are apparently critical elements in the growth process.

As with the discussion of the incorporation of non-economic variables in explanations of economic development, this last point once more reminds us that the central questions of long-run economic development involve functional relationships rather than particular institutional arrangements. At the same time, however, such relation-ships exist *only* in particular institutional embodiments: they are in a sense the conceptual artefacts which we impose upon reality to help us to a systematic understanding of it. We do this because the apparent uniqueness of historical institutions and events can only be adequately understood with the use of 'theory'. But in so doing it is important to bear in mind that it is a necessary ab-straction which we bring into the argument. Even more important, the tension between conceptual generalization and the analysis of 'real' institutions can never (and should never) be completely resolved. The utility of our concepts and general hypotheses is based upon their selection and refining in actual use. And it is this which shapes the distinctive role of the economic historian in the study of economic growth: not to formulate theories or test hypotheses (although he will do both of these) nor to counter every theory with a bogus appeal to reality, but to play the honest broker between the two contradictory yet essentially correct views of long-run economic development: on the one hand, a patterned process amenable to useful generalisation and explanation; on the other, a sequence of unique events only comprehensible in terms of particular historical settings and institutions.

1799859

3

The Nature and Diffusion of Technology

S. B. SAUL
University of Edinburgh

I

In what follows I have simply tried to make some general observations on the question of technological change and diffusion based on the experience of Europe, and, in a minor degree, of the United States in the nineteenth century. Two aspects of the subject have received most attention. One is the processes by which countries learned about and took up new ideas, and the other – which is not really a separate issue at all – is the vexed question of the nature of particular technologies and their relevance or adaptation for countries other than these in which they originated. I have not pursued the wider question of the origin of inventions but rather I have examined what part different factors have played in the emergence of new technologies or in the change of factor-mix within given technologies, and what happened when the question arose of their adoption in circumstances where the economic environment was quite different.

I have deliberately written about technology in a purely technical sense. I have looked at questions of skills, knowledge, opportunities, relative prices and the like. Of course technological change is very much part of and dependent upon change in whole patterns of social behaviour. There are those who would argue that technological change should only be viewed in this wider context. I cannot agree with them. There is much to be said for trying to clarify the technical/economic aspects on their own so far as this is possible. Then and only then will we be able to see the question more accurately in its total environment. Inevitably there are limits to the extent that one can do this, but it is worth the attempt otherwise too much of the literature on economic development will be concentrated on social and institutional problems which are by no means the whole story.

It is now widely accepted that any analysis of technologies conducted simply in terms of the labour/capital ratio is unhelpful historically;

though the addition of other factors makes the problem less amenable to quantitative study. For example, it is essential to divide labour into various skill groups and to take cognisance of the notion of relative differences in the effectiveness of human capital. As we shall note later, much of the American industrial success derived less from substitution of capital for labour than from the more effective use by its labour of the same capital equipment. Account has to be taken of the differences in resource endowments. For example, a new process may be developed to save a factor short in one country but abundant in another. The reluctance to adopt coke-smelting on the Continent, initially anyway, was due not to inertia but was a proper reaction to the fact that it was an expensive process producing poorer iron and only worthwhile when the supply of charcoal, or the labour to process the wood, was very expensive to come by. Much of the early American machining technology reflected above all a resource endowment where wood was cheap and could be economically processed in ways that wasted a great deal of it. Such a technology was less attractive in Britain. From the first, steam engines on the Continent far surpassed those made in Britain in fuel economy. French locomotives tended to have high first cost because they were designed to economise on fuel more than did the British or German. This involved giving a more accurate finish to certain parts, and installing more devices and gauges so that the driver would know more precisely what he was doing. He got a fuel-saving bonus, too – unthinkable in Germany, where he simply had to get there on time.

A product may require peculiar market conditions present in one country but not in others. The mass production techniques which emerged in the United States after 1850 were relevant only where there was a mass demand for a homogeneous product. It was therefore simple to introduce sewing-machine manufacture in all parts of Europe, using American manufacturing methods, but much more difficult with the more costly motor-car. A process may call for special patterns of industrial organisation. Thus, new textile technologies such as ring spinning and the Northrop loom were, for technical reasons, not easy to accommodate in an industry where cotton spinning and weaving were carried on in separate establishments. New products such as artificial dyes and pharmaceuticals required that high skill in both research and development which Keesing, among others, sees as a major element in explaining world trading patterns; while machine tool making required a rare degree of skill from the machinists.[1]

[1]D. Keesing, 'The Impact of Research and Development on U.S. Trade', in P. Kenen and R. Lawrence (eds), *The Open Economy* (New York, 1968), pp. 175–89.

There are sometimes real problems in discovering precisely what it was that a product or process had to offer. Take, for example, interchangeability. The specific method of achieving it by developing machine tools for the mass manufacture of small parts for later assembly came from American gun-makers, but the idea itself was obvious enough. It was most desirable where the servicing of similar equipment on any scale was involved. This, rather than cost, was the first motive for making rifles that way, and, early in the 1840s, locomotives in Britain had interchangeable features for the same reason. The problem was how to do it? The evidence shows that the new milling machines were devised in New England not to save labour costs, but to achieve a technical end which had for several decades been eluding the gun-makers. So it was that whenever interchangeability was adopted on the Continent – to make sewing machines for example – the same tools were used regardless of relative costs; for what other way was there of making them? This is not to ignore costs but to deny them a completely dominant role. Similarly, when the Crystal Palace was erected in Britain in 1850, it was made by quite unique interchangeable building methods because that was the only conceivable way of meeting a remarkably tight building schedule. Paul David has shown that the effectiveness of the mechanical reaper in saving labour was greater on higher-yield land, and that on farms of a given size the profitability of its use was directly affected by terrain and field lay-out. Indeed, in certain physical conditions the use of reaping machines would not have made sense, no matter what factor prices had prevailed.[2] The advantage of threshing lay not so much in saving labour, for the permanent employees of a farm were, if anything, underemployed at that time of the year, but in speed in getting the crop to market before prices began to fall.[3] The steam plough was useful if it saved temporary hired labour, but rarely if it replaced the services of the permanent labour force of the estate for much the same reason.

Perhaps most important of all, new technologies as often as not changed significantly the quality of the product. No true sportsman would use an interchangeable rifle in preference to the much more accurate handmade gun with a stock shaped to his own specific requirements. On the other hand, the cream separator, besides saving

[2] P.A. David, 'Mechanization of Reaping', in H. Rosovsky (ed.), *Industrialization in Two Systems* (New York, 1966), pp. 26–7; and 'The Landscape and the Machine . . .', in D. N. McCloskey (ed.), *Essays on a Mature Economy*, (London, 1971), pp. 147–155; and the following discussion, especially David's reply to the comments by E. H. Hunt.

[3] E. J. Hobsbawm and George Rude, *Captain Swing*, (London, 1969), Appendix IV.

time on one of the most tedious jobs on the farm, had two other major advantages; it produced butter of higher and more homogeneous quality and, unlike earlier machines, would cream milk that had been transported and shaken up over some distance, so making possible processing in central creameries. The threshing machine, too, produced a grain of better and more regular quality. It is significant, as Dovring has pointed out, that no progress was made at all in Europe before 1914 towards devising what were potentially the most labour-saving machines of all – potato and beet lifters – but which had little, if any, 'crop saving' functions.[4] Alternatively, the same basic techno-logical end might be achieved in very different ways. Ford sought to increase the effectiveness of the engine's power by reducing the weight of a car. Renault attacked the problem by technically transforming the efficiency with which power was transmitted from engine to wheels. The resulting end-products were of course quite different, and the very approaches were functions of different traditions of engineering and of different market structures.

Equally one must emphasise the serious technical limits that existed in the degree to which substitution of factors could be brought about. It is usually assumed that the production function is continuous and that marginal adjustments are possible, but in practice this was rarely the case and the curve was in fact kinked. I have already suggested that for interchangeable manufacture there was just one technique. It seems likely that for steel-making, alternative techniques were bunched at the capital intensive end, so that whatever the relative factor prices, it had to be a capital intensive technology with only minor modifications available, say by employing less mechanical handling devices. Sometimes the situation shown in Figure 1 must have arisen where the curve had two production possibilities relating to very different factor ratios. Obviously it requires a big change in the factor price ratios to make it worth while shifting from a to b. This may have been the case with the Norwegian fishing industries, for example.[5] Norwegian fishermen continued to rely on small coastal fishing boats for their cod and herring catches, and exported these fish dried and salted to low-income markets such as Spain, Portugal, West Africa and South America. The really profitable trade was satisfying the rapidly growing demand for fresh frozen fish from high-income markets, but this required bigger vessels to fish for cod, say, on the Dogger Bank and off Newfoundland, and investment in quick-freezing plants; there was no half-way house.

[4]*Cambridge Economic History of Europe*, Vol. VI, Part II, (Cambridge, 1965), p. 646.
[5]S. Lieberman, *The Industrialisation of Norway 1800–1920*, (Oslo, 1970), p. 157.

Other constraints on technological choice derived from the fact that the machine-making industry was slow to emerge in the less developed countries, and they had to buy what was available or go without. Modernisation of iron-making in the Urals after 1800, for example, was slow in coming about partly for institutional reasons, but also because, before the building of railways, the cost of getting Western equipment to the area was prohibitive. What was available to late developers tended to be based on Western practice, and insofar

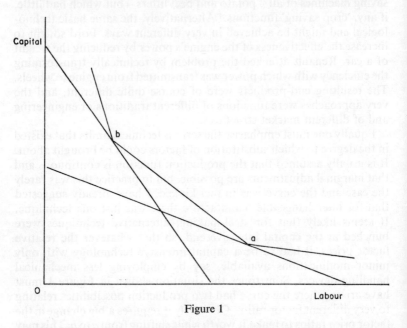

Figure 1

as new industries in the less developed countries were managed by Westerners, they not unnaturally chose the techniques they understood best. McKay tells us that in the Russian steel industry it was good existing practice that was transferred, but the latest ideas and experiments were almost inevitably confined to the home plants.[6] In any case it would be wrong to argue that transfer was based on ignorance, inertia and fixity of technology. There is evidence that the heavy use of capital implied in the modern techniques was more than offset by the low cost of labour operating the plant. The argument that this low cost simply reflected low productivity is incorrect; it reflected also its

[6]John P. McKay, *Pioneers for Profit*, (Chicago, 1970), p. 120.

inability to reap the rewards of its productivity. An American observer noted in 1907 that the Singer plant at Podolsk near Moscow, which used only American techniques and machines, had costs well below those of the parent in New York.[7] Unit costs of the Singer plant near Glasgow, where only the most modern machinery was used, were also lower than those in the United States.[8] The Pneumatic Tool Company at St Petersburg, equipped entirely with American tools, produced at costs much below those of the equivalent American plant. Another report put costs of making 32-count cotton yarn in the United States as 20 per cent above those in a good Russian factory using the same kind of equipment.[9] The most modern machines were not only in many instances the only available, but more often than not they offered substantial cost advantages.

It is suggested that one reason why underdeveloped countries adopted the latest technologies was that labour, in the sense of a stable, reliable, disciplined work force, was still very scarce in such countries: not expensive in terms of wages, perhaps, but very hard to come by. It is not clear how true this was for the simple type of repetition work carried on in textile mills or in operating the more modern automatic machine tools. In the Podolsk Singer plant it was thought that the firm benefited from a labour force that was happy to carry out the same routine task, day in day out, all the year long. Certainly there was a shortage of the highest skills, though in part this may have arisen because such labour was already very productive in the traditional craft trades, and so there was much to be said for using such skill to best advantage by employing the most up-to-date technologies in the new industries. But we should be careful not to attribute too many of the difficulties of industrialisation to labour problems. It is striking what could be achieved with an ill-trained labour force when other conditions were right. Also we should note that in the countries of Eastern Europe, above all, there were wide differences in the supply price of labour from one area to another, and this makes generalisation difficult. The Donets Basin was very sparsely populated, and labour was scarce for this reason alone. It was in the smaller towns of the north that the cheapest labour was found, though its quality would not be high. In the big cities – Moscow and St Petersburg – it

[7] U.S. Department of Commerce and Labour, Bureau of Manufactures, *The Machine Tool Trade of Austria–Hungary, Denmark, Russia and the Netherlands* (Washington, 1910). p. 135.

[8] R.B. Davies, 'The Singer Manufacturing Company in Foreign Markets, 1854–1889', *Business History Review*, Vol. XLIII (1969), p. 317; and S. B. Saul, 'The Market and the Development of the Mechanical Engineering Industries in Britain, 1860–1914', *Economic History Review*, Vol. XX (1967), p. 124.

[9] U.S. Bureau of Manufactures, *op. cit.*, p. 131.

would be dearer but more accustomed to the routines of factory work.[10]

In their recent path-breaking work, Dupriez and his students have been analysing the circumstances in which prices and wages reached much higher levels in developed than in undeveloped countries, and have been considering how far this of itself was a significant motivating force for technological change.[11] In the eighteenth century, for example, prices in Britain and the United States were already relatively high. But, as we have just said, labour-saving technologies are by no means always motivated by high labour costs. What would have happened if the industrial revolution had begun in a country with a relatively low price level? Possibly it is a pointless question because low prices indicated a social structure in which such a rapid change was impossible, but one can see the problem today where a relatively low-wage country such as Japan has been in the van of technological change. It may be that it was this combination of cheaper labour with the most advanced technologies (in a technical sense) which made Germany such a fearsome competitor at the end of the nineteenth century. The theoretical literature is full of references to cheap-labour countries using labour-intensive techniques and dearer-labour countries offsetting this cost disadvantage by employing more capital-intensive techniques. All too often in practice it has not been like that. In part the notion is misleading because American labour was far more efficient than European *using the same capital equipment*. As Leontief put it, the input of labour in productive terms was much higher than appearances suggest.[12] Even so, this greater effectiveness did not offset fully the higher cost. American manufacturers have been competitive in world markets not because their production costs are lower, given the same market conditions, but because the products have had a technical edge or because the home market has offered peculiarly favourable production conditions. Today American aircraft-makers dominate world markets on the basis of the huge runs they derive from home orders in an industry dominated by immense launching costs and a learning curve. Run

[10]Tugan-Baranovsky suggested that wages in St Petersburg, a sparsely populated area, were higher than those in Moscow. This led to differences in technology for St Petersburg factories were better equipped. Their owners were also less opposed to factory reform. M. Tugan Baronovsky, *The Russian Factory in the Nineteenth Century*, (Homewood, Ill., 1970), p. 322.

[11]L.H. Dupriez, *Diffusion du progrès et convergence des prix*, Vol. I, (Louvain, 1966). especially Ch. 1.

[12]W. Leontief, 'Domestic Production and Foreign Trade: The American Capital Position Re-examined', *Proceedings of the American Philosophical Society* (September 1953), p. 334.

for run, their different technology – in the widest sense – gives the Americans a 50 per cent advantage in labour productivity over British makers, compared with labour costs some 200 per cent higher.[13] Similarly, E. A. G. Robinson eliminated differences in size and product by studying the experiences of big international companies producing identical goods. He found a labour-productivity advantage for the United States over the United Kingdom of 1·5 to 1; not the general 2·8 to 1 that Rostas and Frankel have shown.[14]

As regards the role of capital, it is possible that the price of capital has in many instances been far less important than its availability. American and some European railways were built in a capital-saving manner for no other reason than that only a certain amount of money could be raised at any one time, and any railway has a minimum size below which it simply cannot be worked. Equally the existence of only rudimentary knowledge of capital costs may have predisposed industrialists to save on the bills they met every week for wages and materials. Alternatively, as price structures adjusted themselves upwards, there was a reasonable presumption that wages would go on rising, never mind what happens to capital, so yet another bias inserted itself. In all countries where we take account of the requirements of working capital, the less mechanised and slower techniques implied a longer lag and therefore a greater use of capital.

But of course some degree of modification of technologies was often possible, and it was more particularly in consumer-goods industries that intermediate technologies were adopted. The use of second-hand equipment was the obvious course, though unfortunately we know all too little about it. Steel-making in Holland began shortly after 1900 with the purchase of a second-hand Bessemer furnace from Germany.[15] When the Great Western Railway in Britain abandoned its wide-gauge system in 1892, the rails were sold to an Italian railway. In Russia Nikopol-Mariupol, the main tube manufacturers, bought an entire tube plant, second-hand, in the United States.[16] It was more common to buy second-hand machine tools and textile machinery, though to be sure the best manufacturers in the less developed countries rarely did so. It was probably more a means of saving on initial outlay than of maximising profitability. The use of the second-hand

[13]See generally the Elstub Report, *The Productivity of the National Aircraft Effort*, H.M.S.O. (1969).
[14]E. A. G. Robinson (ed.), *The Economic Consequences of the Size of Nations* (London, 1960), p. 345.
[15]R. M. Westebbe, 'The Iron Age in the Netherlands', *Explorations in Entrepreneurial History*, Vol. IX (1956–7), p. 177.
[16]McKay, *op. cit.*, p. 128.

equipment was most common in shipping. Table 3.1 shows the striking differences in practice in Europe in this respect.

TABLE 3.1

STEAM VESSELS ADDED TO NATIONAL FLEETS, 1914

	Tonnage added ('000 Net tons)	Percentage of new vessels
United Kingdom	955	97
Germany	387	85
France	137	61
Italy	137	12
Norway	152	59
Sweden	66	62

Source: *Shipping and Shipbuilding Trades after the War*, p. 56.

Rapid technological advance and the differential requirements of routes and cargoes gave the used vessel this major role. On the other hand, ring spinning was such a new technology in the 1880s when many of the less developed countries in Europe began building up their cotton industries, that there were very few spindles available second-hand anyway.

Another variation was that adopted in the making of footwear where many firms used American machinery for part of the process but left to the traditional outworkers the sewing of uppers to the soles. In textiles, modification of technologies came by varying the number of machines any worker tended and by altering their speed. For example, just before 1914 on much the same counts of cotton yarn, the number of operatives per thousand spindles was 9 in Italy and Silesia, 6 in France on average, $3\frac{1}{2}$ in Westphalia, and possibly $2\frac{1}{2}$ in Lancashire. In the 1890s, Schulze Gaevernitz estimated that for spinning yarns of count 60, spindles in Alsace were run 25 per cent slower than those in Bolton. The French workers also had more breakages and were slower at repairs, so that their spindles operated for only 80 per cent of the theoretically possible time, compared with 95 per cent in Lancashire. The situation was not always simple, however. The Russian cotton industry ran its spindles faster than the German, and used at least twice as much labour to tend the broken yarns. Possibly the British engineers there had their own special prejudices. Looms varied in speed too: for weaving plain cotton goods 80–85 cm. wide in England, they were typically set at 240 picks a minute in 1890, compared with 190–200 in Switzerland, and 150–160 in France. In Italy it was stated that female workers were so slow

44

at piecing the ends that almost 40 per cent of their time was lost this way.[17]

Diffusion varied, of course, according to the age composition of existing plant and the rate of growth of demand for new capacity. It was also affected by the state of the market for second-hand equipment, since sale of the old obviously reduced the capital costs of the new. For replacement to be justified, total costs of the new had to be less than variable costs of the old, and in these circumstances diffusion depended heavily upon the gains to be expected from the new technology as well as the certainty of these gains. Sometimes the new completely crushed the old. The Héroult process for making aluminium, developed during the 1880s, reduced costs immediately by something like 75 per cent, and there was no survival for the old technology under such conditions. But the Solvay process for soda manufacture had nothing to offer the older Leblanc makers. They were able to reduce their own costs markedly; they had a royalty charge to face; the price of their main by-product, bleaching powder, was buoyant. Given their capital charges, at no time until a new process for chlorine manufacture in the 1890s destroyed the market for the by-product, was a changeover through scrapping existing plant in any way viable. The charge of entrepreneurial lassitude is non-proven. For these reasons, and also, of course, through pure ignorance and inertia, the gap between best and average practice everywhere was wide. Mansfield shows for example, that pig-iron production per manhour in the U.S. in 1911 was 0·313 gross tons best practice and 0·14 average.[18]

II

Now let us turn to look more carefully at the international diffusion of technology. The first thing that strikes the historian must surely be less the problems of transfer than the incredible ease with which it came about. In 1850 modern technology was in its infancy on the Continent of Europe and yet, half a century later, sophisticated products such as steam-turbine and diesel engines were being made in a number of leading works spread all over the Continent, and almost every country was just about to have a shot at making its own cars. Why was this?

As I have already suggested, one can easily exaggerate the problem of labour skills. There were, it is true, certain key workers, such as

[17]See generally G. von Schulze Gaevernitz, *The Cotton Trade in England and on the Continent* (London, 1895), pp. 83–107.
[18]E. Mansfield, *The Economics of Technological Change*, (1968), p. 26.

puddlers, who were in very short supply, and the difficulty was not easily overcome because the best workers were unwilling to emigrate. Why should it have been otherwise? Why leave the centres of technological excellence where rates of pay were as high as anywhere else and industry seemed to assure a lifetime of work and in a well-understood environment? Georges Dufaud, ironmaster from the Nivernais, wrote of this from London in 1823: 'Le Pays de Galles et Cyfartha surtout a et conserve les meilleurs puddleurs du monde, un puddleur ordinaire et non soigneuz n'est pas admis, et malheureusement, c'est la rebut qui nous vient.'[19] A similar comment came from J. C. Fischer of Schaafhausen: 'English workers who are efficient and well-behaved can earn a good living at home. It is not uncommon to come across English workers in foreign countries who are far from competent in all branches of their trade.'[20] There was also a real need for trained supervisory staff; for local labour might have the necessary dexterity but not the initiative and experience to act when something went wrong. But apart from this there is little evidence that skill was a major problem and, indeed, in some industries, such as cotton-spinning, the level of skill required was extremely low. Labour might not be amenable to discipline and the rate of turnover might be high, but these were problems that seemed to resolve themselves fairly quickly.

The basic point is that there existed or were soon created all over Europe important reservoirs of skill. The first source was the indigenous craft industries. It is significant that Matthew Boulton, for example, recruited many such skilled foreign workers. For engravers he went to Vienna and to Sweden, and the most valued workers at the Soho Foundry around 1800 were a Fleming and a Frenchman.[21] In fact a number of French workers, skilled at luxury metal trades, were tempted to take employment with Birmingham firms at this time.

More important was the need everywhere for repair and maintenance facilities. Wherever metal equipment of any kind was in use there were men skilled to some degree in its modification and repair. For wood-working – and many of the early technologies developed in the United States came in wood – the required skills were obviously very widespread, and hence the speed with which in every country local manufacture of railway coaches and wagons developed. There

[19]G. Thuillier, *Georges Dufaud*, (Paris, 1959), p. 225.

[20]W. O. Henderson, *J. C. Fischer and His Diary of Industrial England, 1814–1851*, (London, 1966), p. 14.

[21]A. E. Musson and E. Robinson, *Science and Technology in the Industrial Revolution*, (Manchester, 1969), p. 220.

were local jobbing shops for all kinds of metal work; iron ploughs and later more sophisticated agricultural machinery extended the needs. This kind of technological advance tended to be cumulative, for the higher the level of internal demand, the more widespread was this type of local manufacture. At a more advanced level of development, textile manufacturers needed repair shops to adjust their machines; gradually the experience gathered there, together with the growth of specialisation of the textile industry itself, led to their transformation into machine and machine tool making establishments and from these centres of learning a whole engineering industry would be born. It happened in New England, in Leeds, in Manchester, in Mulhouse, in Switzerland. Such firms then developed into those general engineering concerns which were such a typical feature of nineteenth-century industrial centres. In fact they became centres of technological transfer within themselves, for these firms could apply the same basic techniques for a variety of outputs. It was some time before demand grew sufficiently to allow specialisation to emerge from this pattern. Escher Wyss and Sulzer in Switzerland, Cockerill in Belgium, Sharp Stewart and Fairbairn in Britain, Koechlin and Schlumberger in France, all followed this course, the last two retaining for longer their links with textile manufacture.

So the supplies of skill and knowledge were accumulated. Of course, once production was under way in Britain, it was not difficult to buy machines and copy them or, more commonly perhaps, to buy the more difficult bits in Britain and copy the easier. At the Chaillot Foundry, the Soho of France, Jacques Constantin Périer made his first steam engine in 1779 in this way, with parts supplied by Boulton and Watt.[22] In any case, the technology was not so precise that ingenuity and adaptability could not work wonders in trying to make a steam engine that would at least work. The tolerances were still considerable. It was not like the later turbines and diesels where anything but the near perfect simply would not work at all. Franz Dinnendahl described the problems and achievements of a pioneer steam-engine maker early in the nineteenth century, in his memoirs: 'I was obliged to do my own forging without ever having learned the job. However, I succeeded in forging with my own hands all the machine and even the boiler.' The absence of skilled help in forging the plates explained the fragility and imperfection of his boiler, and some parts of the engine such as cylinders, pipes and pumps left much to be desired too.[23] Still,

[22]M. Daumas (ed.), *Histoire générale des techniques*, Vol. III, (Paris, 1968), p. 69.
[23]P. Benaerts, *Les Origines de la grande industrie allemande*, (Paris, 1933), p. 388.

it worked, and Dinnendahl had never had the advantage of a stay in Britain to see how it was done there. It may be, as Landes says, that the French made some use of second-hand steam engines from Britain, but it is wrong to emphasise this and not to see how quickly indigenous manufacture grew up.[24]

A major step in the acquisition of engineering skills emerged from the servicing of locomotives and other railway equipment. Even before unification in Italy, for example, railway construction had brought with it those typical beginnings of a future industrial complex in the Genoa, Turin, Milan areas. Ansaldo of Genoa was just the most famous of the firms to be boosted along the path of becoming a major engineering complex through locomotive repair. Reference to this firm reminds us of the role of ship repair in creating the same traditions. It was from such roots that engineering emerged so quickly and easily in Holland and Denmark, for example. The influence of railway engineering in Europe was truly remarkable. Not only did the railways need workshops of great size but they had to have them spread all over the network, bringing new skills and possibilities to the remotest areas. New towns were created at places like Crewe, Swindon, and Horwich in Britain, and taking the country as a whole, there must have been at least thirty different large workshops stretching right up into the Highlands.

The effectiveness of these technological transfers can be seen from the speed with which locomotive manufacture itself was undertaken. In France, for example, despite a very slow start at railway construction, already there were three firms in Alsace able to make engines by 1834, together with two other firms, at least, at Arras and Le Creusot. The role of the foreign-made locomotive quickly declined, and by 1854 French output was running at about 500 per annum. For all its alleged industrial retardation, French makers were soon numbered among Europe's major exporters, helped, of course, by French overseas investment. Of 602 engines imported by the Piedmont railways before 1878, for example, 372 came from France, mainly from Koechlin in Alsace. Another 90 came from Austria, over 100 from Belgium, and only 25 from Britain.[25] In Germany, where industrial development was less marked, the same sequence is apparent. In 1842, of 245 locomotives in all the states, 38 were German made: by 1851 there were 1,084 locomotives of which 679 were locally made.[26] Such was the spread of the industry that by the end of the century large

[24]*Cambridge Economic History of Europe*, Vol. VI, Part I, p. 376.
[25]G. Luzzatto, *L'economia italiana dal 1861 al 1894* (Turin, 1968), p. 62.
[26]H. Mottek, *Studien zur Geschichte der industriellen Revolution in Deutschland* (Berlin, 1960), p. 45.

works were to be found all over Europe, even ignoring those in Britain, France and Germany. In Vienna the State Locomotive Works were turning out 140 locomotives a year, and the Budapest works half as many again; Borsig, the great German maker, was making 300 at this time. In Russia the Kolomna works were producing 200 locomotives a year; near Nijni Novgorod there was a works second only to Kolomna, set up by an American syndicate and with the entire stock of machinery shipped from the United States.[27] Hartmann, the German, and Bouhey, the French makers, had works there too. In Switzerland the Winterthur works made its two thousandth engine in 1909, and a high proportion had been exported. In Italy the Breda works had 2,000 men making engines for home railways, and exporting them to countries such as Denmark, Romania, France, using wheels and axles imported from Germany. In Belgium there were four well-known works. There were works in Sweden and Holland too.[28]

Possibly an even greater impetus to growth for the less advanced nations came in the manufacture of coaches and wagons. Such a trade offered few serious technical problems and considerable opportunities to benefit from the economies of batch production. A lot of woodworking was involved, and wheels and axles could be bought out if necessary. In Sweden, to give a particularly significant example, railway building enjoyed its first long boom only in the 1870s, and yet after 1877 no more coaches and wagons had to be imported. Before 1878 in Piedmont the railways had imported just under 7,000 carriages, but almost 10,000 had been made at home; to 1865 a third of the freight cars in Russia had been locally built.[29]

Another industry which had a similar impact in helping to spread industrial skills was the manufacture of agricultural machinery both for cultivation and for processing, for although there were in Britain and Germany, as well as in the United States, firms carrying on a large export trade in such machinery, it is striking how quickly local manufacture expanded and local specialities were created once demand began to build up. Sometimes powerful protection and subsidy helped. This was particularly true in Russia, where the International Harvester Company had a large plant in Moscow employing 3,000 men in 1913; a resumption of high tariffs on harvesting machines was one of the baits offered to them. There were also at least three very sizeable German plants, and in 1913 there were altogether 40,000

[27]U.S. Bureau of Manufactures, *op. cit.*, pp. 41, 184.
[28]U.S. Bureau of Manufactures, *The Machine Tool Trade in Germany, France, Switzerland, Italy and the U.K.* (Washington, 1909), pp. 173, 191.
[29]Luzzatto, *loc. cit.*; and J. N. Westwood, *A History of Russian Railways* (London, 1964), p. 57.

men employed in the whole industry, not including local peasant producers.[30] High duties also forced British makers of threshing machines to set up their own plants within the Austro-Hungarian Empire. More interesting were the effects of locally important agricultural activities in encouraging the emergence of particular manufacturing concerns. In Sweden the manufacture of railway rolling stock of the 1870s, which we mentioned earlier, was carried on by existing firms – not new creations – most of which had grown up on the basis of supplying steam engines, steam saws and other equipment for the forestry industry. In Europe the most successful manufacturer of cream separators was de Laval in Sweden, and it was soon to develop into a much more widely based engineering concern. The great metal rollers required for the new grain mills in Budapest from the 1840s onwards were made locally and exported all over the world by firms such as Ganz, which was soon to establish an international reputation in electrical engineering. To dismiss such a firm as an isolated, untypical example, is totally to misunderstand a process of diffusion of which this was a prime example, for such 'isolated examples' were to be found everywhere.

So, for all these reasons, the progressive transfer of technology came about with remarkable speed. But it was progressive: it depended upon the establishment of a succession of routes through which skills of all kinds were accumulated. Because of such channels of transfer, the newer products such as electric generators, steam turbines, diesels – all articles of high precision but not of mass production – came to be made in many parts of the Continent very soon after their invention. Ignoring the great German works, one can think of Sulzer, Brown Boveri, Escher Wyss in Switzerland, de Laval and Atlas in Sweden, Burmeister in Denmark, Werkspoor in Holland, Carel in Belgium, Ganz in Hungary, Fiat and Tosi in Italy (the latter described at the Paris Exhibition of 1900 as the finest steam-engine manufacturer in Europe). Given these processes of diffusion, given these reservoirs of skill, it is hardly surprising.

In such new industries there was no reason for ideas to be concentrated; indeed, with the shift away from traditional engineering, there was every reason to expect them to be dispersed. As in chemicals, high standards of performance and frequent innovation weighed as heavily with the market as price. It was, for example, Ganz engineers who in 1884 developed the first commercially practicable transformer system, and who after 1900 offered to London Underground a

[30]A. C. Sutton, *Western Technology and Soviet Economic Development 1917–1930* (Stanford, 1968), p. 132.

radically new propulsion system that attracted wide attention. New ideas were basic to such a firm. So although scale of production and rich sources of finance were powerful allies, they were not everything. The Germans might produce the solidly-made, competitively-priced equipment; the Swiss and Hungarians offered these other qualities. By and large, too, the machine-making industry itself was not capital intensive, and the economies for very large-scale production were not all that significant. It is curious how the literature on Switzerland concentrates on the need for exports so as to achieve economies of scale, whereas the obvious point is that except for watch manufacturing, her industry was dominated by processes where such economies were distinctly limited.

But if the skill of the bulk of the workers was easily come by, the experience and knowledge of the chief technical men was a different matter. There was no substitute for first-hand knowledge and practical observation. Whether or not they went to technical schools, on the Continent, just as much as in Britain, most engineers trained in the works of other engineers. Some frequently followed their fathers, and the value of a thorough understanding of very technical business clearly outweighed in many cases the disadvantages of nepotism. It was for these reasons that Frenchmen streamed across the Channel at every opportunity during the lulls in the Revolutionary and Napoleonic Wars, and why the English were so hostile to them. Where innovation depended less on practical experience and more on scientific experimentation, the situation was different, and the wars gave Britain less advantage – in chemical developments in cotton bleaching and dyeing, for example. But the more common problem of first-hand practical experience was still there a century later, though the roles were by then somewhat reversed. Possibly the greatest single triumph in chemical engineering before 1914 was the Haber-Bosch process for ammonia synthesis. In 1919 Brunner Mond raided the B.A.S.F. plant at Oppau to take the technology as war booty, but it was no use to them; they could not make the process work until out of the blue two chemical engineers from Alsace, who had operated the plant for the Germans, offered their services at a high price.[31] It was well worthwhile.

The spread of technical and entrepreneurial experience through personal connections can best be illustrated by a quick look at the growth of engineering in Switzerland; for the career of C. E. L. Brown, the father of Swiss engineering, gives a fine example of the transforma-

[31]W. J. Reader, *Imperial Chemical Industries: A History*, Vol. I (Oxford, 1970), p. 364.

tion of a whole industry, through the transmission of such knowledge. Discovered working at Maudslays in London in 1851, he was persuaded to move to the Sulzer works at Winterthur, and there designed the epoch-making steam engine, the ventilmaschine, which swept through Europe and first made Sulzers one of the great names in European engineering. In 1871 he left to manage the Winterthur locomotive works for thirteen years, and they too grew into major exporters. His son, at the age of twenty-three was made director of the electrical department of Oerlikon, then a small foundry, and there pioneered long-distance transmission of electric power. In 1891 he founded Brown Boveri, and on his father's advice took up manufacture of the Parsons steam turbine, and in a decade this firm too had become a great name in European engineering.[32] Such was the value of genius and experience. Elsewhere the fame of outstanding works in training skilled men caused budding engineers to travel far and wide to work with men such as Maudslay and John Penn in London, and Egells in Berlin.

There were exceptions of course. Machine tools required an unusual degree of skill in their manufacture and the industry was largely confined to Britain and Germany. The importance of this industry for the diffusion of engineering skills has frequently been noticed, but one should take care not to exaggerate its role. It was beneficial to industry if one was present: its absence was no disaster. Thus the comment on industrial growth in Italy that 'it is widely accepted that the absence of this industry was itself a causative factor in the generally slow economic growth of the nation' is an absurd overstatement of its role.[33] The most remarkable industry in respect of skill requirements, however, was the making of cotton-spinning machinery, which was concentrated in Lancashire to an amazing extent, so that even large producers of yarn, such as Germany and France, imported most of their machinery. For all but the most specialised equipment there was a virtual world monopoly outside the U.S.A., and American manufacturers had no export trade at all. The reason seems to have been a combination of very specialised skills, since handwork was dispensed with to only a very small extent before 1914, and a very high degree of specialisation and sales service based on large export markets – to India in particular. The refusal of British firms to cater for special requirements also helped in their control of the bulk market.[34]

[32]Derived from various obituaries.
[33]D. L. Spencer and A. Woroniak, *The Transfer of Technology to Developing Countries* (New York, 1967), p. 13.
[34]Saul, *op. cit.*, pp. 112–3.

III

Countries were much helped to a higher manufacturing status by the impact of arms manufacture. By its very nature this was an unusually widespread trade, and well before 1880 had been responsible for the creation of important centres of special skills – towns such as Birmingham and Liège, for example, the latter almost inevitably becoming one of the earliest of the modern nineteenth-century manufacturing centres on the Continent. Possibly the most striking example of this kind of technological diffusion occurred in Turin. In 1862 the city had four military establishments employing 2,000 men. There the latest machinery was to be found, local private firms began to supply these arsenals with pumps, tools, hydraulic machinery and above all they proved to be the source of skilled labour for firms such as Fiat and Ansaldo, one of the few significant machine tool makers in Europe in the less advanced countries.[35] But as regards the general stimulus to technological diffusion in the nineteenth-century military demand had certain more general aspects.

In the first place it was often very large, though equally it could be variable. Size had the advantage of offering economies of scale which could spin over into other associated uses as well as giving a good profit base, for normally one lost money on military contracts only with some difficulty. Such large orders gave early opportunities for mass, or at least, batch production. This was true for interchangeable arms-making and a bulk order for small naval vessels gave the first chance for standardised manufacture of marine engines in Britain during the Crimean War. Secondly, cost was by no means always the crucial factor; it might be outweighed by the need for quality, or innovation. This brought the benefits now known as 'technological fall out'. Military requirements were often of a very advanced kind and with this relative disregard of cost and sometimes the large scale of the requirements, new products, processes and tools which were of eventual use for civilian needs were developed or taken up far sooner than would otherwise have been the case. It was Maudslay's machinery for making ships' blocks at Portsmouth Naval Dockyard that saw the first use of machine tools for mass production. The incredible efforts of Krupps and Vickers to produce large steel castings by the crucible process resulted from demands for new types of artillery. Several hundreds of these small furnaces were organised for their tiny output to be poured into the mould one after the other, a feat of staggering industrial organisation and staggering cost. In France the first import of modern machine tools from Britain came around 1820 for use in

[35]P. Gabert, *Turin: Ville industrielle* (Paris, 1964), p. 83.

53

the naval arsenals. The Ministry of the Marine bought the world's first three steam hammers, made at Le Creusot before Nasmyth ever got around to actually producing one from his own sketches: a naval corvette, *The Sphinx*, was the first successful sea-going vessel made in France.[36] Jacob Holtzer made high-quality steel for arms-makers in St Etienne from the 1820s and brought chromium and manganese steel to France in the 1870s, but a generation later he had a special shop turning out such steel for motor car manufacturers. At the end of the century the use of steam turbines in ships was first encouraged by naval demand because of the potential gains in speed that were offered. When B.A.S.F. wanted equipment for the Haber-Bosch process which would have to work in very exacting conditions, they turned to Krupps whose guns had to resist even higher temperatures and pressures, if only for an instant. 'Without Krupps' technology it seems unlikely that Haber and Bosch would have got their process working anything like so quickly, if at all.'[37] It was the equipping of the Terni Arsenal by the Leeds firm of Greenwood and Batley that brought knowledge of altogether new types of machine tool techniques to Italy. The two naval vessels of over 20,000 tons each, built by Ansaldo, were by far the most remarkable engineering feats accomplished in that country before 1914.

Possibly most important of all, in the second half of the nineteenth century anyway, military and naval demand gave a great boost to the firms that enjoyed the orders, providing a powerful financial as well as technical base for their civil work. Krupps in Germany, Vickers in Britain, Schneider in France, Ansaldo in Italy, Putilov in Russia were just the greatest examples. There was, too, a great deal of international investment on the part of the armament companies which was of real technological value to the less advanced countries. Armstrongs had links with Ansaldo and Vickers with Terni in Italy; Schneider took charge of the Putilov works in 1905; Krupps were associated with Skoda.

This is not to say that arms making was 'a good thing' but that it had not altogether undesirable side effects. In the nineteenth as in other centuries before, most countries felt the need to keep up to date in this area of industry above all others and so for many there was at least one island of modernity which formed the basis for further industrial advance when the time became ripe, though on occasion for strategic reasons it might be located in a relatively remote area – Terni for example – and its overall influence limited by this fact.

This interaction of technologies across industries was crucial

[36]Daumas, *op. cit.*, p. 341.
[37]Reader, *op. cit.*, p. 350.

because, as Schmookler points out, most industries produce for other industries, not for final consumers, so although military demand may have been highly significant, it was only one aspect of a general situation.[38] The chemical industry provided bleaches, dyes, new textile fibres, processes for wood-pulp manufacture, insulators, lubricants, coatings for electrical engineers though the electrical industry contributed even more in return through the new electro-chemical and electro-metallurgical techniques. Progressiveness in one industry in part at least determined the growth of others. So an industrial structure where electrical engineering and chemicals were important got an added impetus of its own and this contrasted with the position in Belgium, for example, where the high dependence on standard steel processes, heavy engineering, coal mining and textiles offered little opportunity for this self-reinforcing type of techno-logical advance.

IV

I have no time to discuss the transfer of technology through direct international investment though undoubtedly it was very much more extensive than is sometimes recognised, especially in the newer electrical and chemical industries. The electrical engineering industry in Italy in 1914, dominated by three foreign companies – Thomson Houston, Siemens and Brown Boveri – is not an untypical example to quote. But one special aspect of policy affecting such international diffusion was the operation of patent laws.

Patents were originally closely linked with the use of an invention within the country or with a desire to attract foreigners, but as international trade developed they were increasingly used to protect foreign markets. Sometimes chaotic laws or the absence of any law helped diffusion; in Germany, before unification, ten states had no patent law and the other twenty-nine had different laws, so the cost to an outsider of trying to patent was prohibitive and German manufacturers copied at will. Switzerland had no law either to 1887 and it was for this reason that French dye-makers crossed the border to take up the manufacture of the fuchsine dye in the 1860s when they were being frustrated by the activities of the patent-holders in their own country. The Swiss law of 1887 excluded inventions which could not be represented by a model, so effectively leaving all processes unprotected. The concentration of the Swiss chemical industry on specialty dyes depended on the fact that German firms were unable to patent their own processes which were an essential feature of the

[38]J. Schmookler, *Invention and Economic Growth* (Cambridge, Mass., 1966), pp. 174–5.

manufacture of all dyestuffs. The manufacture of aluminium had made little progress in Germany to 1914, basically because certain American patents were upheld there over those for the more efficient Héroult process. Consequently the A.E.G. group, which held the Héroult rights, purchased the plant of an existing manufacturer at the Rhine Falls in Switzerland where all process patents were ineffective and later established other works in the Tirol and the French Alps. Once again the patent system worked to the Swiss advantage. With the Swiss manufacturers well established and developing new processes of their own, they welcomed more effective patent protection when it came at last under heavy diplomatic pressures in 1907. One might wonder, indeed, why small developing countries felt it worthwhile to have a patent law: Holland abandoned such protection from 1869 to 1910 altogether. But patent protection abroad could be vital and so the small countries tended to offer it at home as a *quid pro quo*, to put aside this kind of political pressure. After all in the last decades of the nineteenth century the Swiss took out more patents in Britain per head of their population than almost any other country.[39]

The German patent law of 1877 protected processes only, not products, and so gave a powerful stimulus to firms to discover alternative routes to the same end. In France the product was covered, so leading to a more rigid monopoly position and inhibiting the search for processes which was the essence of cost-reduction in chemicals; the fuchsine affair rose because an alternative route to the same end was held to infringe the original patent. In Britain the situation was similar. B.A.S.F. held a dye patent there, and when Levinstein developed a new process in 1883 they were unable to use it as it infringed the product patent. Eventually it was used in Holland where B.A.S.F. had no protection.[40] French law over the working of patents held by foreigners was extremely lax and German firms with branches in France satisfied the requirement by importing dye concentrates from their home factories and simply diluting them for sale in France.

The sale of patent rights became a major form of technological diffusion by the end of the nineteenth century. Solvay & Cie of Brussels kept control of their soda process by maintaining large holdings in the companies granted the rights, and with the passing of rights often went agreements over market sharing too. Where he could not protect his process – in Switzerland – Solvay built a plant at a very favourable location just over the border and effectively crushed any possible competition from within the country. Nobel on

[39]Edith T. Penrose, *The Economics of the International Patent System*, (Baltimore, 1951), p. 121.
[40]*Ibid.*, p. 106.

the other hand maintained absolute control through a central holding company. If rights got into the wrong hands the consequences could be serious. Diesel, for example, sold his British rights for a very small sum to a small manufacturer of sugar machinery in Stockport. For several years very little happened, as the company simply had not the resources to develop manufacture of a very intricate engineering product. In the U.S.A. the rights went – for a much larger sum – to Adolphus Busch, a beer magnate in Milwaukee, who made virtually no progress with the engine and inhibited all use of diesels in the United States for over a decade until the patents ran out and Busch in 1911 formed a combination with Sulzers.[41]

But it would be wrong to attach excessive importance to patents. Very deliberately the technical knowledge embodied in a patent was only half the story. Know-how, rather than a particular technology was what was required for there to be any hope of further development, and under this head one includes all the engineering aspects of production and the management skills. Without these, mere knowledge of the Haber-Bosch process availed Brunner Mond nothing; with them Brown Boveri bought the rights to Parsons' steam turbine and went on to develop it and its associated generating equipment to a degree of refinement that Parsons himself never achieved.

V

We can now turn to discuss in more general terms the role of smaller countries or those disadvantaged by resource deficiencies in the exploitation of modern technologies when faced with the competition of the industrial giants. The success of the Swiss was certainly most striking, given the need to export a high proportion of their output. A relatively advanced textile industry gave a good basis for the engineering industry through repair and machine building, and the Swiss developed a substantial export trade in specialised textile machinery and the associated power equipment. The vital element for Swiss industrialists was their ability to concentrate on high-quality production and constant innovation both in engineering and in chemicals. There was no question of following the ideas of others, for there the big men came out on top most of the time. Irish textile machinery makers lacking the huge home market of the Lancashire firms, were likewise able to concentrate on special types of flax-spinning machinery, helped by the fact that cotton machinery, the preserve of Lancashire, did not lend itself to preparing and spinning flax, though flax machinery could be used for spinning hemp and jute

[41]Busch-Sulzer Bros., *The Diesel Engine* (St Louis, 1911), p. 12.

which are also bast fibres.[42] So the Ulster industry enjoyed both a shelter and a source of expansion. The Swiss chemical firms were also able to make use of cheap German labour across the borders, in the end taking their plants to that labour. Even so, as Haber points out, it is doubtful if the Swiss chemical industry could have survived outright German competition. It seems likely that the Germans found it convenient to live with the Swiss, to sell them their bulk chemicals and to keep in touch with the quality end of the market through agreements rather than through competition.[43] In some sense the German chemical industry used the Swiss as research units, indulging in what one might consider a form of venture capital investment there.

Purchase of semi-manufactured inputs was, of course, a common feature of the activities of industries in smaller countries. Bulk dye chemicals we have mentioned; engineering works imported gears and forgings in the rough state and finished them – in other words doing the labour-intensive part for themselves. Despite the absence of any but the smallest local steel industry, Dutch shipbuilding was the fourth largest in Europe in 1923. They took in rough forgings and steel plates from Germany, as did British yards for that matter, above all Harland and Wolff in Northern Ireland who faced much the same resource pattern as the Dutch. The quality of engine-building was high and Dutch shipbuilders were responsible for some notable innovations, most of all with regard to motor ships. Burmeisters in Denmark operated in much the same way, though they made a speciality of forgings, using up to 80 per cent Danish scrap in making the steel and even exporting the finished, very high-quality, product to British yards. Good shipyards in the smaller countries could flourish, sometimes with an underpinning of local orders, partly because labour costs were a high proportion of total costs in an industry where the economies of scale in any one yard were not great, and individual as opposed to batch building remained the rule everywhere. Yards in northern Europe could get their steel easily enough and their ability to build high-performance engines was a great asset.

The flexibility of some technologies was a great advantage too – nowhere more than in steel-making. All too often the steel industry is considered solely in terms of the great concentrations in the Ruhr and the Donets Basin and for the bulk trades this provides an accurate enough picture, but the technology admitted a range of other suppliers too. Sweden, for example, was able to concentrate solely on the supply

[42]W. E. Coe, *The Engineering Industry of the North of Ireland* (Newton Abbot, 1969), p. 67.
[43]Haber, *op. cit.*, p. 163.

of charcoal steel right to 1914. The Austrian steel industry in Styria began to overcome its relatively poor resource endowment by establishing a reputation for technical ingenuity and inventiveness that it has maintained ever since. The ability to use scrap in the Siemens Martin process and the high efficiency of relatively small furnaces was a godsend to small producers and to countries deficient in coal. Martin steel was good for shipbuilding too. On such a technology the Italian steel industry grew up, locating its furnaces near the markets and the sources of scrap – at Milan for example – rather than near the coast. Electric furnaces offered further opportunities, though to 1914 the technology was still in its infancy everywhere.

Many of the smaller and less developed countries got their footing in the industrial world through the processing of primary products – pulp, paper, butter, cheese, margarine, chocolate, sugar beet, beer, flour – the typical resource-based industries of the development literature. But they did not stop at that as we have seen. Manufacturers in these countries had an advantage in that they found it relatively easy to insert themselves into world trade by carving out special niches not requiring very large markets. With a total market of perhaps 200 a year it was impossible for the Danes to make ordinary lathes competitively, but it was possible to build an export trade through series production of a very specialised type of machine tool or, as in Sweden, to make the most accurate tool gauges in Europe.[44]

In some ways the nature of world trade favoured these countries. Tariffs were generally very low, and there were many important industries with a high labour content. Smaller countries were also helped by the high-income elasticity of demand for their electrical engineering and chemical products and the rising share of these goods in world trade. By and large in European trade in manufactures, the smaller countries made their impact felt in capital rather than consumer goods. They might protect their home consumer industries, but rarely did they create an export trade from such a base. Possibly the economies of scale that were present in the manufacture of most consumer goods were less significant for capital goods, and this, together with the rapid rate of innovation in capital equipment, frequently offered convenient points of entry.

An interesting exception was motor-cars. At first the industry spread rapidly because capital needs were low, demand active, and the technology relatively conventional. But it soon became apparent that cars could only be made competitively within existing industrial complexes because the wide variety of bought-in parts could only

[44]U.S. Bureau of Manufactures, *The Machine Tool Trade in Austria-Hungary, Denmark, Russia, and the Netherlands* (Washington, 1910), p. 105.

with difficulty and great cost be brought together from distant suppliers. So Paris, Turin, Birmingham soon became the focal points, and in Switzerland, Holland, Sweden and Denmark there was no manufacture of any significance at all. Here the small countries faced one of their inevitable problems – real disadvantages in industries where external economies were important. Of course as internal economies of scale grew more and more significant the smaller countries suffered from their small home base too. So the Belgian car industry had a brilliant start before 1914, but one which proved very short lived. It was fortunate that the motor-car industry was by no means typical in its engineering economies.

VI

As I indicated at the outset, I have deliberately viewed my problem from a narrow angle. The general drift of my argument has been that the actual transfer of technology and the acquisition of the necessary labour skills were much slighter problems than the achievement of a state of society in which these changes were called for. There were certain patterns of activity which were especially helpful in promoting transfer. Probably of greatest significance were the reservoirs of skill that already existed before industrialisation, and the depth of these in large measure depended on the nature and patterns of prior development. For example, it has been persuasively argued that investment in the American South was inhibited by the absence of local skills.[45] This arose because the area lacked a pattern of demand for those manufactures where the technology permitted production on a modest scale in small shops widely scattered. In Europe, too, one may suggest that the supply of local skills varied according to these patterns of demand; this was one critical advantage that Britain and France and the richer German states enjoyed when rapid growth became technically possible.

But it might be useful to end on a note of caution by stressing that these patterns did not always work as one might expect. In his recent Presidential address to the American Economic History Association, Professor Parker was asking how we are to explain those 'lucky' sequences of events that made things work out – the successive discoveries that kept the gold standard working, that came up with uses for the oil that had been found, and so forth.[46] It seems an odd thing

[45]W. N. Parker (ed.), *The Structure of the Cotton Industry of the Antebellum South* (Washington, 1970), p. 117.
[46]W. N. Parker, 'From Old to New to Old in Economic History', *Journal of Economic History*, Vol. XXI (1971), pp. 8–9.

to be concerned about, for, after all, there are all those cases that do not get into the history books because the lucky sequences did not come about. So with our patterns of technology. How odd it is that with all those wonderful entrepreneurs, marvellous technical schools and generous bankers, and having pioneered the internal combustion engine through Daimler and Benz, the German motor industry limped along so miserably right to 1939. How odd it is to contrast a city like Turin following the classic patterns – coach makers, arms makers, machine tool makers, to become a major area for the making of motor-cars – with St Etienne. There was a place for motor-cars, with its old firearms tradition, its cycle component shops, its local steel mills, its markets in Lyons and the south: a real French Birmingham – horrible thought! Yet among all those many optimistic car-makers in the leading country in Europe before 1914, we find only one in St Etienne, and that a short-lived, miserable failure.[47] In their way these are some of the most intriguing elements of economic history. But as I said at the outset the paper is about technological potentials. How fast they worked themselves out was only partially a technological question.

[47]This point about St Etienne is made by Professor Laux in his forthcoming book on the French industry, to be published by Liverpool University Press.

4

Technology, Resources, and Economic Change in the West

WILLIAM N. PARKER
Yale University

This chapter is a restatement of a paper which I published nearly ten years ago under the title 'Economic Development in Historical Perspective'.[1] It fell at once into almost instant obscurity, furnishing only the title, like an outworn locust's shell, to Professor Gerschenkron's enlightening book of essays. Since I am sure he was ignorant that he had borrowed my title, his use of it only emphasised the obscurity of my piece. This summer, however, Professor Rosenberg has been astute enough to reprint the article in an otherwise notable collection of essays on technological change, by various hands. Rereading it there, I had the feeling that I might try again to make its points in a somewhat more orderly fashion and at the same time to stir into the outline of a history of Western economy and technology the results of some reading and work done since its appearance.

This is perhaps a suitable place and occasion at which to make such an attempt. I think it is the sort of effort which might have pleased a Scottish philosopher of the eighteenth century. It is, in effect, an effort to deduce the path of technological development and from it the path of economic development in the world economy since the mideighteenth century, from what such a philosopher might have called the 'basic postulates of the human mind'. We all know what Adam Smith did with the human propensity to truck and barter. Perhaps I can do the same thing with the propensity to invent.

My basic postulate is that things which are simple to invent get

[1]W. N. Parker, 'Economic Development in Historical Perspectives', *Economic Development and Cultural Change*, Vol. X (October 1961), 1, 7, reprinted in N. Rosenberg (ed.), *The Economics of Technological Change* (Penguin, 1971). Gerschenkron's book is *Economic Backwardness in Historical Perspective* (Cambridge: Belknap Press of Harvard University Press, 1962).

invented first. Discoveries that do not require an elaborate science, complex instrumentation, or subtle theory precede in time those that do. The latter build on the former; they furnish to later inventors the ideas, tools, mathematical formulations, which become part of the stage-setting for more complex syntheses. Nature gives out her secrets *seriatim*, though the rate of disclosure is affected by the level of training of technicians, the social organisation of their efforts, the economic resources devoted to invention, and the economic climate stimulating it. When this simple truth is realised it would appear that inventions and the fundamental science accompanying them have followed a certain time path which in turn has had strong economic effects.

In the first section of my paper I restate once again the picture of the inventive activity and process drawn for us by my teacher, Professor Usher, extending his model of the inventor beyond psychology and out into sociology a little farther than he made explicit. In the second section I provide a consideration of the relation of this activity to the development of fundamental science, and try to show what effect the movement of science had in guiding the direction and types of inventions as a continuous chain-reactive process of invention got under way and continued in the West. In my third section I finally come to the point: the effects of these sequences on the sequence of economic opportunities offered in the economic development of the West – in particular the effects on the various industries and locations in which dynamic economic change has centred. In a final section I get around to what I have been most recently interested in: the development of agricultural technology as Western industrialisation has occurred. What the implications of all this may be for today's underdeveloped countries I leave to those who hear or read it. My own concern is in trying to set in order our understanding of the elapsed economic history of the last two hundred years, and in making economists and sociologists, who tend to economic and sociological interpretations of history, face squarely the problems of interpretation posed by the physical world and the sequence of our attempts to understand it and to use it for our purposes. If this be determinism, let them make the most of it.

I

Nature of the inventive process
To understand the natural or logical controls on the course of invention, we must consider the nature of this activity as it has been exhibited in history. I wish to begin, then, by restating A. P. Usher's

well-known theory of invention[2] with a few new wrinkles. The new wrinkles relate, first, to the function of the community of inventors and entrepreneurs, and of communication links among them in accelerating the inventive process within society; and, second, to the relation of invention as a form of engineering activity to the simultaneous development of fundamental science.

Usher identifies four elements in the mental and physical act of creating an invention. First, there is the seizure of the mind by a problem, the identification of a need in the existing technology toward whose satisfaction activity may be directed. The second is the assembly in the inventor's mind and environment of the ideas, materials and components necessary for the solution. Next comes the act of insight, the selection and combination in the mind of the elements that constitute invention. Finally, Usher identifies a stage of critical revision, in which the bugs are ironed out, the engineering of the invention is completed, and its adoption in various uses is made.

Usher's concept of invention is a psychological one, and no doubt its psychological basis could be improved and refined from the *Gestalt* theory to which he linked it. What makes it useful as a construct in historical analysis is the readiness with which it can be linked to a sociology of inventive activity. The inventor is obviously the product of a surrounding culture, nurtured in its values, endowed with its skills and technology. His mental stage is set with facts and theories from the engineering of his time, with knowledge of materials, mechanisms and natural processes and properties. His 'greatness' as an inventor consists in a certain intuition or luck which leads him to focus on a problem which is both economically important and technically capable of solution by a novel combination of the means at hand.

Now let me make an important point about the relation of the 'economy' to this activity. Obviously 'bottlenecks' in the economy – where the movement of demand is not readily matched by a re-arrangement of productive factors – may serve to attract the attention of inventors. Where factor mobility is perfect – regardless of the

[2]A. P. Usher, *A History of Mechanical Inventions*, 2nd ed (Harvard Press, 1954), Ch. IV. See also the interesting analysis of Vernon Ruttan, 'Usher and Schumpeter on Invention, Innovation, and Technological Change', *Quarterly Journal of Economics* (November 1959), 596–606. Reprinted in N. Rosenberg (ed.), *op. cit.* The development of the subject by Homer Garner Barnett, *Innovation: the Basis of Cultural Change* (1st ed, New York: McGraw-Hill, 1953) is somewhat different, but might equally well be linked to a social environment and a communications network in the ways suggested here. Interestingly, mathematicians have had something to say about creativity in their field which is closely akin to Usher's theory. See Jacques Solomon Hadamard, *An Essay on the Psychology of Invention in the Mathematical Field* (Princeton: Princeton University Press, 1945).

relative rates of growth of the productive factors – such pockets of high returns do not appear. The bottleneck theory of invention implies a measure of factor immobility which is more readily solved by a movement of inventors to the point of high returns than by a movement of workers or of capital, or an adjustment in their rates of growth. A sticky economy, then, may reward a fluid inventive process. This is what Mantoux is really suggesting about the alternation between spinning and weaving in the eighteenth-century textile sequences. More often, one would suppose, inventors have been attracted not so much by relative factor scarcities as by the whole state of production taken in relation to the whole stage of technology. Given that a latent demand exists for all sorts of things in the economy, the state of technology – the evidence that certain inventions are ripe for the picking – serves as the focusing force on the inventor and gives him the problem with which, in Usher's first stage, his mind is seized. Professor Rosenberg has recently emphasised this point in an illuminating article.[3]

It is important to consider, then, not so much relative factor supplies as the general level of wealth, its distribution and demand in the economy. And it is of first importance to consider the supply of inventors and the communication among them which diffuses the ideas that set the stage. It is here that one can identify in northwestern Europe after 1700 a critical mass, and a set of chain-reactive relationships. The essential elements are: (1) a flourishing economy, offering prospect of financial success to improvements and new products; (2) a body of entrepreneurs ready to put inventions into production (this is important not only in order to realise the rewards from inventions, but even more importantly, to give inventive ideas the concrete embodiment needed to incorporate them into the existing technology and to communicate them to other inventors for use in further inventions); (3) a body of inventors, of tinkerers and experimenters, equipped with knowledge about some areas of existing technology and searching to acquire more knowledge and to use it in the solution of specific problems (one may note that it is in use that knowledge is most effectively acquired); (4) effective means of communication among inventors and diffusion of knowledge both about successes and about failure, so that the limits of the possible can be known to an inventor with his focus on a specific problem. Communication is of course by word of mouth, by written information, or by direct observation of embodied results. A 'critical mass' of

[3]N. Rosenberg, 'The Direction of Technological Change; Inducement Mechanisms and Focusing Devices', *Economic Development and Cultural Change*, Vol. XVIII (October 1969), Part I, 1–24.

inventive activity forms a locality among men who can talk to each other, but the relevant intercommunicating space is not truly a geographical concept, but a zone of cultural diffusion. Since technology is involved in such diffusion, the interaction between invention in transport and communication, and the extent of the area in which inventive activities can react on one another is an important feature in the cumulative character of the process. Finally, for a modern process to be initiated, it is necessary to have (5) a distribution of both entrepreneurs and inventors among the various types of categories of inventions discussed below, so that inventions which combine materials, power source, and energy transmission are not held up by a lag in technology of any one type.

As these five elements became increasingly present in the eighteenth and nineteenth centuries in western Europe, the continuing technological revolution began and with it begins the economic history of modern times.

II

Relation to science and controls on inventive sequences
Underlying what has just been said is an assumption that invention has occurred through a kind of random collision of ideas and materials, with inventors seeking solutions to problems. A discovery sequence occurring by trial and error may be pictured as the bombarding of nature with many missiles – a buckshot approach, as it is called. The rate at which useful discoveries can be made depends, then, on the number and construction of missiles fired at the target, and the sighting mechanism employed. What I have said to this point is that from the eighteenth century on, the number of missiles has increased, and the ammunition – the ideas and materials available to hurl at the target – has improved in power and variety. For much of the modern period, the sighting mechanism for invention has still been the inventor's mind, memory and observation, relatively unaided by theories about how the world is constituted or even by engineering formulae and measurements which quantify forces and qualities of substances and show the expected effects of changes in a technical process.

Now the seventeenth and eighteenth centuries in western European science are, as we well know, the period of perfection in the science of mechanics. Chemistry was in its infancy, electricity and atomic physics hardly thought of, and the life sciences were not much beyond the stage of magic. In the progress of natural science, a succession may be observed, from mechanics to the more complex and obscure sciences of matter and natural forces. Newtonian mechanics begins with the world as we observe it; it does not analyse the sub-

66

stances with which it deals, or seek to explain from their inner construction their physical properties or their influences on one another. Its greatest discoveries were made by observation, some simple experimental controls, simple instruments, and the invention of calculus. It states regularities in nature and provides powerful formulae for predicting them. But in its level of penetration into why levers, gears, falling objects, and planets behave as they do, it is at about the level of the science of biology before the discoveries in biochemistry. Following mechanics, nineteenth-century science developed the penetration of nature one step further in the essentials of a science of chemistry and electromagnetism, and has moved in recent decades into those atomic and genetic discoveries that have so disturbed our existence.

One may sympathise with – and even espouse – sociological theories of scientific activity. Science, it may be said, develops as it is used and needed; without the accompaniment of a vigorous technology and a vigorous economy, its speculations would have remained vapid, and its progress short. Despite a certain priestly role that it assumed in a secular but aristocratic culture in Europe, it was required ultimately – and certainly from the Victorian age onward – to prove its utility, to secure respectability and support. Nevertheless, it is very hard for me to understand a sociology of knowledge which would specify more closely economic or social controls on the actual course of science, once it acquired the status of a kind of sub-culture in the West. In particular, it is hard to see why the order of events in scientific development occurred as it did – going from the mechanical to the chemical and electrical to the sub-atomic and biochemical – because of economic necessity or social structure. Rather, I would suppose that an internal logic exists here in the way the human mind has attacked nature. The human senses and brain have a certain physical character and capability: turning to the general task of understanding external nature – whether for curiosity's sake or in order to use that nature – the course of its activity must be controlled, as an economist would say, largely from the supply side, i.e. from the existing constraints on what can be known rather than by what society needs to know.

Considerations of this sort lead us a certain way into questions of the history of science. They also lead a mere economic historian rapidly out of his depth. One must wait for historians of science to tidy up the bibliography of the world before Newton before we can expect much help. The important point in my present argument, however, should be apparent: a developing science furnished a powerful instrument – a sighting mechanism (to revert to my original analogy) – for a technology. We know that it is very hard to trace the links between science and technology, especially before the age of so-called organised science and the research laboratory. But surely it is no accident, as Marxists like to say, that the science of mechanics developed alongside the flourishing of mechanical invention. Both occurred when they did for similar natural reasons, lodged in human perceptions, but at least by the time of Smeaton's work on the water wheel, the one development aided the other. As mechanical invention entered the stage of engineering, it was most important for scientific principles and measurements to show just what could and could not be done, and so to guide the inventor's hand and fancy. The same is true *a fortiori* of the chemical and electrical inventions as they developed.

A cross-classification of inventions

To set up a framework for the modern history of technology, then, let me now classify inventions both by their mechanical function, and by the type of science to which they relate. There appears to exist in nature, observed and reflected on by men, a certain order of precedence in the unfolding of what we call 'her secrets'. Now the natural phenomena dealt with by science and technology appear to group themselves around three classes which we call 'mechanical', 'electrochemical', and 'biochemical'. And the problems of technology may be classified into four groups: those relating to (*a*) the transmission of power, (*b*) the release of power in usable form, (*c*) the alteration in the physical qualities of materials, and the recombination of substances, and (*d*) the control of life processes. We may call these two groupings, respectively, the scientific bases of invention and the technical function of invention. The combination of these classifications produces the following matrix.

CHART 1: CROSS-CLASSIFICATION OF INVENTIONS

Technical Function		Scientific Basis		
	Mechanical	Electrochemical		Biochemical
	(*a*)	(*b*)		(*c*)
		(b_1)	(b_2)	
Power transmission	1	x	x		
Power creation	2	x	x	x	
Materials	3			x	
Life processes	4			x	x

The boxes in the table may be identified with certain historical groupings of inventions: 1*a* for example, with the development of gears, moving and turning bars, belts; 1*b* with the transmission of electric power, radio-waves, and other forms of non-mechanical energy; $2a$ with the windmill, water-mills, and the steam engine, where mechanical 'power' is captured; $2b$ with the dynamo, the electric motor and (between b_1 and b_2) the release of atomic energy; $2b_2$ with fire power and the gasoline engine; $3b$ with smelting and refining operations, and the separation and recombination of chemical elements; and $4c$, of course, with the inventions involving genetics and plant and animal nutrition. The x's in the table show where invention of each scientific type has its greatest technical use.

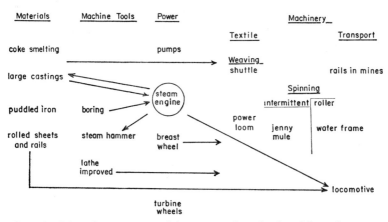

Chart 2: Selected sequences and interconnections in the eighteenth century (1710–1820).

Now for inventive activity to procede without impediment, enabling inventions must be made along one or more of the four lines represented by rows in the table. A sketch of the technical interconnections (Chart 2) among the inventions of the Industrial Revolution shows this to be the case. It is common knowledge – at least among economic historians – that the steam engine required improvements in castings and in the machining of cylinders. Indeed what we mean by 'a technology' is a set of interdependent inventions along different lines: characteristic raw and structural materials, fuels and power sources, characteristic ways of harnessing and transmitting power, characteristic tools and specific machines. So in the eighteenth century, chemical technology – at least of the cookbook kind used in iron smelting and working – and an agricultural technology able to borrow and develop the cotton plant were essential parts of the textile technology whose more prominent feature was mechanisation with applications of water and steam power.

The problem of quantifying the history of technology is still a very elusive one; certainly, a mere counting of patents or of inventions actually put out is not satisfactory. Nevertheless, the impression is surely justified that technology, like science, has shown a certain drift across our Chart 1 from 1750 onwards to today – from mechanical inventions to inventions of materials, on through to the electrical and biochemical inventions so prominent today. At every stage, inventions along each line and purpose have appeared. Enough materials inventions occurred in the nineteenth century, for example, to create vulcanised rubber, Bessemer steel, and various alloys. But the main thrust of invention moved in machinery, and then in the adaptations of electric power. And, if this is true, there can be little doubt that its cause lies in those logical and psychological controls on the movement of science itself.

III

Economic implications of the movement of inventions
All this may seem but a curiosity to one interested in the subject of the Conference: 'Economic Development in the Long Run'. So long as the stream of inventions pours forth, what difference does it make in what lines it concentrates its abundance from one time to another?

What I am conceiving of here is a whole body of technology which grows in its different parts at different times, as encouraged and controlled by the growth of science, and by those same relations between man's perceptions and brain on the one hand and nature on the other, by which scientific progress has been controlled. In such a development, one may conceive of leads and lags along certain lines, of bottlenecks, and breakthroughs. In the industrial inventions, materials, power source and transmission techniques are all required to complete a technology. Technologies have come into being because enough enabling inventions have occurred along all these lines to permit their development and application in a variety of uses.

The state of technology, then, may be said to set the basic level of cost or productivity around which an economy may operate. Around that level, and within certain physical limits, resource mobility may compensate for the failure of invention at certain points to adjust resource use to the structure of demand. But neither knowledge of techniques nor economic resources are perfectly mobile. The course of development of technology, therefore, has set a succession of problems for mankind, the adjustment to which constitutes the main path of modern economic history. These problems have been both technical and economic in character. The technical problem posed by the uneven development of science along various lines is apparent from the matrix. The development of a mechanical technology based on the steam engine and the water wheel rendered immensely profitable the invention of transmission mechanisms, and all this in turn made special demands on materials – both structural materials for machinery construction, and fuels, lubricants and raw materials for processing. These latter might have been filled by advances in chemicals technology or, as in fact occurred, by drawing on the world's supply of mineral and agricultural resources. The composition of demand for materials on international markets then was set by the structure and focus of inventive activity. The economic problem then derives from this. Given an exogenous movement of technology across the various operations and components of production, how could factors move – or grow at differential rates to make maximum use of the opportunities offered for the growth of output? This is, I believe, a wholly new way of looking at the problem of economic dynamics, and its thoroughgoing application in economic history may serve to clarify many of the puzzles facing economists in elaborating a theory of economic growth and fitting it to history.

To show more closely what I mean, let me apply to the matrix given above the usual sectoral categories used by development economists: manufactures, transport and communications, agriculture and mining. I omit the problem of the service industries, and ask: Into which boxes in the matrix do the techniques used in these industries largely fall? It is interesting to note that this division of technology, so familiar and natural to an economist, in fact compounds two standards of definition: definition according to natural process and operations involved, and one according to human use to which the output is put. Manufactures involve the shaping of materials to a variety of uses: transport and communication, the movement of materials or messages through space; agriculture; the provision of basic materials themselves. All three sectors require progress along the lines of invention that make up the boxes in the chart: but manufacture, mining and transport have depended more strongly on lines 1 and 2; communications on column b_1, and agriculture – though using power and chemical inventions is unique in its involvement with c_3 in our matrix.

Now the Industrial Revolution of the eighteenth century was, first of all, a mechanical revolution in the processes of manufacture; it did not expand the resource base of the industrial sector, but, by immensely raising the productivity of processes, especially in terms of labour and capital inputs, it expanded its demand for materials inputs to be furnished by conventional techniques. In particular, expanding demand for coal in western Europe – and by the mid-nineteenth century in the northeastern United States – was able to be filled from local sources, and this, together with the wastefulness of the industrial use of coal and the high labour productivity of the mechanical techniques, served to fix industrial location in the complexes at coal beds.[4] It is interesting to speculate on what might have happened in technology had oil been as readily available as coal in eighteenth-century England. Would the gasoline engine have developed a hundred years before it did? Some of its components – in particular an electrical firing mechanism – were not present in the technical environment and might have lain beyond the reach of invention.[5]

The shape of nineteenth-century development, its distribution among industries and over space, was set partly by the impact of the industrial technology on the patterns of resources in the world economy. But the reaches of that economy were themselves set partly by techniques of transport and communications and partly by techniques and modes of agricultural development. I wish now to turn to specific applications of the generalisations developed above to those two sections of technology and the economic activities derived from them.

IV

Communications techniques and the diffusion of inventions
Coal and water power served as the industrial fuels in the Industrial Revolution. Ordinary locational analysis shows that cost minimisation over a wide geographic area gave strong advantage to industries located at water-power or coal sites. The accident of coal location thus gave strong advantage for industrial location to those areas where in fact also inventive activity was taking place. Invention works with problems and resources local to the inventor. But, as we have seen earlier, the definition of local is not, for inventive ideas, strictly a geographical one. The zone of communication for inventors is set by communications technology, and resource-based locational patterns for industrial activity are also strongly conditioned by the techniques of transportation. These technologies are also those utilised for factor movement: communications for the diffusion of information about investment and settlement opportunities; transport for the movement of capital goods and of men.

[4]Will Bowden, Michael Karpovich, and Abbott Payson Usher, *An Economic History of Europe since 1750* (New York: American Book Company, 1937), Ch. I.

[5]On the early history of the gasoline engine, see Arthur F. Evans, *The History of the Oil Engine* (London: Sampson, Low, Marston & Co., Ltd, 1932), pp. 3–69; and Dugald Clerk, *The Gas, Petrol, and Oil Engine* (London: Longmans, Green, 1909), Vol. I, 1–50.

Now the sequences of nineteenth-century invention had a very peculiar impact on these techniques, and thus on the economic activities utilising them. Essentially, mechanical invention improved the techniques of transporting goods by land, i.e. particularly the bulky non-perishables that had always moved in long-distance trade. The railroad, set on top of a resource-using, labour-saving technology with a strong locational pull to concentrated coal-based locations, gave a means of collecting resource products from the interiors of the world's land masses and of redistributing a manufactured product.[6] Railroad and steamship were important helps, too, in the once-over migration of labour.

The effect of transport and communications techniques on capital movement and the diffusion of the knowledge and tastes of an industrial culture before World War I was less striking. To be sure, capital equipment could be shipped to remote destinations, and workers moved to migrate to use it. Business messages, too, could be sent by cable and telegraph after mid-century to join capital and commodity markets and permit some central control of far-flung operations. One might add to these techniques as instruments of control the development in the Western countries of a superior weaponry, thanks to mechanical invention.[7] Nor is it clear that

[6]The railroad and steamship also made possible the movement of coal from coal sites. Even by 1900 in the United States, the Pittsburgh location was overshadowed by the zone from Gary to Youngstown based on lake and rail transport from the Minnesota ores. Electric-power generation and transmission had the effect on coal-site local that the grave-diggers in Hamlet noted for alcohol: 'It makes 'em and it mars 'em, it puts 'em on and it takes 'em off.' It extended the local dominance of coal over light industry, while at the same time it permitted water-power sites, remote from Europe's industrial sectors, to dream of industry.

[7]The state may be defined as the agency with a sanctioned monopoly on violence. Then scale economies in the technology of violence should set an optimal size for the state. We know that the national states of western Europe and the principalities in central Europe in the sixteenth and seventeenth centuries maintained themselves by gunpowder and the massed use of foot soldiers. The difference in power between the king of Poland and the king of France rested, then, on the latter's superior access to finance, through an active bourgeoisie, just as the large firm's advantage rests today on its access to capital. In both cases, military technology set an optimal scale of plant, producing oligopolistic conflicts and further concentrations based on enterprise and financial resources. Sea-power in the nineteenth century appears to have shown similar advantages to scale. D. C. North has shown its interesting effects on the productivity of ocean shipping through the elimination of piracy – a policing action whose large externalities could only be captured by a world-wide empire. (See D. C. North, 'Sources of Productivity Change in Ocean Shipping, 1600–1850', *The Journal of Political Economy*, Vol. LXXVI (September–October 1968), 953–70, reprinted in Robert W. Fogel and Stanley L. Engerman (eds.), *The Reinterpretation of American Economic History* (New York: Harper and Row, 1971), pp. 163–74.

decisive obstacles existed to the movement of knowledge about production techniques. These, after all, are either transmitted by written documents or they are carried in the minds of migrating technicians. The component missing from the nineteenth-century techniques was the means of social communication, the ready transmission of the intimate aspects of a culture. But, as we have seen, inventive activity requires a strong surrounding culture – to socialise a class of investors, to provide access to immediate economic problems on which to focus invention, and to furnish a varied inventory of materials and ideas with which to solve them. Herein lay the cultural advantage of western Europe and the source of its technical dynamism.[8] It was an advantage which it could keep so long as it kept the inventors and scientists and the institutions and ways of thought which trained and motivated them. A resource base in coal for industrial technology, which specialised in mechanical, and eventually the electrical transmission of that coal or water-based power, a transport technology that made it cheap to bring in materials and food, and a communications technology that made for rapid economic connections, while still keeping a social distance – by these routes the movement of nineteenth-century technology and science shaped the contours of a world economy. By the same token, the shifts in the main direction of thrust of technology in the twentieth century has caused those spatial patterns to fade, if not to disappear.

Features of the agricultural development
Agriculture, and particularly agricultural technology, has a rather curious role in modern economic history. The complexity of its techniques has made this branch of activity the last to be affected by scientific technology. Before considering the implications of that fact in detail, however, let me get out of the way another matter which affects our consideration of agricultural history. Since agriculture's technology does not appear at first glance to have been as dynamic as that of industry or transportation, there is a temptation to connect the relatively slower rise of incomes in agricultural regions to this fact. This, of course, is a mistake. Even if the growth of agricultural productivity has lagged behind that of the other sectors, we know that its income growth need not have done so. These matters are all

---

[8]The direction given to experimentation in tropical agriculture by the location of the science and stations in England and France has been remarked by S. H. Hymer and R. H. Green, in 'Cocoa in the Gold Coast: A Study in the Relations between African Farmers and Agricultural Experts', *The Journal of Economic History*, Vol. XXVI (September 1966), 299–319.

arranged by that wonderful equilibrator: the terms of trade between industry and agriculture. If agricultural regions have been backward in some sense, if the impulses to further growth have not come from them, if they have been playing a passive, almost feminine, role in Western development, the reason must lie not in agricultural techniques themselves, but in the fact that agriculture continued to occupy space and that that space was only incompletely mastered by the technical developments in the arts of war and of social and commercial communication. Suppose, for example, that the path of technological change had been reversed. Suppose that the great revolution in the eighteenth century had been in the life sciences rather than in machinery, and that the second wave of revolution had been in communications techniques rather than in the transport techniques of railroad and steamship. Then a dynamic well-educated and progressive agricultural sector might have been the source from which technology spread, perhaps first to chemicals and finally to machinery. In that case land-saving inventions would have come first, and a thrust of technology might have developed which put less emphasis on saving human labour for frivolous occupations and more emphasis on conservation of the natural base of life on this planet.

Or, again, had the productivity gains emanating from industrial techniques been diffused quite perfectly through the price system, agricultural regions would not have been disadvantaged, whatever their technical progress. Indeed, given the undesirable externalities of industrial growth, the growth regions might have been looked upon as the exploited ones, bearing with all the discomforts and pollutions of modern industry and the dull routines which it imposes in order to produce a flood of products enjoyed by the happy peasant population of the rest of the earth.

Going now to a direct consideration of the evolution of agricultural technology, it must be first remarked that it does appear to have lagged. This lag is the result of two factors: (1) the great diversity and specificity of technical problems in agriculture, and (2) the difficulties in arriving at the underlying theories of genetics and life processes. The former of these meant that the application of trial and error in agriculture rarely produced dramatic breakthroughs as it did in manufacturing processes. Peasants are always trying and erring, and in the course of centuries they make small improvements in specific localities, adaptations to specific conditions of soil, terrain, and climate, which are carefully preserved in the traditions of the locality. This process of trial and error was applied in new regions wherever agricultural techniques were implanted. The difficulty of breaking through from it to an agricultural science was markedly greater than in the branches of manufacture or even in the common applications of chemistry to non-living materials. This is borne out by the fact that in agricultural technology, of all the various branches, a specific stage of statistical methods was introduced. The presence of many small causes influencing the outcome of an agricultural experiment, in the absence of any good underlying theory of why things occurred as they did, proved a great boon to the development of statistics. A rich field was offered for the calculations of the effects of chance, the development of probability limits, the application of regression analysis and analysis of variance. In agriculture, too, just preceding and overlapping the statistical stage in its technical development, was a marked age of quackery found elsewhere only in the history of that other life science – medicine. Where the conditions for finding the truth are extremely complex, and the drive to find out is exceedingly strong, the development of premature syntheses inadequately tested and put forward with too much assurance is a characteristic phenomenon.

However, we know that ultimately the science of genetics and plant and animal nutrition has been opened up. The effects have been so spectacular that a new question has been set for agrarian history: how did agricultural productivity manage to keep up at all before these recent spectacular breakthroughs? The answer is a mixed one. First it should be noted that mechanical invention helped the most, but still not very much. Wherever agricultural operations could share in the development of manufacturing techniques, that is, in Column 1, a and b in our matrix, improvement occurred. The positive nineteenth-century gains came in the reaper and the thresher, and finally in the tractor and the use of new and industrially produced materials, steel and industrial chemicals. But the lag in the development of the gasoline engine, following the eighteenth-century improvements in power sources, was a serious matter for agriculture, and one which appears to be conditioned by almost purely technological considerations. Steam ploughs did not work well, except for a while on some large English estates, and the heightened development of horse-drawn machinery contributed to the social separateness of agriculture and to the sense of self-containment. Secondly, the world-wide expansion of trade and settlement drew large new regions and large old regions of increasing population density into world trade. Western Europe could then concentrate on itself, like the sun's rays in a glass, an ever larger exchange with the agrarian surplus product of the other continents. And following this expansion of inter-continental trade, there occurred the specialisation according to a region's natural

76

advantage and the wider diffusion of known techniques and genetic materials among the continents. And finally, within Europe itself, that shift which we know as the agricultural revolution occurred in response to market growth, and spread from England across the Continent throughout the nineteenth and early twentieth centuries.

That productivity gains should have been notable from these sources leaves the implication that there was considerable slack in the agrarian economy of seventeenth- and early eighteenth-century Europe. Increases in the length of the working day, and diversion of peasants from rural to industrial occupations may both have contributed to keeping up agricultural output and adjusting it to new patterns of demand. The growth of demand for livestock products had complex effects through the provision of draft animals and fertiliser on the productivity of the agrarian sector. These various subtle sources of productivity growth permitted agriculture to supply food and materials and also labour to the growing industrial sector, even in advance of the striking scientific improvements of recent times. Finally, as we know, the social separateness of the agrarian and urban sectors of the nineteenth century must have kept the terms of trade turned against agriculture compared to what they would have been with easy mobility from the countryside. The not-so-subtle imperialism of the industrial areas was no doubt partly a sheerly political and military dominance over the world's peasant populations. But it was also an advantage permitted by communications techniques and the course of invention.

Summary

I have suggested in this paper that a course of technological change underlies much of the reasons why Western development has taken the path among industries and regions that history records. That course has depended on the relation of the human mind to nature in the activity of scientific discovery. Given the structure of the world, the structure of our perceptions, and the structure of our needs, the path of economic opportunity for output and productivity growth has made itself manifest. The problem for population growth and for saving has been to adjust factor supplies to the relationship between technology and resources on the one hand and demand on the other. It is these, I would insist, and not technology which are the adjustable and adjusting elements. A technological determinism can only make itself felt in a society where inventors as well as scientists are active, and where entrepreneurs, whether in business or state service, carry on a lively investment activity. There is nothing in science or technology to require that this should occur. That does depend indeed almost wholly on man and the personality development of masses of men in an evolving social structure. Into these questions, which perhaps are the important ones for economic development, technological determinism does not reach.

5

Russia as an Emergent Country

A. NOVE

University of Glasgow

I did not invent the title of this chapter: the organisers of the
Conference did. It is challenging, but opens boundless vistas. A book
on the economic history of Russia, reinforced by long commentaries
on various historical interpretations of Russian development, might
meet the bill – 700 pages, say. Time is a scarce commodity, however,
and the patience of conference participants and author alike wears
thin. So what I shall do is to discuss a few selected aspects of Russian
history which bear on the theme represented by the chapter title.

By age-old tradition, Russia was a country of potential anarchy
and relatively weak spontaneous social forces, and so the state had
to be strong and to some extent to act as a substitute for weak or non-
existent enterprise. The state and territory of Russia were exposed
to powerful enemies: Tartars in the south and east, Poland and other
culturally and economically more developed powers to the west. In
1571 the Crimean khan burnt Moscow and took away great numbers of people to sell as slaves. In that same period Ivan the Terrible
was raging a hard and generally unsuccessful war against the Poles.
Like many Russian rulers after him, he saw the underdevelopment of
his country primarily in military terms – scattered population, low
level of literacy and know-how, inability (despite the magnificent
'tsar cannon' still to be seen in the Kremlin) to produce adequate
supplies of what were then modern weapons. Ivan also saw the threat
to stability posed by the power of the landed nobility, and did much
to weaken it by the organised terror of the *Oprichnina*,[1] transferring
many of the lands of the nobles to his own servants. His centralising
and military policies increased the burdens on the peasants, who
sought to evade these burdens by migration into the open spaces to
the north and east.

[1]A special body of the tsar's servants, sustained by land confiscated from the
nobility.

People in such a situation cannot easily be 'exploited' by conventional economic means, a point noted recently by Samuelson: 'But actually this [exploitation] hypothesis is absurd in the context of Smith's early and rude state. What hold does the capitalist there have on the worker? . . . What that is useful can the employer withhold from the rude worker, who hunts where he pleases on superabundant acres . . . ?' What indeed except slavery, as Samuelson also notes, can enable a surplus to be exacted?[2] Substituting the state for the capitalist, there is here the rationale of state serfdom in a sparsely populated and vast land with an open frontier. So the strengthening of central autocratic power was accompanied by the gradual attachment of the peasants to the land, land mostly held by the tsar's servants on condition of service. It is hard to consider Ivan as a moderniser, in that he was superstitious, cruel, barbarous.[3] Yet Stalin was surely right to treat him as one of his great precursors. One sees in him some key elements of a repetitive theme: forced development by the state, the 'hypertrophy of the state' (to use a phrase of the philosopher Berdyaev), the great importance of military *raison d'état* as a motive for development, and finally the close association of the growth of state power with enserfment.

Ivan's autocratic rule was followed by a period of confusion and anarchy, establishing in the minds of people another element of their consciousness: the danger of anarchy; the need for a strong centralised autocracy to prevent chaos. This is still an important factor in the political culture of the country. Of course, order, as against disorder, facilitates economic development in all times and places, not least in developing countries of the twentieth century. Or the nineteenth, for that matter: the unification of Germany has evident developmental consequences, for instance, and Prussian and German governments took military questions very seriously indeed. There are, no doubt, parallels elsewhere for many features of Russian history. However, it is still arguable that the interlinkage between autocracy, the state as an agency of change, fear of anarchy, serfdom (or forced labour), and military-strategic questions, were peculiarly and even uniquely important in understanding Russia, from the sixteenth century to the twentieth century.

The seventeenth century saw the restoration of order under a new dynasty, the Romanovs, the further regularisation of serfdom, a

[2]P. A. Samuelson, 'Understanding the Marxian Notion of Exploitation', *Journal of Economic Literature* (June 1971), p. 406.

[3]He had about as many wives as Henry VIII, but, unlike Henry, he executed none of them, since he could obtain annulment by sending them to a nunnery. In this respect at least he was *less* barbarous than some of his contemporaries.

series of wars with Poland, expansion eastwards to the Pacific Ocean across sparsely-peopled Siberian wastes undertaken by relatively small groups of cossacks and adventurers. Some advanced statesmen were deeply concerned at the cultural and economic gap separating Russia from the rest of Europe, but it was not until Peter the Great's reign that a leap forward was attempted.

Russian industry was at this time based on scattered and mainly rural handicraftsmen, with few urban workshops, and no guilds. Merchants played a vital role in linking these mini-producers with the market. In his classic work on *The Russian Factory*, Tugan-Baranovsky emphasises the role of merchant capital, some of it very large-scale, in contrast with the small-scale, unorganised and poor producers. 'Our first capitalist class, the merchants, showed no propensity to take production of goods into its hands. Controlling the market, the merchant preferred to buy the goods made by the petty producer and keep the latter dependent upon him, without turning him into a hired labourer.'[4]

Some traditionally-minded Russian economists in the latter half of the nineteenth century 'blamed' Peter for not using the comparative advantage of small-scale handicraft industry, and forcing instead an 'unnatural' growth of factories. Tugan-Baranovsky rejects the category 'unnatural' (or 'artificial'), and points out, very properly, that the kind of products Peter needed could not be made by petty handicraftsmen: iron, guns, broadcloth, sailcloth, and the like. Nor could the small producers hire foreign experts or purchase instruments abroad. What the handicraftsmen could not do, and the richer merchants would not do of their own volition, was done by the state. Peter ordered the construction of manufactories. Some were built by the state, and then handed over to private entrepreneurs. In other cases the state subsidised would-be manufacturers, granted then interest-free loans, exempted them from taxes; but Tugan showed that much of the capital came from the rich merchants as well as from the state. The main customer was the state itself. The new entrepreneurs came, in the main, from the merchant class. Some of the factories were large indeed: examples cited include one employing 1,162 persons in making sailcloth. At this stage foreign entrepreneurs were relatively few, but of course imported specialists and know-how were of the highest importance. Peter also sent Russians to study abroad, and himself learnt about shipbuilding in Holland and England.

Peter's motives in speeding development were predominantly

[4]M. Tugan-Baranovsky: *Russkaya fabrika* (6th edn, 1934), p. 8. The first edition appeared in 1898.

military. Early Western commentators on Russia, such as Scherer (1788) and Herman (1822), in referring to Peter's policies, attributed them to 'Peter's need for a regular army, artillery, a fleet', and his unwillingness to be dependent on other countries for 'soldiers' uniforms, firearms, powder, ships . . .'.

These policies of technological westernisation might have been accompanied by some move towards social westernisation, in the sense of greater freedom of movement and the relaxation of serfdom. It is one of the paradoxes of Russian history that what actually occurred was the exact reverse: Peter's policies reinforced serfdom. True, the upper classes now wore 'German' clothes and learnt to speak French, but they were also mobilised to serve the state for life. This can be explained in several ways. Firstly, the strain of waging war, setting up factories, building ships, greatly added to tax burdens and also required the mobilisation of society, from the gentry to the common people, for the purposes of the state. Far from relaxing serfdom, it was necessary to strengthen it as a means of providing a supply of forced labour, and also to sustain the gentry in the service of the tsar. Secondly, the new factories themselves could only be manned by serfs, for there was no free labour force on which to draw. The population of whole villages was turned over for compulsory factory labour, along with rogues and vagabonds, and even 'public women'.

Tugan-Baronovsky contrasts this situation with west-European factory work, where skilled workers and old guild tradition provided a reservoir of relatively well-trained labour, and of course people could move more or less freely from the villages. Russia had serfdom, and a grave shortage of labour of any kind of skill, and so forced labour seemed inescapable. But only the *dvoryane* (gentry) were allowed to keep serfs, and few of the gentry were operating factories at this time. Hence a decree by Peter (January 1721) allowing merchants to own and purchase serfs, 'under the condition that these villages will always be attached to the factories'. So, quoting Tugan again, 'instead of capitalist industry which was then developing in the West, we had large-scale production based on forced labour'. By 1736, decrees issued by Peter's successors bound even the hitherto-free factory workers 'for ever' to their factories. Factory-owners were allowed to punish their workers, and those who proved difficult could be handed over to the state (the *Kommertskollegium*) for deportation to remote areas 'so as to cause fear in others'[5] (the words are in the decree).

Indeed it is a feature of early Russian economic thought, especially

[5]*Ibid.*, pp. 23, 24, 25.

that of the pioneer thinker I. Pososhkov (1670–1726), that they believed in the necessity of the whip rather than the carrot. Pososhkov advocated flogging as a cure for overcharging, for malfeasances by state officials, and for idleness by common people.

Much space is sometimes devoted to the existence or non-existence of feudalism in Russia. It all depends on definitions. There was in Peter's Russia a unique kind of universal service state, with lands and sometimes factories held on condition of service. As in feudal Europe, the obligation to serve gradually disappeared (in Russia 'the freedom of the gentry' was decreed in 1762). However, the differences are profound. The Russian hereditary aristocracy did not have regional power-centres, had no private armies of retainers, no fortifications. Peter merged them with the untitled serving-men in the civil and military service, and long after 1762 they still owed everything to the tsar: status, influence, rank. In this sense it was possible for the great poet (and excellent historian) Pushkin to assert in 1830 that the Russians had no hereditary aristocracy in the European sense. He deplored what he considered to be the resultant 'slavish obedience' to the monarch. So an important qualitative difference was the lack of countervailing forces, the more so as the towns remained poorly developed, with little corporate and guild life. (Novgorod, which had such life in association with the Hanseatic league, was almost destroyed by Ivan III and Ivan the Terrible). The autocracy, the state, had perforce to play the decisive role in economic development, and the specific interests of the state and its administrative machine deeply affected the policies adopted, in ways to be further discussed below.

Another feature of Russian life distinguished it from Europe (and still does so). This is the control exercised by the state over movement of people. It is extraordinary to read that, as early as 1734, a resident of a small provincial town was registered as a merchant and then 'his passport was endorsed for Moscow' where he worked in a factory, 'with his passport endorsed every year'. He then left his employment, and his factory-owner claimed that he was attached to his work 'for ever'. The case went to the Senate (which acted as a kind of administrative high court) for decision, on the issue of whether, as a registered merchant, he was exempted from the law binding factory labour to their factories. The point of interest here is the passport.[6] In the nineteenth century it was still common practice to deny even gentry the right to reside where they pleased, or to travel. Pushkin was reprimanded for travelling to the Caucasus without the permission of the chief of the gendarmes, and the latter ordered two

[6]Tugan-Baranovsky, *op. cit.*, p. 24.

gentlemen to leave Moscow because they made a noise during a theatrical performance.[7] The right to reside in cities is limited by police regulation to this day, and the citizens need to have their passports endorsed for change of residence. This affected, and still affects labour mobility. It can be an economic nuisance, but seems administratively convenient.

However, to return to the eighteenth century, in the second half of that century there was a most unusual politico-economic conflict, which can have no Western parallel. The gentry (*dvoryanstvo*) began to see advantages in setting up factories, and a challenge to themselves in the rise of rich factory- and serf-owning merchants. So they petitioned the monarch to stop merchants who had become manufacturers from buying serfs. They wished to confine factory-owners of the merchant class to the hiring of wage-labourers, partly to maintain the gentry's monopoly of serf-ownership, partly because the employment of their serfs as wage-earners might give them (the gentry) money via quit-rents, and firstly to give themselves an advantage as factory-owners using slave labour. For the same reason (quit-rents), the gentry wished to encourage handicrafts and also trading activities by their peasants, while the merchants complained bitterly of peasant competition, asking the state to forbid peasant enterprises which competed with the hereditary functions of the merchant estate. There was a very Russian tendency to appeal to the state, to the monarch, to determine such issues. There was also widespread resentment at the monopolist privileges granted to big factory owners, to some of the merchant class, and also to some foreigners. Many products made by unfree labour were of very poor quality, despite many decrees and orders defining what ought to be produced.

Catherine II came to the throne with the help of gentlemen guards officers (who murdered her emperor husband for her), and during her reign the interests of the gentry estate were furthered. Serfs lost such vestigial rights as they had held to appeal against their masters. The ideas of the physiocrats suited the landed interest, and so official statements (for example, the famous *Nakaz*, or legislative instructions) extolled agriculture and encouraged handicrafts. There is a reference in the *Nakaz* to the danger that machines (*makhiny*, in the antique Russian) would threaten employment. Their use was recognised, however, in exporting industries, where competition requires costs to be kept low.[8]

[7]Pushkin's historical and other notes (Vol. V of Russian 1887 edition).

[8]*Nakaz* (1768 edition). Two Russian graduates of the University of Glasgow, Desnitsky and Tretyakov, may have had some influence in the drafting of this document. They had attended Adam Smith's lectures.

Catherine stopped the merchant estate from acquiring serfs by purchase, but, interestingly enough, by a decree of 1763, allowed foreigners to do so if they set up factories in Russia.

The net effect of Catherine's measures was to increase not only handicraft production but also the number of factories, the latter being due largely to the lifting of restrictions which had protected the monopoly position of large establishments set up under Peter. A decree of 1775 authorised the setting up of industrial establishments by anyone. The supply of wage-labour increased, many of the labourers being serfs who left the village on paying their masters a quit-rent (*obrok*). Under Catherine there was a little more scope for free enterprise. Peter's system involved minute regulation of the factories, justified no doubt both by their monopoly privileges and by the fact that their products were made to the orders and requirements of the state. Indeed, the operation of a factory was regarded as a species of state service, under close supervision undertaken by various *kollegia* (ministries). Catherine eliminated some of these controls and controllers, though the state continued to be the principal customer of the large factories, and in her reign, too, there were many examples of obligations imposed on factories to deliver specified types of product (e.g. cloth) to the state, with a ban on sales to anyone but the state.

When Catherine died, her son Paul took steps against the privileges of the gentry, and authorised merchant factory-owners once again to buy serfs, though this was not done on a large scale, owing no doubt to the growing advantages of employing wage-earners. (Paul was assassinated in 1801, by a conspiracy of the gentry.)

Russia's mining and manufacturing in the first years of the nineteenth century was part slave and part free (the latter category including wage-earners of serf status paying quit-rent). The large factories primarily supplying the needs of the state were predominantly slave; the smaller-scale workshops supplying the needs of the market were mainly free. There were many intermediate situations in practice.

The growth of capitalist enterprise conflicted with serfdom, and a variety of expedients were devised to get round it. Tugan-Baranovsky cites the remarkable case of the textile town, Ivanovo-Voznesensk. Factories were set up there by serfs, who began as handicraftsmen and accumulated large profits, paying their 'owner', Count Sheremetev, a share of their earnings. Some of these serf capitalists bought serfs for themselves (theoretically they were the Count's serfs) and employed hundreds of other serfs and some free men as wage-earners. This was so profitable for the Count that he demanded a very high price when these now-rich capitalists wished to buy them-selves their freedom: 20,000 roubles was not untypical, and only a very rich man indeed could raise such a sum. Other capitalists were former artisans of non-serf status, as well as merchants and, less often, gentry.

By the 1820s there came to an end the purchase of serfs to work in so-called 'possessional factories', i.e. those operated with forced labour; but the existing forced labourers and their progeny were still bound to factory work. A series of decrees sought to regulate their status. They included provisions for limiting hours of work on a scale laid down, an obligation to provide work and also medical services; rates of pay and holidays were also determined. The fact that these were 'possessional' factories entitled the state to interfere also in determining what these factories should produce. They were not allowed to change their product mix without permission. The result of all this was greatly to diminish the advantages of forced labour, which was anyway unsuitable for work with machines. Factory-owners tried to evade their obligations. A decree adopted in 1840 gave the right to entrepreneurs to let their 'possessional' (i.e. serf) workers go, with compensation if they had paid for them, and to go over to production with free wage-earners. Many took advantage of this. An ex-serf-worker, now freed, had the choice of registering as a state peasant or as townsman (*meshchanin*). Some workers preferred to stay in their factories and there were cases of their having to be expelled from their homes there by force. Some had to be flogged to persuade them to go and be free men; they had a paid job and some sort of security and housing at the factory, and had nowhere else to go.

Was the use of slave labour profitable? Adam Smith's *Wealth of Nations* was translated into Russian on the orders of the Minister of Finance (typically this too was a state initiative!), and his ideas were used to strengthen the case for a free labour force. Despite this, serfdom survived unaffected in the villages. As for industry, in 1825, of the 210,568 workers in factories, 114,515 were wage-earners, the others virtually slaves. The slaves still predominated in industries supplying the state (primarily the army): thus, in manufacturing wool cloth for uniforms, the slaves outnumbered the free by five to one, in metallurgy by four to one.[9] By contrast the new and rapidly growing cotton industry was almost totally 'free'. It is the 'free' industries which grew in the period 1800–60, while metallurgy, notably, stagnated. Tugan-Baranovsky argues that this was due in large part to the fact that the state provided privileges and forced labour, and thereby removed any incentive to improve technique and

[9]Figures cited by Tugan-Baranovsky, *op. cit.*, p. 73, from an industrial census.

productivity. This is a stimulating paradoxical idea: the interest of the state in metallurgy was itself the cause of its failure to grow. One must add other reasons, especially remoteness and lack of communications, and cost reductions abroad. The lag in metals production set Russia very far behind the West, not least in the military sphere: the Russian navy in the Crimean War had neither steam nor ironclads, and could only be scuttled to prevent the Allies from sailing into Sebastopol harbour.

In this war, Russia had to sustain her army in the Crimea by bullock cart, which explains why sufficient forces could not be deployed. In 1854 the only railway of consequence completed was from St Petersburg to Moscow.

Why so little progress between 1815 and 1860? Russia seemed so strong at the end of the Napoleonic wars. Did the emperors not know that military strength required economic modernisation?

They were certainly told of this. Histories of economic thought ought to pay some attention to the Russian statesman and economist, Count S. N. Mordvinov, admirer of Adam Smith, who corresponded with Bentham. Years before Friedrich List he put forward ideas of national economic development, and (despite his admiration for Smith) he argued for protection to defend Russian industry against British competition.[10] He looked forward to Russian economic penetration of Asia. He urged the spread of education and saw that 'the brains and hands of slaves cannot bring riches to a nation', though he also saw the need for caution in liberating the serfs. One of his works, *Some considerations on Manufacturing in Russia and on Tariffs*, (Russian edition, 1815), was translated into French.

Then why so little progress? Two reasons suggest themselves. One is the survival of serfdom, a survival partly due to the reliance of the state on the land-owning gentry (which provided the civil service, army officers, local government, and which gathered the taxes), partly to fears of what might happen if serfs were set free – the belief that peasants were children who might wreak havoc unless told what to do. Serfdom stood in the way of labour mobility and removed incentives to efficiency, productivity, mechanisation. The other reason is the intense conservatism of Nicholas I (especially) and his ministers. They were real reactionaries, genuinely taking pride in preventing progress and change, considering these as undesirable in themselves. Kankrin, the tsar's Minister of Finance, knew about railways and thought that they were bad: they concentrated large numbers of potential rioters in one place, and helped people to move about in uncontrolled ways, as well as 'increasing

[10]He argued in vain: low tariffs were then the rule.

87

equality among social estates'. Industry itself was a potential source of trouble and commotion. The Western commercial spirit was alien to the tsarist bureaucracy, as it was alien also to the gradually-emerging radical opposition to autocracy. The landed gentry were interested in cheap imports from the West, and were hardly likely to be a pressure group in favour of industrial development. Nicholas I was no Peter the Great, and showed no will to enforce industrialisation upon his minister-bureaucrats. In any case, Russia's immediate neighbours (Prussia, Austria, Turkey) were not then in the throes of an industrial revolution. The dominant industrial power, Great Britain, was far away. There was also military over-confidence.

The shock of the Crimean War changed this situation. It is tempting to say simply that the abolition of serfdom in 1861, and the other reforms of that decade, showed that the government became committed to rapid industrial development, and that serfdom was abolished because it stood in the way. This is tempting – but over-simple (though the government did learn that railways *were* necessary). The liberation of the peasantry was accomplished in a manner not in the least conducive to industrialisation. The peasants remained in effect bound to the land, with a communal system of land tenure reinforced by a joint responsibility for taxes and redemption dues, with no right for the individual to sell his land and get out, and indeed with severe restriction on movement out of the village. The form in which the landowners were compensated (state bonds) did not help them to raise capital which might be invested in industry.

Why was such a policy followed? Because the stability of the state and its administration had top priority. The liberation of the serfs was a complex and risky undertaking. State revenues needed safeguarding. Fear of peasant revolt, itself a major cause of the liberation, led to much concern about minimising the social disruption of so major a change in human relations. The peasants felt dissatisfied by what they regarded as an inadequate share of the land. Their folk memories saw all land as theirs, with serfdom as part of a universal obligation of service to the tsar. But since for a hundred years the gentry had held no obligation to serve, were they still entitled to own any land? Rapid population growth caused increasing pressure on the peasants' land in the decades that followed. Many landlords found it difficult to readjust to the new situation, and financial difficulties were common. Thus the poet Nekrasov was right:

The great chain burst asunder, and one end hit the master,
the other – the peasant.

Alexander II must have felt he had little room for manoeuvre, that fiscal and police reasons stood in the way of assuring full mobility of labour and giving the right for the peasants to own and sell their land as private property; he may not have understood that such policies were desirable anyway.

Industrialisation was discussed, but opinion was very mixed. The followers of free trade doctrine, already strong earlier in the century, still reasoned against protectionism, urging that Russia's comparative advantage lay in agriculture. The internal market for industrial products was weak because the peasantry was poor. Some argued that to raise agricultural production was a precondition for a healthy development of Russian industry. Others pointed to the horrors of Western capitalism, and saw in the village commune the precursor of a Russian road to socialism. A relatively liberal tariff policy was followed until the end of the 1880s with little opposition from influential groups. The Russian industrial bourgeoisie was still a feeble and dependent infant.

The real industrialisation boom did not begin until 1890. It was preceded by state-supported railway-building, which greatly increased demand for rails and other equipment, at first imported from the West, and for mobile labour. There was also much naval and military investment. The imposition of heavy tariffs on imports in 1891, and the role of the railways both as consumer of industrial goods and linking together products and markets, was of key importance in the process. The government, especially the Ministry of Finance under Witte, became conscious at this period of the need to stimulate industry, not least on grounds of national defence. Witte's many writings and speeches show clearly that he was an economic nationalist, and indeed he was the author of a work on Friedrich List. The lack of entrepreneurial ability and of capital was recognised, as also was the need for a modern banking system. Witte, particularly, did his utmost to make Russia attractive for foreign investors. Witte, and also his predecessor Vyshnegradsky, must be seen as pursuing a vigorous and conscious policy of industrialisation, with a strong bias towards heavy industry. All this was doubtless facilitated, or made possible, by the abolition of serfdom. But Gerschenkron is surely right in stating that it did not stand high on the list of the conscious motives of those who carried out the liberation in 1861.[11]

By the 1890s Russia was launched on the road of capitalist

[11]See his contribution to the *Cambridge Economic History of Europe*, Vol. VI, Part II.

industrialisation. True, in the launching and in much of the navigation, the state had to play a major role. In the words of Portal,

'Spontaneous growth of national consumption . . . could not have provided its industrialists with customers enough, had it not been for the orders for military equipment and the works undertaken or guaranteed by the state. Railway construction stimulated the economy generally, not only by ending the isolation of a great many regions of the immense empire, but also by bringing about a sudden increase in metal production and coal mining, which until then had been negligible.'[12]

(At the end of the eighteenth century Russia had been one of the world's largest producers of iron, but by 1860 had fallen very far behind.)

The state had constant financial troubles, and its ability to finance development directly was limited; and Witte's tariff policy was designed to create profitable opportunities for domestic and foreign capital. This no doubt partly explains the gradual withdrawal of the state from *direct* involvement in industrialisation, in the sense of leaving actual management and entrepreneurship increasingly in capitalist hands.[13] Adam Smith and free trade may have been fashionable in 1820, but the needs of the state seemed plainly to require serfdom, forced labour in factories, and a close link between these factories and the state as consumer of the bulk of their products. It could easily be shown that the evils of serfdom, social and economic evils, were known not only to Mordvinov or to the Decembrist rebels, but also to both Alexander I and Nicholas I, but they did not feel able to dispense with it. The internal market was exceedingly small: the upper classes used mainly imported manufactures; and at first it was only the cotton industry which supplied goods primarily to the market rather than to the state, the other needs of ordinary people being met by handicraftsmen and artisans. By the end of the century 'national economics' had replaced belief in free trade, but direct activity by the state was declining relatively. Under shelter of protective duties, sometimes with state guarantees and credits, domestic and foreign-owned capitalist enterprises grew rapidly.

One institutional obstacle remained. The restrictions on peasant mobility were somewhat eased in the last years of the century, and

[12]R. Portal, 'The industrialization of Russia', *Cambridge Economic History of Europe*, Vol. VI, Part II.
[13]Though foreigners in Russia in the second half of the century complain repeatedly of petty regulations of various kinds.

migration to Siberia was even encouraged when the great Trans-Siberian railway was begun in 1893. But the communal forms of tenure remained, and were an obstacle to growth. Evidently the preservation of medieval-type strip-cultivation, with (in many areas) periodic redistribution of the land, was not conducive to land improvements and productivity. If the holdings could be consolidated, if the poorer peasants could sell out to their more efficient and ambitious neighbours, it would greatly stimulate the development of commercial agriculture among the peasants, lead to the emergence of a peasant bourgeoisie who would be conservative supporters of political stability, and speed up migration from villages to town. Witte favoured such measures, which were certainly a logical part of the spread of capitalism in Russia.

They were opposed by the conservatives, who still saw the peasantry as in need of special 'parental' supervision. They were opposed by Slavophils of radical hues, because the communal institutions were a Russian road to a Russian species of socialism. They were opposed even by the political party closest to representing the urban bourgeoisie, the Constitutional Democrats, when the proposals reached the stage of legislation, for reasons hard to fathom. Marxist socialists opposed them too, because of their total opposition to tsarism, and because political stability and a peasant bourgeoisie hardly suited their interests. So it was not until after the shock of another defeat, in the war against Japan (1904–5), and major land riots in villages (1905–6), that a shaken monarchy finally resolved to support the able prime minister, Stolypin, and to reform rural land tenure. At long last, in 1906–11, laws were passed making it possible for peasants to opt out of the commune, to sell their land, to consolidate their holdings. The process of change speeded up, to be interrupted all too soon by war and revolution.

So, within a relatively short time, Russia moved from an economy dominated by serfdom and the state to something which was visibly taking the capitalist road to development. Until almost the end of the nineteenth century the growth of Russia as a great power was closely associated with serfdom and slavery. The state mobilised scarce resources in a poor country to keep up with Europe, and so peasants were enserfed; the gentry were largely confined to the service of the state (after 1762 they could also vegetate on their estates if they chose); the first factories were run for the state if not by the state, by men who could hardly be called entrepreneurs without stretching the meaning of words. Russia entered the capitalist road with a political structure left over from the earlier autocratic-bureaucratic stage, with the masses' psychology still deeply affected by serfdom ('We are squeezing the slave out of ourselves drop by drop,' wrote Chekhov), and with a bourgeoisie lacking numbers, confidence, political influence, and a sense of independence *vis-à-vis* the state bureaucracy on which it was so long dependent. Perhaps somewhere here can be found some of the principal causes for the contrasts between Russian and Japanese patterns of modernisation. It is important to note how strong were the currents of opinion hostile to the logic of European capitalism: the intelligentsia of almost all hues was opposed to it from various socialist points of view; the gentry was divided; the bureaucracy was unimaginative and often highly conservative, as poor Witte found to his cost. The peasants still wanted the landlords' land, resented heavy taxation; many clung to the old communal forms and opposed the Stolypin reform, as may be seen by the speed with which they reversed it during the revolutionary chaos of 1917–18. The workers in factories were largely composed of uprooted ex-peasants, living in slum conditions and prone to angry riot and strike. It was an explosive mixture, which, under stress, duly exploded. It was not the absence of industrialisation, but the strain of industrialisation which, along with the war, brought down the Empire.

The 'Witte' period of industrialisation brought some interesting problems to the surface.

One of these was the role played in industrialisation by the peasant masses in a predominantly agricultural country. In the eyes of many economists it was the low purchasing power of the peasants which held back industrial growth, because the internal market was too small. But Witte's policy greatly increased Russia's import bill (first for railway equipment, then for many other capital goods), and foreign investors and bondholders had to be paid. The government's own expenditures required increased taxes. This policy required a large increase in sales of farm produce, and the burdens on the peasants were designed to force them to sell grain. In the words of Tugan-Baranovsky, exports were based on 'the *muzhik* not eating his fill'. So, paradoxically, deliberately-sponsored industrialisation actually tended to impoverish the peasants, and this contributed to political instability. No adequate statistics exist to show whether or how far their incomes actually fell, but it seems clear that official policy was not concerned with enlarging the market for industrial goods among the peasants; but was very concerned indeed with the balance of payments. Stalin in the 1930s also collected food for export while the peasants tightened their belts. It must be added that the reforms of 1906–11 gave a powerful impetus to agricultural productivity; a marked upward trend was

RUSSIA AS AN EMERGENT COUNTRY

interrupted by the war, with peasants buying not only more industrial consumers' goods but also farm equipment in rapidly increasing quantities.

The second feature of the period was a highly-marked contrast between the old and the new, between modern large-scale manufacture and antique workshops and handicrafts. Why was the modern sector so modern, so capital-intensive? There is a considerable literature on the subject of labour-intensive investments, and it is there frequently implied that the existence of abundant labour and scarce capital in developing countries proves the irrationality of labour-saving investment. If in a 'dual economy' such investments are made in the modern sector, this is often ascribed to unreasoning preference for having the latest equipment, or to protective labour legislation which artificially increases labour cost. Indeed, it is pointed out that within the modern sector itself many tasks (e.g. materials-handling) are carried out by medieval methods, and this too is taken to be evidence of irrationality.

It is therefore important to note that in Russia under Witte it was found advantageous to instal the latest machines, although this was not a consciously-pursued policy, and although labour legislation was rudimentary and wages were very low. The reasons have been pointed out not only by Gerschenkron but also Tugan-Baranovsky, Hexthausen and others: Russia had plenty of unskilled peasants, but reliable factory labour was scarce, inefficient, and, despite the poor wages, *expensive*. Even if it were technically feasible, it would not have paid to substitute labour for modern metallurgical equipment. But where there were opportunities for the 'Volga-boatmen' type of mass physical labour, these opportunities were often taken, even in the modern factories themselves. The irrationality is only apparent, and the appearance is due to wrongly treating labour as homogeneous.

The 'dual economy' in Russia, as elsewhere, must be seen as part of the process of change, since it is plainly impossible to alter methods, organisation, equipment, or human attitudes, within a very few years. By 1913 it could be argued that Russia was moving towards a European-type economy, though with still a long way to go. Despite the interruption due to depression and disorder in 1903–6, Russia's industrial growth rates in the period were impressive, 5 per cent per annum in 1888–1913 according to Raymond Goldsmith's computations. There is much controversy as to whether she was in fact catching up with the West. Such authors as Grinevetsky and Prokopovich, writing fifty and more years ago, argued that progress was insufficient and that Russia was not keeping pace with Germany, who was very far ahead and drawing away. Others have pointed out that growth rates on the scale of 1890-1913, if continued over thirty to forty years, would have brought Russia to a high level of industrial development (which is no doubt true, but assumes that the social-political breakdown and the First World War had not taken place). Still others point to the heavy Russian dependence on foreign capital, and the difficulty which would have been encountered in keeping up the flow. Let us not pursue these 'what-might-have-beens' of history. Let us simply assert that Russia was on the capitalist road, that this caused strain, that the tsarist régime was slow to adjust, that the opposition to the tsar was also, in the main, opposed to the capitalist road, and that industrial and social weaknesses led to disaster when the challenge of the war was faced. Despite Witte's industrialisation strategy, Russian industry could not sustain an army in modern war, and in fact was greatly dependent on Germany for machinery. The revolution was caused by, indeed itself was, a social breakdown. With no faith any longer in the divine attributes of tsardom, the masses had no faith either in the middle-class liberal and moderate-socialist alternative.

The breakdown having occurred, Lenin and the Bolsheviks succeeded, after a bitter civil war and much anarchy, in re-establishing order. They faced the problem of continuing the industrialisation of Russia, a problem complicated by the rural revolution, which destroyed not only the landlords but most of the consolidated 'Stolypin' peasant holdings also, thrusting the villages back into the era of medieval strip and communal tenure from which they had begun to emerge. Russia could not now depend on private enterprise, since the entrepreneurs were destroyed and driven out by revolution (the petty 'Nepmen' of the New Economic Policy period were very petty indeed, and played no part in large-scale modern industry). So once again, as in the distant days of Peter the Great, modernisation and factory-building was to be the responsibility of the state. No one else could do it.

'Peter the Great was the first Bolshevik', thus wrote a poet, Maximilian Voloshin, early in the 1920s. They were to be despotic modernisers. Addressing Lenin's successors, another poet, Sergei Yesenin, exclaimed, in 1924:

> Oh you, whose task it is to tame the wild waters
> of Russia between banks of concrete.

Stalin himself understood the parallel well, and insisted on Peter (as well as Ivan) being presented favourably in history books. Gerschenkron, too, has argued: 'The resemblance between Soviet and Petrine Russia was striking indeed.'

Is all this far-fetched? I do not think so. Stalin's collectivisation, with forcible deliveries at nominal prices, was the imposition of a kind of developmental serfdom. Those who went to town to work in the new industries could be said to be paying quit-rent (*obrok*) to the state in the form of turnover tax. Forced labour was widespread. The managers of state enterprises, producing largely to the orders and for the purposes of the state, bore some relationship to the factory managers of Peter's time, who also were ordered what to produce in a kind of primitive version of a planned economy. The universal service state was re-established under Lenin and Stalin, with the hierarchical Establishments structure run by the party (the *nomenklatura*) replacing Peter's 'table of ranks'.[14] Stalin of the 1930s was as concerned as was Peter with the military aspects of economic development. Stalin mobilised society to create the basis of a modern war industry, and so justified the high tempos he imposed. Terror was used by both to maintain order and discipline. The revolution had destroyed the classes capable of autonomous economic and social initiative; and collectivisation ended the peasants' control over land and produce. 'Lenin destroyed the factory-owners and merchants. But the nature of Russian history caused Lenin . . . to retain the curse of Russia: the association between its development and unfreedom, serfdom.' Thus wrote Vasili Grossman, Soviet novelist and publicist, in an unpublished and unpublishable analysis of the post-revolutionary era. Stalin was, from his standpoint, a logical follower of Lenin and of Peter. Just as Stalin's penal system had nothing in common with the comparative liberalism of the last tsars, and was a throwback to earlier and more barbarous ages, so the state resumed under him the task of modernisation which, under Witte and his successors, it was sharing with private enterprise. Foreign know-how and technicians were imported by Stalin, as by Peter, but in the form of imports by the state itself, rather than direct investments by foreigners.

There is much else that could be written on this subject of 'emergent' Russia. Bolshevik economic strategy could be analysed. So could the concept of primitive socialist accumulation. The fascinating arguments about development in the 1920s can be, and have been presented as pioneering the doctrines of development economics.[15] Centralised planning, its use in a period of rapid change, and its limitations in a modern industrial society, could also be dis-

[14]This thought is developed in A. Nove, 'History, Hierarchy and Nationalities' *Soviet Studies*, Vol. XXI, No. 1 (July 1969).
[15]See J. M. Collette, *Politique des investissements et calcul economique*, (Paris, 1964); and A. Erlich; *The Soviet Industrialisation Debate* (Harvard, 1961).

cussed. People have written books and articles about the relevance of the Soviet model to other countries. I have deliberately taken another and more 'historical' road – not because this is the only way to look at things, or necessarily the most useful, but because it is less frequently attempted.

Surely there are insights to be gained from observing the role of slavery in early Russian industrialisation, and the role of the state as organiser and customer of industrial production. It may well be that the problems faced by the development of capitalism in Russia were a function of this unhappy past association of industry, state and serfdom, in a way and on a scale unknown elsewhere in Europe, and very different from Japan also. Some sceptics may ask: what has all this to do with the behaviour of economic men in the twentieth century? Is this not an overstress on historical continuity, or national character? I do not think so. Culture and tradition affect what happens and how it happens. It does so through the behaviour pattern of the leaders, and also through what ordinary people consider right or are prepared or accustomed to accept. Who can doubt that Japan's present-day industrial performance is influenced in some important degree by Japan's social-historical traditions, altered though they have been by the passage of time? Or that it is easier for Soviet leaders to impose an internal passport system and police registration because control over free movement has existed in Russia for centuries?

Stalin has been dead for eighteen years; Russia's industrialization has made great progress; the mass terror is no more. Yet would-be reformers make little headway; political-cultural controls are as tight as ever, and the economy remains centralised. Political or economic pluralism remains unacceptable. Change towards market socialism is resisted for a number of reasons, practical as well as political-ideological. However, among the latter one should include as a factor the specifically Russian political climate and her traditional way of organising the economy and society for the pursuit of state purposes. So while life has become easier, and the use of such emotive terms as 'state serfdom' increasingly misleading, the heritage of historical experience remains a factor highly relevant to an understanding of contemporary Soviet economic and political reality.

Russia's past is in many ways more relevant than Marxism to an understanding of Soviet political and economic structure. This is certainly the case in the field of politics. The phraseology is Marxist, but the one-party state, the bureaucratic controls over movement and the printed word, and much else besides, owe nothing to Marx's ideas. Indeed, even Lenin put forward no theory of the one-party state either before or during 1917. The economy too is encompassed by the party-state system. It is surely the case that under any government capable of establishing and maintaining order Russia would have been a major 'emergent' country in the present century. Development plans as such were devised also by non-Bolsheviks: thus a far-reaching set of ideas on industrial growth was put forward by the talented Grinevetsky in 1917–18, and he was strongly opposed to Lenin. Lenin knew of his work, and used it, and that of other experts, in his own first ideas on the reconstruction and electrification of Russia: the so-called C.O.E.L.R.O. plan put forward in 1920. Grinevetsky also envisaged an active role for the state, but in his mind there would also be a market and capitalist entrepreneurs. The fact that it was the Bolsheviks who imposed order on anarchy made a difference to the pace and direction of industrial development, and the successive destruction of the landlords, bourgeoisie and a landowning peasantry obviously owed much to the Leninist ideology. However, once they were destroyed, the state organs alone could be agencies of economic growth, and the traditions of Russian statehood soon gave to Marxism a distinctly Russian translation. Naturally the state planned production and investment, for no one else could do so. This made politics of economics, or rather linked the two indivisibly together. Russian political culture thus became a vital factor in economic organisation, and this political culture certainly owes more to Peter the Great than to Karl Marx.

NOTE. The statistics quoted on p. 86 above on the proportion of free to slave labour in the factories are challenged by some scholars. For example, some quite different figures have been quoted by Strumilin and others. Apart from the statistical inadequacies there are complex conceptual problems. Thus some adscripted peasants spent only a part of the year at factories and the rest on the land, and some workers who were treated by their employers as free wage earners were in fact the servants of a distant master to whom they paid a quit rent.

6

Western Europe and Great Britain: 'Catching Up' in the First Half of the Nineteenth Century

F. CROUZET

University of Paris—Sorbonne

The aim of this volume is to avoid those hasty generalisations, from random examples, without much regard to time and place, which have been drawn too often from the historical experience of advanced nations and presented as lessons to be used by contemporary underdeveloped countries; instead it is to concentrate on concrete cases which can be analysed in some depth. This is why I suggested that I might deal with the experience of Continental Western Europe – France, Belgium, the Netherlands, Germany and Switzerland[1] – during the period from 1815 to about 1850. This leaves aside the disturbances of the war period prior to 1815 and stops at mid-century, when there is a definite turning-point in the economic development of the area. These countries were (along with the United States) the first 'followers' or 'late-comers' who tried, during this period, to emulate Britain and to introduce the new technology which she had invented. The sample is relatively limited, homogeneous and yet varied. The study of the problems facing these countries in their attempts to catch up with the leader of the Industrial Revolution may possibly throw some light upon the questions which beset us at the present day.

However, an important qualification must be made from the start: there are enormous differences between the relative situation of Western Europe after the Napoleonic wars *vis-à-vis* Britain, and that of today's underdeveloped countries *vis-à-vis* the industrially advanced nations – so that one might wonder if this study is really relevant to contemporary problems.

The range of current measures of *per capita* incomes in the present world shows differences of a factor of 10, 20 or more between

[1]For brevity's sake, these five countries will henceforth be generally referred to as 'Western Europe'.

98

the richest and the poorest nations.[2] But among European countries, income differences between the economic leaders and the backward economies were never so pronounced. Some writers have estimated that in the early nineteenth century, *per capita* income in France was half that of Britain, but this is an under-estimate and it is more likely that the French figure should be put around 20 per cent below the British one;[3] income *per capita* may have been higher in the Low Countries than in France, and it was certainly lower in Germany, but overall the gap between Britain and the Continent was undoubtedly narrower than the one presently existing between, say, the United States and Western Europe. Moreover, despite the snags inherent in such comparisons, it can be maintained that real income levels in Western Europe were markedly higher before 'modern economic growth' began than they are in many underdeveloped countries today.

In addition, the countries under consideration were, by 1815, in possession of a wide range of industries, the output of which was considerable. J. Marczewski has estimated (though not quite convincingly) that up to around 1820 the real value of industrial production was higher in France than in Britain[4] (but of course France had a larger population). Some Swiss writers assert that as early as the late eighteenth century, their country was more 'industrialised' than England – in the sense that a larger share of the labour force was employed in manufacturing activities. Belgium had also a relatively large industry, which had made some remarkable progress before 1815, to the point that some scholars maintain that the Industrial Revolution had started there in the late eighteenth-century. And if Germany was more backward, it was far from destitute of manufactures. Western Europe had thus a wide basis of 'proto-industrialisation'.

Thirdly, many of the preconditions of the Industrial Revolution,

[2]Depending upon the conversion by specific price weights or by currency exchange rates: S. Kuznets, *Modern Economic Growth: Rate, Structure and Spread* (New Haven, 1966), pp. 360–1, 374–86; also G. Ohlin, 'Remarks on the Relevance of Western Experience in Economic Growth to Former Colonial Areas', *Journal of World History*, Vol. IX, No. 1 (1965), pp. 31–2.

[3]According to a calculation by the U.S. Bureau of the Census (quoted in *The Economist*, 20 October 1966, p. 495), in 1870 the French real product per head was 80 per cent of the British, and the German 71 per cent. My own wild guess is that the relative difference between French and English incomes *per capita* did not change much between the late seventeenth century (when Gregory King put it at 20 per cent) and the 1950s. See also J. Marczewski, 'Le produit physique de l'économie française de 1789 à 1913 (Comparaison avec la Grande-Bretagne)', *Histoire quantitative de l'économie française*, Vol. IV (Paris, 1965), p. lxxix.

[4]*Op. cit.*, p. xlv.

which had been realised in eighteenth-century Britain, were also achieved (though less completely) in Western Europe by 1815; whereas it would be optimistic to assume they exist in most under-developed countries in 1971. Some of these existed thanks to the French Revolution and to its exportation to neighbouring countries, especially by Napoleon. A whole deadwood of time-honoured institutions (such as the guilds[5] or the manorial system), which had been hampering economic progress, had been wiped out; and a bourgeois, laissez-faire social and economic system, much more akin to the British than to that of the *Ancien Régime*, had been established – and was not much tampered with by the post-Waterloo 'Restorations'. Western Europe had also rather efficient and orderly systems of government, and the short revolutionary upheavals or the limited wars recurring here and there between 1815 and 1850 cannot be considered to have seriously hampered economic growth; while there was nothing like the heavy burden of military expenditure which many underdeveloped countries of today impose on themselves.

Western Europe had also some supplies of capital of indigenous origin and was well provided with human capital: a largely (and increasingly) literate population, an industrial labour force well trained in the skills of traditional crafts, some reservoirs of entrepreneurs and managers, as well as numerous communities of scientists, many of whom were up to the best British standards.

A last contrast with the present situation of underdeveloped countries lies in the field of population. Western Europe had no population explosion,[6] with its depressing effects on *per capita* income levels and on savings. During the period under consideration, the rates of natural increase of population never reached the levels common today in the Third World. Between 1800 and 1850, they range from 0·54 per cent per year in France to 0·79 per cent in the Netherlands; and for the five countries taken together the population increased from 58 to 81 million, a mean rate of growth of 0·66 per cent per year, as opposed to an average rate of 2·2 per cent per year for the present underdeveloped countries, some of which (in Latin America for instance) go up to 2·5 per cent, 2·8 per cent or even 3 per cent.

On the other hand, it would be wrong to draw too optimistic a picture of the Western Continental countries' situation in the post-Waterloo era; and Maurice Lévy-Leboyer has even stressed that

[5]However, the guilds survived in Germany until after 1850.
[6]Largely because death rates, though falling, remained at high levels.

their prospects of economic development were quite dark.[7] Though ahead of the rest of Europe – and of the world – in relation to Britain these countries were backward and underdeveloped; the lag behind this happy island, which had become obvious in the 1780s, had been seriously aggravated by the wars, blockades and internal upheavals of the Revolutionary and Napoleonic period. While the Technical Revolution was in full swing in England – not only in industry, but in agriculture and in transport – it had hardly started on the Continent, which retained an essentially eighteenth-century or *Ancien Régime* pattern of economic structures. Agriculture was archaic, with many regions living in isolation upon the produce of a quasi-subsistence economy; industry, except in a very few cases, was pursued on a handicraft and domestic-system basis; the transport networks and the banking systems were quite inadequate.

To be sure, during the Napoleonic era, the first rumblings of the Industrial Revolution had been heard, and some English innovations had been introduced in a few industries, especially cotton-spinning. Cotton mills had been set up in various parts of France and Germany, as well as in Belgium and Switzerland; and a small machine-building industry had emerged to supply them with machinery. But even these new 'advanced' industries were suffering from a considerable lag behind England. Continental cotton mills of 1815 were equipped with the type of plant that had prevailed in Britain in the 1780s or at best the 1790s, and they were driven by horse-gins or water-wheels, very rarely by steam-engines. This small 'modern' sector, which had grown in the hothouse atmosphere of the Continental Blockade, was therefore quite weak, and unable to withstand British competition; and in fact many concerns which had prospered under Napoleon were wiped out when British goods flooded the Continent after the Emperor's fall.[8]

The Continental countries were thus faced with a problem of backwardness, just like that of today's underdeveloped countries; but, unlike them, they had to *transform* existing industries, to 'modernise' them by the large-scale introduction of the new techniques which had been invented and perfected in England, and did not need to build up completely new industries from scratch.[9] This

[7]M. Lévy-Leboyer, *Les Banques européennes et l'industrialisation internationale dans la première moitié du XIXᵉ siècle* (Paris, 1964), pp. 27–32, 49 (quoted *infra*: M. Lévy-Leboyer).

[8]F. Crouzet, 'Wars, Blockade and Economic Change in Europe, 1792–1815', *The Journal of Economic History*, Vol. XXIV, No. 4 (December 1964), pp. 567–88.

[9]This problem was akin to the one which they faced after World War II, in relation with the United States – with Britain by their side this time.

may seem in some ways an easier task,[10] inasmuch as the Continentals, once peace and normal relations with Britain had been reestablished in 1815, were theoretically able to take advantage of the experience accumulated by the British during the preceding decades, to tap their reservoir of technical expertise, and to borrow straight away the best British practice. And there were powerful commercial and official influences, both in Britain and on the Continent, to encourage the diffusion of the new technology.

However, in many other respects, the process of modernisation ran into some serious obstacles. Those which were 'internal', i.e. related to conditions within the Continental countries themselves, will be discussed later; but we must mention from the outset the 'external' barrier which resulted from Britain's lead, and from the position of strength – and a constantly growing strength – which she had secured *vis-à-vis* the Continent.

Britain had superabundant supplies of cheap coal and of capital; she had a large and skilful labour-force, which moreover was already partly trained to factory work; her equipment and plant were much larger in quantity, better in quality and constantly improved by cumulating innovations; her industrial districts were provided with a full panoply of ancillary services; thanks to high productivity techniques, her costs of production were markedly lower; and she was in a position to take advantage, almost alone, of the increase in demand which was to be expected.[11] Not only could England exclude the Continentals from third markets,[12] she threatened also to invade their own home markets, and one could well wonder in 1815 if Continental industries had much chance of survival in the face of British competition. Moreover, the threat of the overwhelming economic power of Britain, which was hovering over Continental industries, was by itself a brake upon modernisation, as it created among manufacturers an inferiority complex which crippled their initiative. Of course the British challenge could be also a stimulus, an incentive to modernise, to improve produc-

[10]As a matter of fact, in France, traditional industries – especially wool and linen – grew at a snail's pace, and this was a major factor in the relatively slow growth of aggregate industrial output; while 'new' industries, like mining, iron, engineering, chemicals and cotton progressed much more rapidly. See F. Crouzet, 'Essai de construction d'un indice annuel de la production industrielle française au XIXe siècle', *Annales E.S.C.*, XXV, No. 1 (January-February 1970), p. 85 [English translation in R. Cameron (ed.), *Essays in French Economic History* (Homewood, Ill., 1970), pp. 245–78]. In Belgium and Germany, there was an absolute decline of the linen industry.

[11]M. Lévy-Leboyer, *op. cit.*, pp. 32 ff.

[12]This point will be developed below, p. 5–6.

tivity in order to lower costs, but, during the early post-Waterloo period, the balance between its stimulating and discouraging effects was still not settled.

There was of course a simple parry to the British threat: protectionism – to which, for instance, France reverted after the short-lived attempt at a liberal customs system under the First Restoration. The policy of protection has been strongly criticised, both by contemporary and by recent writers, who have seen it as one major factor making for slowness in the modernisation and growth of the French economy. It is more reasonable, however, to recognise that protection was absolutely necessary to the survival of most Continental industries.[13] The French mistake was to carry it to extreme lengths – to downright prohibition of most foreign manufactured goods. But even this 'Second Continental Blockade' did not allow archaic industries to lead a quiet life, owing to smuggling, to the long-term fall in industrial prices, and to a sharpening inter-regional competition. On the other hand, Switzerland is an interesting example of industrial progress under free trade conditions, but at the price of successive and sometimes painful adaptations and of extremely low wages for labour. Belgian industry undoubtedly suffered from the low customs duties it had to labour under during the Dutch period, up to 1830. And in the 1830s and early 1840s, the German market was flooded with imported pig and bar iron (as customs duties on these products were low), and this competition was so disastrous for German ironmasters that they were unable to modernise; they started to do so only after the duties had been raised in 1844. This is proof that a free trade policy was no sure receipt for modernisation. One must add that up to the 1840s, Britain retained a system of protection and prohibition, which would in any case have prevented the Continent from specialising in primary production, or in the few industries – such as the silk industry – in which Continental countries were able to compete on favourable terms with English manufacturers. However, protection was no complete solution, and could even make things worse as far as foreign markets were concerned; and such markets, especially in overseas countries, were those where demand was to rise the most spectacularly after 1815. To give them up to the British was to accept a slow growth, based on home markets only.

[13]P. Bairoch, *Révolution industrielle et sous-développement* (Paris, 1963), pp. 126 ff., 205–6, stresses that the 'isolation' of the national market allowed forward and backward linkages to play their full part, and stimulated induced growth. Protection, by high tariffs and by high transport costs, would have greatly helped the diffusion of the new technology.

Modernisation was thus an inescapable necessity for Western Europe; she had to 'catch up' with Britain,[14] and I shall now consider how this challenge had been taken up by the mid-nineteenth century. I shall say at once that the Continent's drive towards modernisation and growth had been partly successful – with an equal stress on those two words.

Western Europe had built up a 'modern' industrial sector, which used machinery and processes borrowed from England. The mechanisation of Western Europe's textile industries and the renovation of her metallurgical industries had made some remarkable progress: she had coke-burning blast-furnaces, puddling furnaces, rolling mills, textile mills equipped with spinning machinery and power looms; she had an engineering industry, which made a wide range of machinery, including railway engines and steamships. She had extended and improved her roads and internal navigation, and had started to build a railway network. Banking facilities had been improved and some forerunners of the post-1850 Banking Revolution were already to be seen. There were a number of industrial districts with complex and diversified activities, which could be compared, on a smaller scale, with Lancashire or the Black Country.

Such qualitative changes had been accompanied by a relatively high rate of economic and especially of industrial growth – at least according to nineteenth-century standards (P. Bairoch, some years ago, pointed out that the long-term growth rates of Western economies in the nineteenth century never exceeded 2 per cent per year for aggregate national product, and 1·3 per cent for real incomes *per capita*).[15] Unfortunately, we are rather short of good quantitative data. For France, to be sure, three indices of industrial production are now available, but they display growth rates which are markedly different. For Belgium, a major quantitative research is in progress under Pierre Lebrun,[16] but its starting point is in the 1840s. And we are quite destitute for Germany and still more for Switzerland, except for some isolated figures. However, we do not need at the

[14]But rather to prevent the decay of her existing industries and the flooding of her home markets by cheap British goods, and to regain a foothold on third markets, while today's underdeveloped countries have first of all to raise their people out of the abject poverty in which they lie.

[15]P. Bairoch, 'Le mythe de la croissance économique rapide au 19e siècle', *Revue de l'Institut de Sociologie* (1962), No. 2, pp. 307 ff.

[16]P. Lebrun, 'L'industrialisation en Belgique au XIXe siècle. Première approche et premiers résultats', paper presented at the International Conference on *L'industrialisation en Europe au XIXe Siècle. Cartographie et Typologie*, held at Lyon, 7–10 October 1970, under the auspices of the C.N.R.S. (the proceedings will be published in 1972).

moment more than very rough estimates, and in this respect all the evidence suggests that the rates of growth of industrial production, and very likely also of national product, were lower in Continental countries than in Britain, at least in the aggregate. (On a *per capita* basis, the picture would be different, owing to the much faster increase of the population of Britain – at a rate of 1·34 per cent per year from 1801 to 1851.)

Some years ago, M. Lévy-Leboyer computed an index of French industrial production, which grew between 1815 and 1850 at practically the same yearly rate as Hoffmann's index of British industrial output (3·25 per cent as against 3·5 per cent).[17] But this optimistic view is not supported by other writers' calculations. For instance, a careful comparison by Jean Marczewski gives the following growth rates per year.[18]

		FRANCE	GREAT BRITAIN
		1815–24 to 1845–54	1811–21 to 1841–51
Agricultural product,	aggregate	1·2%	1·5%
Agricultural product,	*per capita*	0·7%	0·2%
Industrial product,	aggregate	2·5%	3·7%
Industrial product,	*per capita*	2·0%	2·3%
Material product,	aggregate	1·9%	2·7%
Material product,	*per capita*	1·4%	1·3%

I have also built up an index of French industrial production, which shows a still lower rate of growth: 1·6 per cent per year between 1815 and 1850; but for various reasons, this figure may be too low, and moreover, this index grows at a faster rate during the later part of the period under consideration: 2 per cent for 1830–50, 2·3 per cent for 1830–60. Undoubtedly, French industrial growth and change accelerated in the 1830s and the early 1840s to reach a peak, after the depression of the late 1840s, during the 1850s, and therefore the gap with the British growth rate narrowed (a fact which appears also from Marczewski's calculations).[19] This acceleration (which

[17]M. Lévy-Leboyer, *op. cit.*, p. 410; see also his 'Les processus d'industrialisa - tion: le cas de l'Angleterre et de la France', *Revue Historique*, Vol. CCXXXIX, No. 2 (April-June 1968), pp. 282, 284, 297; 'La croissance économique en France au XIXe siècle. Résultats préliminaires', *Annales E.S.C.*, Vol. XXIV, No. 4 (July-August 1968), p. 793, with a different index and a growth rate of 2·98 per cent for French industrial output, 1815–45.

[18]J. Marczewski, *op. cit.*, pp. cxxxvi, cxxxviii. Products are computed at constant prices, from Deane and Cole's figures for Britain, and from Markovitch's for France; adjustments were made to take into account differences in price levels.

[19]F. Crouzet, 'Essai de construction. . . .', *op. cit.*, pp. 85-8, 96.

would be still more pronounced in the case of Germany (whose industries had been seriously depressed in the early part of the period, but progressed sharply later), heralded the unprecedentedly rapid growth of the post-1850 years – what David Landes has called 'Continental industry's coming of age'.[20]

The idea of a slower rate of growth in France than in Britain is supported by the available data for some key industries – an approach which can also be used for the other Continental countries, for which aggregate indices are lacking. For instance, raw cotton consumption increased between 1815–17 and 1849–51 at a mean rate of growth of 5·6 per cent per year in the United Kingdom, and 4·4 per cent in France. For Belgium, Germany and Switzerland, taken together, the available statistics plus a number of rough guesses would seem to show a rate of growth in cotton-inputs of 6·2 per cent during the same period; but for the total consumption of the four Continental countries, the rate of growth would be 5 per cent only.[21]

As for the output of pig-iron, between 1815 and 1847 it seems to have increased at a mean rate of 6 per cent per year in Britain and of 5·4 per cent in France. If one adds Belgium and Germany to France, and if one takes the years 1830–47, the rate would be 4·75 per cent as against over 6 per cent for Britain.[22]

It seems therefore that the industrial production of Continental Western Europe grew more slowly than that of Britain between Waterloo and the mid-nineteenth century; there is of course a strong possibility that Belgium[23] and Switzerland achieved higher

[20]D. S. Landes, *The Unbound Prometheus: Technological Change and Industrial Development in Western Europe from 1750 to the Present* (Cambridge, 1969), p. 193. One can note that the deep crisis of the late 1840s hastened change by devastating archaic rural/domestic industries.

[21]Calculations from *Ibid*, p. 165, completed by various figures, estimates and guesses, for which I ask the reader to take my word, as full references would be too lengthy. For Switzerland, I have calculated cotton consumption from the spindleage, and its relation to French spinning capacity. An acceleration in the growth of the cotton industry in Belgium, Germany and Switzerland in the 1830s and 1840s seems certain. Their cotton consumption would have grown from about 5,000 m.t. around 1815 to 42,000 in 1849–50; with France included, the figures would be 19,000 and 100,000 m.t.

[22]In addition, raw wool consumption seems to have increased in Britain and in France at the same rate from 1815 to 1850 (and it was of the same order of magnitude in both countries); the coal output of Belgium, France and Germany progressed *pari passu* with England from 1830 to 1850 (and possibly faster before 1830).

[23]According to P. Lebrun (see footnote 16), industrial production in Belgium grew at a mean rate of 4·1 per cent per year from 1847 to 1872; but I would hesitate to extrapolate this figure for the earlier period, owing to the sharp fluctuations in Belgian manufacturing activity.

growth rates than France, and perhaps also Germany at the end of the period (but on the other hand, the Netherlands obviously failed to industrialise); and average product *per capita* would seem to have grown at about the British rate, if not faster. But, even on the most favourable interpretation, Western Europe as a whole had, by 1850, failed to catch up with Great Britain, from the quantitative point of view; and as a result, in absolute terms, the gap between England and the Continental countries had enormously widened since 1815 and was now formidable, especially in the 'modern' sectors such as coal, iron, engineering, cotton. Britain was responsible for over half of the world iron output, and in 1850 made 2,249,000 metric tons of pig-iron, against 763,000 for Belgium, France and Germany (in this last country, pig-iron output *per capita* was 6 per cent only of the British figure). Britain's steam-power capacity was 1,290,000 H.P., against 700,000 for the three Continental countries.[24] Her cotton-spinning industry had 21 million spindles, and Western Europe had a little over 6 million. With a much smaller territory, her railway mileage was equal to that of the five Continental countries taken together. The scale of the British economy, and especially of its industry, had become unrivalled; British predominance seemed overwhelming (and it was still more so in international trade and shipping). As Peter Mathias puts it, there was an impressive list of collective criteria of the process of industrialisation by which Britain could claim by 1850 to be 'unique by being first';[25] she had become 'the first industrial nation', and no Continental country, not even Belgium, was approaching that stage.

From the qualitative, technological point of view, things might look somewhat better for the Continent, owing to the widespread introduction of British technology, but this must not conceal serious persistent lags and backwardness. Very few of the Continent's most progressive concerns were up to the best British practice. Machinery was generally less advanced (for instance, in cotton-spinning, the self-actor, invented in 1825, had come into general use in Britain after 1830; it was introduced in France in 1836, but did not become common until after 1847; in Germany it appeared in the 1840s only, while some hand-spinning survived for wool and flax); steam-power was far less used than in England; the size of firms and of plant was smaller, the large-scale, power-driven factory being still the exception; the productivity of labour was lower, costs higher;

[24]D. S. Landes, *op. cit.*, p. 194.
[25]P. Mathias, 'The Industrial Revolution in Britain – Unique or not?', paper delivered at the Lyon conference (see footnote 16).

industry was also more scattered and often retained rural locations. Moreover, many sectors remained deeply archaic, both in their techniques and in their modes of production. Power-loom weaving in factories was not common in France, and was very rare in Germany and Switzerland; in 1847, whereas the British cotton industry had 250,000 power-looms, the Continental countries had about 45,000,[26] and a few thousands more in their other textile industries. In the iron industry, France made just under half of her pig-iron by coke-smelting, and Germany 11 per cent only; Belgium alone had almost entirely changed to the new process.

Although Western Europe had clearly entered the stage of the Industrial Revolution, this had been belated and was still incomplete by 1850; large lumps of the economic *Ancien Régime* survived. The period 1815–50 is a *Gründerzeit*: a number of industrial centres and of industrial firms of great promise had been established; industrialisation had crossed a first threshold, but nowhere had it attained the massive character it had in Britain, and in the aggregate change remained modest; it was only after 1850 that the great structural mutation took place. Even if a number of new industries *de pointe* grew fast, at rates of 4 or 5 per cent per year, they remained heavily outnumbered within economies which in their bulk were still traditional. As a matter of fact, the development in Western Europe of a 'modern' sector had given to its economy, by the mid-nineteenth century, a dualistic character, which Britain had never known, and which is often considered as characteristic of today's underdeveloped countries. This was especially clear from a geographical point of view: a few regions – in the van were Alsace and the Sambre-et-Meuse axis in Belgium – had achieved remarkable breakthroughs, but each country had to bear the burden of large backward and stagnating areas: Western and Southern France, the eastern provinces of Germany, the Alpine uplands in Switzerland, overpopulated Flanders with its decaying linen industry. These inter-regional differences in productivity and skills – in a word in 'modernity' – were in fact much more pronounced than those between nations 'in the aggregate', which generally are the only ones to be discussed. And the elimination of this dualism was to take a long time; in France one can wonder if it has yet been completely achieved – not to speak of Italy and Spain, if we look for once outside our chosen area.

Moreover, during the 1850–1914 period, Germany was to be the

[26]There were 31,000 in France, under 8,000 in the Zollverein, 4,000 in Belgium, 3,000 (or less) in Switzerland. One can estimate the total number of power-looms (for all textiles) in 1850 as 300,000 in Britain and 60,000 in Western Europe.

only Continental country to 'catch up' with Britain, from the double point of view of the volume of industrial production and of technology, although not for incomes *per capita* (or foreign trade and investment). And this resulted not only from a fast growth on the German side after the mid-nineteenth century, but also from a slowing down on the British side from the 1870s (or even possibly the 1850s) onwards. Likewise, if several Continental countries have now achieved levels of income *per capita* which are somewhat higher than the British, this is due not only to their own exertions, but also to the disappointing rates of growth of Britain during the last twenty years.

These observations (implying that a long stretch of time is necessary to lay the basis for a vigorous industrialisation) might lead to some pessimistic conclusions as to the prospects for today's underdeveloped countries – especially if we keep in mind that a reasonably satisfactory constellation of preconditions had been achieved in Western Europe by 1815, and that the gap with Britain in the matter of incomes *per capita* was quite narrow. It would seem that backward countries have little chance of catching up with the leaders, and even of narrowing the gap, unless economic and technological progress in the advanced countries slows down markedly. On the other hand, one might stress more optimistically Lévy-Leboyer's view that, around 1815, the modernisation of the Western European economy appeared to face obstacles and handicaps which could be thought insuperable, and that they were nonetheless partly overcome; the de-industrialisation which could be feared had not in fact taken place, lags had stimulated progress, and a number of positive results had been achieved.[27]

However, we must now try to explain why Western Europe was not more successful in the competition with Britain during the first half of the nineteenth century, why its rate of economic growth was not higher, and why, in the field of technology, it did not adopt on a large scale the best possible practice, but rather stopped regularly at yesterday's machinery and processes.

To start with this last point, one might think that the introduction of the 'modern' British technology was, by itself, a difficult process. For instance, David Landes has stressed that the technical gap between Britain and the Continent had not only widened during the Revolutionary and Napoleonic period, but was more difficult to fill up by 1815 than in the 1780s. He points out that the 'modern'

[27]M. Lévy-Leboyer, *op. cit.*, pp. 326, 409–14.

type of plant, which was in use in Britain at the time of Waterloo, was much more expensive and complex than it had been thirty years earlier, and that the size of the smallest effective unit of production had greatly increased. The introduction of such plant therefore required more capital and more specialised skills, to build it, operate and maintain it; as such resources were not readily available, manufacturers might have been condemned to a sort of 'voluntary obsolescence', always installing equipment which was less productive than what was theoretically available to them.[28]

For his part, Mathias has suggested that the problems of diffusing innovations already extant and publicised may prove as formidable as those of initiating crucial inventions. The successful utilisation of the British innovations depended upon highly specialised artisan skills, which were essentially 'learning by doing' skills. These were relatively abundant in Britain, because of a peculiarly favourable context of resources and of a long-developing tradition, but their exportation abroad was difficult and slow, for the means of institutionalising them were undeveloped compared with the means of diffusing formal knowledge.[29]

This was certainly true in the eighteenth century, but, during the period under consideration, my own feeling is that the introduction and utilisation of any given machinery or process was never a serious problem, and that they could be successfully operated after relatively short teething-troubles, which might be due, in the iron industry, for instance, to differences in the quality and chemical composition of the raw materials. After all, the complexity of early-nineteenth-century machinery must not be overestimated, and the skills of traditional craftsmen could be adapted to build or repair it.[30] And the abundant references, in British sources, to the awkwardness and incompetence of the Continental workers who were put in charge of the new plants – 'They are all of a lazy turn,' said an English carder returned from France in 1824[31] – are possibly not to be taken literally.

As for the British efforts at prohibiting the export of many types of machinery (especially textile machinery, as well as models and drawings) or the emigration of skilled workers, and at preventing industrial espionage, Dr W. O. Henderson and several other writers

---

[28]D. S. Landes, *op. cit.*, pp. 145–7.
[29]P. Mathias, *op. cit.*
[30]P. Bairoch, *Révolution industrielle* . . . , *op. cit.*, p. 206.
[31]Giving evidence before the Select Committee on Artizans and Machinery; quoted from S. Pollard and C. Holmes, *Documents of European Economic History*, Vol. I: *The Process of Industrialization 1750–1870* (London, 1968), p. 288.

have demonstrated that these were largely ineffective.[32] Hosts of Continental manufacturers, engineers and civil servants came to Britain after 1815 and toured her industrial districts to study the new techniques; a number of British businessmen settled on the Continent and founded there 'modern' undertakings; thousands of skilled workers, foremen and managers migrated also. Although they were not always the best England could provide, though they drank too much, demanded high wages, changed jobs too often and were unpopular with the locals, they played a decisive role in teaching to Continental workers those very techniques, like puddling, which could be learned only 'by doing'; while the British industrialists were specially useful in introducing and developing the most sophisticated of the 'new' industries – machine-building.

However, one can still wonder if the British laws against the export of machinery, which were in force up to 1842, did not hinder technological progress on the Continent: a foreign manufacturer, who wanted to set up, say, a new cotton mill, could not order straight away from Manchester a complete set of the most up-to-date machinery; he had to get hold, by hook or by crook, of some models, blueprints or spare parts, then have them smuggled out of England, and eventually have them copied by his own workmen or by some local engineering firm. Time-lags in the introduction of best practice were thus inevitable. On the other hand, P. Bairoch has maintained that the British bans on machinery exports, plus the tariff protection and the high transport costs which reinforced their effects, had beneficial long-term effects for the Continental countries, which were thus forced to create an engineering industry of their own, while today underdeveloped countries can take the easy path of buying abroad all the machinery they need.[33]

As a matter of fact, Western Europe was able fairly quickly to achieve a sort of technological independence, to build most of the machinery it needed, and to dispense with the help of the British migrants. New generations of engineers, technicians and skilled workers were soon trained, and in the 1830s and 1840s Belgium and France were able in their turn to supply to more backward countries – especially Germany to start with – the skilled cadres they needed. As for the engineering industry, it made undoubted progress; it was said in 1824 that British-made textile machinery was 40 per cent cheaper than French, and steam-engines 30 per cent, but the gap seems to have narrowed later. Several witnesses before the 1841

[32]W. O. Henderson, *Britain and Industrial Europe, 1750–1870* (Leicester, 1965, 2nd edn).

[33]P. Bairoch, *Révolution industrielle . . .* , *op. cit.*, pp. 130–5.

committee on the exportation of tools and machinery stressed the rapid progress which had been made in Belgium and France, and the 'ingenuity' of the French: 'very inventive people . . . they have no longer any difficulty in making any machine . . . [they] make as good machines as we do'.[34] These technical achievements must not of course be overrated; if France, for instance, built all sorts of machinery, its output of each type was relatively limited.[35] Still, it is important that within ten years of the Rainhill trials, Belgium, France and even Germany were able themselves to build practically all the locomotives they needed for their expanding railway networks, and that very few engines were in fact imported from England, except during the early years of railway construction. One can also observe that several important inventions – like the multi-tubular boiler, the steam-hammer, the wool-combing machine – were made simultaneously and independently in Britain and in France.

These technical achievements were partly due to the progress on the Continent of technical and scientific education, which was a noteworthy development of the period – from the French *Grandes Ecoles* and their imitations abroad, to the German and Swiss *Technische Hochschüle* and the numerous 'popular' evening classes in applied sciences. And this remains true, though one may readily concede that the new élite of engineers and technicians remained small in number, that education on the whole was far too 'classical', and that Continental countries could have done much more to develop its technical side.

It seems therefore that there was no *purely technical* barrier to the diffusion of British innovations. In fact, most of them were introduced fairly quickly on the Continent; the trouble was that they came into general use quite slowly, and more slowly than in Britain. For instance, coke-burning blast-furnaces and the puddling process appeared in France in 1817–18, but thirty years later over half the make of pig-iron was smelted with charcoal. Likewise, power-looms were experimented with in France in the 1820s, just at the time when they were catching on in Britain; but they did not triumph, even in the cotton industry, before mid-century. If British innovations were not adopted more quickly and more widely in Continental industry, it was because manufacturers did not want them in a very broad sense, because they did not appear profitable, or because they were not adapted to their lines of production, or

---

[34]S. Pollard and C. Holmes, *op. cit.*, pp. 276–7, 285–97. The 1841 committee recommended to permit the exportation of machinery from Britain, in order to nip in the bud the nascent engineering industry of the Continent.

[35]M. Lévy-Leboyer, *op. cit.*, p. 381.

because they could not be afforded. The problem is therefore economic, much more than technical, and it is linked to the question which has been put formerly – why was economic growth not faster in Western Europe during this period; and why was change not more rapid and more widespread?

This is ground which has been well laboured by many writers, who have unearthed a whole complex of obstacles or 'bottlenecks', which are supposed to have hindered economic growth, especially in the case of France, the favourite whipping-boy of American scholars. The argument has been sometimes carried to the point that one is surprised that any growth took place at all. I do not intend to discuss thoroughly these obstacles, inasmuch as new economic historians have made lists of factors unfashionable, and I shall concentrate on a few points which seem to me of special importance, and also relevant to the present problems of underdeveloped countries.

I shall start with the demand side, which is often neglected, wrongly in my view, as I think that the narrowness of the markets which were available to their industries was one major factor in the Continental countries' slow growth and change.

The narrowness of the home markets is evident in the case of the smaller countries: Switzerland, which had only 2 million inhabitants by 1835 (plus, up to 1848, internal customs and tolls); Belgium, which suffered greatly from the loss of the French market in 1814, and again from the loss in 1830 of her markets in Holland and in her colonies (which had partly offset the separation from France), and which, after her independence, repeatedly sought a customs union either with France or with Germany; also the small German states up to the establishment of the Zollverein in 1834. As a matter of fact, the favourable influence which the Zollverein had upon German industries can be used to support the view I am putting forward. I know, of course, that present-day German scholars do not think, like their predecessors (who believed too much in the providential role played by the Prussian State), that the Zollverein was *the* decisive factor in the economic progress of Germany; but nonetheless, by creating a large 'common market' in 'the Central of Europe', as it is called in *Gentlemen Prefer Blondes*, it gave a strong stimulus to German industry.

In the larger countries, France and Prussia, opportunities in the home market were restricted by several factors: the inadequacy of the transport system (of which more later), the variations from province to province in consumers' habits and tastes, and the low purchasing power of a large majority of the population. This last fact was aggravated, in countries which remained predominantly agrarian, by the fall of agricultural prices from 1817 onwards, which brought about a deterioration in the terms of trade of agriculture towards industry; and some time lapsed before the rise in the volume of agricultural production had offset the fall in prices and had thus restored rural purchasing power. Anyhow, the fragmentation of landholdings which prevailed in France, in the Low Countries, and in western and southern Germany was rather unfavourable to industrial development, as small cultivators were only marginally involved in the market economy, and saved to buy land rather than manufactured goods.[36] There was a sort of vicious circle in which the narrowness of urban markets in countries which had few large towns discouraged agricultural improvements, and the sluggishness of rural demand slowed down industrial growth. That this circle was broken some time after 1820 by the beginnings of the agricultural revolution, with favourable induced effects for industrial growth, has been asserted by several writers. This is true especially of P. Bairoch, who has built a model in which increased demand from the rural sector (consequent upon higher agricultural productivity), both for textiles and for iron products (the latter required for better implements), is the mainspring of the Industrial Revolution.[37] M. Lévy-Leboyer also sees an important engine of growth, in the prosperity of the French countryside in the 1830s and 1840s, owing to the rise in production and the improvement of its terms of trade.[38] However, Michel Morineau has recently pointed out, in the face of opinions which had been hitherto accepted, that as late as 1840 there were very few signs of an agricultural revolution in France, where in most regions agriculture remained deeply stagnant and backward, if not primitive, and where cereal yields had scarcely improved as compared with the eighteenth century.[39]

[36]This is why the 'Prussian way' of abolition of the 'feudal' system through expropriation of the peasantry is often considered as more congenial to modern economic growth than the French (or rather Western-European) system of small peasant-ownership, which pre-dated the French Revolution, but which the latter – and the Napoleonic inheritance statutes – consolidated. It must be kept in mind, however, that a good deal of French land was still owned by large landowners, though their estates were often divided into small farms for leasing.

[37]P. Bairoch, *Révolution industrielle*. . . ., *op. cit.*, pp. 98 ff.

[38]M. Lévy-Leboyer, 'La croissance économique . . .', *op. cit.*, p. 794.

[39]M. Morineau, 'Y a-t-il eu une révolution agricole en France au XVIIIe siècle?', *Revue Historique*, Vol. CCXXXIX, No. 2 (April-June 1968), pp. 299–326. This does not exclude, however, some productivity increases in the progressive areas of northern France. For Germany, W. Hoffmann, 'The Take-off in Germany', in W. W. Rostow (ed.), *The Economics of Take-off into Sustained Growth* (London, 1963), pp. 103–4, mentions an 'extensive growth' of agriculture up to the 1860s, mostly through extension of tillage, with slow increases in yields per acre, but faster progress in labour's productivity.

The fragmentation and inadequacy of the Continental markets made them unsuitable for mass production, and this was one of the reasons for the 'voluntary obsolescence' which has been stressed earlier, of Continental industry, as marginal gains from the best kind of plant over less capital-intensive techniques were smaller than in England and economies of scale an unrealistic proposition. For instance, the few large iron-works, using coke-smelting and puddling, which were established in France around 1820, were for years a disappointment to their owners (many of whom went bankrupt), who found it quite difficult to dispose of an output which was too large for the available markets – just as India today has some very large and up-to-date, but greatly under-employed, steel and engineering works.

On the other hand, Continental countries were not in a favourable position to offset the narrowness of their home markets by developing a strong export trade. During the Napoleonic wars they had been cut off from overseas markets, and had lost practically all those they had enjoyed in the late eighteenth century. Britain had established an almost complete monopoly in these markets (especially in the United States and in Latin America) and she was very largely able to retain this after Waterloo, owing to the lower prices and better quality of her manufactured goods, to the acquired habits and tastes of overseas customers, and to the commercial infrastructure which Britain had set up in many countries. The Continentals found it very difficult to regain a foothold overseas after 1815; those industries which, in the eighteenth century, had been dependent upon sea-borne trade, and which had been badly hit during the Napoleonic wars, went on decaying or stagnating; and for some time Western Europe was not able to take advantage of the fast growth in the volume of world trade, which Kuznets has estimated at 50 per cent per decade between 1820 and 1850,[40] and which was undoubtedly faster than the expansion of demand in internal markets. The counterproof is that those Continental industries which expanded the fastest were precisely those which succeeded in recovering export markets, as we shall see later. To be sure, French exports, for instance increased at a fast rate of 4 per cent per year, but, starting from a very low level, they were between a third and a half of British exports, and equivalent to a small fraction (around 5 per cent) of national product, so that their induced effects on the economy were limited.[41]

[40]Quoted by I. B. Kravis, 'Trade as a Handmaiden of Growth: Similarities between the Nineteenth and Twentieth Centuries', *The Economic Journal*, No. 320 (December 1970), p. 861.
[41]J. Marczewski, *op. cit.*, p. lx-lxiii.

It appears therefore that once a major 'modern' industrialising economy – Britain – had been established, the whole international trading context became unfavourable for other nations, and the mere presence of the new industrial giant restricted greatly the opportunities for them to base a major industrial impetus upon foreign markets.[42] Likewise, without sharing in any way the leftist view that underdevelopment is a consequence of 'imperialism', we must admit that today the very existence of the advanced industrial countries is, in some respects, a barrier to the industrial progress of underdeveloped areas. On the other hand the narrowness of many of these countries' home markets, due to the scanty population of many of them and to their low incomes *per capita*, is also an enormous obstacle to economic growth.

Anyhow, the demand factor seems to have been vital for Western European countries during the period under consideration, while the acceleration of their growth during its later part must largely be accounted for by the widening of the market, by the new opportunities which resulted from agricultural prosperity, the rise of foreign trade, the Zollverein, and, last, but not least, railway building. If the coming of the railway did not have much effect on the transport system as a whole before the 1850s – except in the few areas which were served by the first lines – it created a relatively enormous demand for all kinds of goods, and David Landes sees it as the 'most important single stimulus to industrial growth' in the 1840s.[43]

This brings us to the transport problem which is interrelated to both the demand and supply sides. The inadequacy of the transport network in Continental Europe is often mentioned as one of the major bottlenecks which hindered economic growth and change, and which was not really broken before the large-scale building of railways in the 1850s and 1860s. However, like the shortcomings of the banking system, it is not really a 'primary' factor, in the sense that its deficiencies can be traced either to faulty government policy, or to inadequate private entrepreneurship, or to capital shortage. I wonder also if its influence has not been exaggerated. The high cost

[42]P. Mathias, *op. cit.* As for import substitution, there was not much opportunity in a country like France which had heavily protected its home market from the start (except, in a way, for new products, like locomotives); and in non-protected, or half-protected markets, as in Germany, English competition was too strong for a long time. But import substitution was a likely factor in the spurt of German industry after 1840.

[43]D. S. Landes, *op. cit.*, p. 153; but he observes also (p. 175), that the fast-growing demand for iron products gave to many ironmasters a security of outlets which permitted them to sit back and reap good profits with obsolete equipment'.

of transport was certainly an obstacle to the growth and technical progress of heavy industries, especially iron and chemicals. France is the classic example, because of the distance which separated the few coal-fields which had good coking coal from both the iron-ore deposits and the traditional charcoal-burning iron-works. Owing to the high price of coal, the change from charcoal to coal was not economical for most iron-masters, and this, much more than their supposed conservatism, was the main reason for the relatively slow introduction of English innovations in the French iron industry. High transport costs gave also geographical protection to traditional producers and restricted the outlets for the output of the 'modern' *forges à l'anglaise*, the marketing difficulties of which have been pointed out earlier.

On the other hand, transport was much less of a problem for the textile industries, the raw materials and finished goods of which were far less bulky. It is significant that prosperous and progressive cotton industries developed in Alsace and in Switzerland, very far from the ports which imported raw cotton (while the cotton industry of Normandy, which was close to Le Havre, is well known for its relative stagnation), and also far from any coal-field. On the other hand, the fast rise of a modern cotton-spinning industry in the Lille area took place only when canals linking it to the neighbouring coal-fields had been dug; it could then turn to steam-power on a large scale. And there is no doubt that the slow but regular improvement of transport facilities, which was achieved everywhere in Western Europe during our period, was an important engine of growth.

If we now turn, more briefly, to the supply side, it is clear that, broadly speaking, factor endowment was less favourable in Continental Western Europe than in Britain, and, in addition, each country, with the exception of Belgium, was labouring under some serious deficiency in this respect.

From the point of view of natural resources, Belgium and Germany had rich coal-fields (though the richest deposits in the Ruhr basin were not discovered until 1838). But France was poorly endowed, at one and the same time as far as the quantity of reserves, the quality of the coal and the mining conditions were concerned. Switzerland and Holland had no coal whatever, although the former had plenty of water-power and the latter could import coal easily. I know it has become unfashionable to assign any importance to the scarcity of coal as a brake on industrialisation in the nineteenth century, but I think this is going too far, and that in the case of France the coal factor was important, inasmuch as the distribution of the coal resources was unsatisfactory in relation to other resources (especially iron-ore) and to established industrial districts.[44]

As for capital, it was undoubtedly less abundant and more expensive on the Continent than in Britain, partly owing to the two decades of costly wars before 1815. Moreover, there was a tendency to invest in land, buildings and government securities rather than in industrial ventures, or just to hoard. Also, the banking system and the capital market were in an embryonic state; they were not able and even did not try to drain available savings towards industrial long-term investment. However, it would be wrong to think of a capital 'bottleneck' as a decisive obstacle to industrialisation. Even for Germany, which was undoubtedly the 'poorest' country, K. Borchardt has maintained that there was no absolute shortage of capital and that commercial interest rates were quite reasonable.[45] In France, within a few years from the end of the wars, the ability to save had been restored; and M. Lévy-Leboyer has convincingly refuted the traditional accusations levelled against the malthusianism of the Paris *Haute Banque*, by showing that it in fact supplied a lot of risk capital to the new industries, and channelled savings towards progressive sectors.[46] In Switzerland there was an abundance of capital and a willingness to invest it in industry, while the pioneer role of the *Société Générale de Belgique* in investment banking, as well as the important role it played in the rise of Belgium's heavy industries, are well known. Moreover, recent research and thinking has tended to eliminate the key role capital was formerly supposed to have played in the beginnings of modern economic growth and in industrialisation. The stock of capital and its rate of increase are no longer considered as the crucial determinants of a country's rate of progress, and capital appears to many economists as a result rather than a precondition of industrialisation. Nonetheless capital remains a permissive factor, and I think it was not unimportant that in the 1830s and 1840s the investment proportion was probably a good deal lower in Continental countries (5 per cent or somewhat more) than in Britain (10 per cent). And at the micro-economic level, one

---

[44]English iron remained the cheapest until the large-scale exploitation of Ruhr coal and Lorraine *minette*, i.e. in the last third of the nineteenth century. One can also mention the poor quality of most of the raw wool available to Continental manufacturers.

[45]D. S. Landes, *op. cit.*, p. 155, who, however, asserts that the supply of capital was limited in the aggregate, as was proved by the tension on capital markets during the railway boom of the 1840s.

[46]M. Lévy-Leboyer, *op. cit.*, pp. 699–704, 707–10.

can note the important results which occurred from relatively small investments by Basel capitalists in the Alsatian cotton industry,[47] by British capital in the French railways, by French and Belgian capital in several German industrial undertakings. The support given to the Belgian economy and state by the Paris house of Rothschild is also worth mentioning. But it must be stressed that these investments were either made in a favourable environment, or accompanied by the technical and organizational skills to put them into effective use.[48]

It was in the matter of labour that the Continent had its only comparative advantage in relation to Britain, as the level of wages was everywhere inferior to the British (roughly by a third in Switzerland around 1830); and, as a matter of fact, labour became cheaper from west to east: it was cheaper in eastern France (for instance Alsace) than in western France (Normandy), and cheaper still in Switzerland and Germany.[49] Of course, this was not an un-mitigated advantage: low labour costs were undoubtedly a major factor in the protracted survival of handwork in many Continental areas, especially of hand-loom weaving. Moreover, although the Continent had some large pools of labour which was both skilled and cheap, it had also a lot of workers who were poorly trained, not accustomed to and even hostile to factory work; and generally speaking, using the same kind of plant or machinery, the produc-tivity of labour was inferior to that which prevailed in Britain.

It remains to point out that, from the point of view of the supply of entrepreneurship, of the socio-cultural environment and of the social values (which remained imbued with the anti-capitalist, anti-business tradition), the Continent was in an inferior position to Britain. In Germany, especially in its eastern parts, society remained deeply aristocratic, the middle class was weak, lived in mediocrity, and suffered from feelings of inferiority. In France, on the other hand, the bourgeoisie had been well integrated by the Revolution and by Napoleon into the system of land-ownership and of govern-ment, with the result that there was a steady drain of talent away from business; and if the timorous and conservative frame of mind of the French business class has been exaggerated by many writers (recent research has stressed many cases of flexibility and innovating

[47]They invested also later in the cotton industry of the Grand Duchy of Baden. It seems that capital was quite abundant in Alsace, and that it was one of its advantages over Normandy and le Nord.

[48]R. Cameron, 'Some Lessons of History for Developing Nations', *The American Economic Review*, Vol. LVII, No. 2 (May 1967), pp. 313-16.

[49]M. Lévy-Leboyer, *op. cit.*, pp. 286–7.

ability), this reputation is not entirely undeserved.[50] Moreover, although there was much more laissez-faire on the Continent after 1815 than in the eighteenth century, governments and bureaucracies had not completely given up the colbertist tradition, and their interventions, which used to be loudly praised by old textbooks, seem in fact to have been quite often inept and harmful. In France, for instance, civil servants, who were afraid of the power of large-scale capitalism, opposed the development of joint-stock companies, with harmful results on the progress of banking and railways. And Schumpeter has suggested that the Prussian state would hardly have followed a different policy from the one it chose, if it had wanted to prevent any sort of economic growth!

It is clear therefore that none of the Western European countries, except Belgium, had, during our period, a complete and satisfactory constellation of factors. Germany had coal and cheap labour, but lacked capital, was not united economically up to 1834, and had an unsuitable social structure. Switzerland had capital and cheap labour, but no natural resources, except water power; her home market was very small and she was geographically isolated and surrounded by protectionist neighbours. France, despite all appearances, was in an unfavourable position; at a time when, to be able to withstand British competition, one needed either cheap coal and iron, or very cheap labour, coal was more expensive than in Britain, Belgium and Germany; and wages, though lower than in Britain, were higher than in Germany and Switzerland; her only advantages were some capital resources, and the skill of part of her labour force.[51] As for Holland, she stagnated during the whole period, owing to a mistaken policy which tried to restore her old staple trade, and owing to the sclerosis of her upper classes. In contrast, Belgium had coal and iron ore, cheap labour, capital (partly from French sources); she built very early the main lines of her railway network, and was thus the pioneer country on the Continent in industrialisation, investment banking and railways; and yet she had difficulties in finding markets, and her activity underwent sharp cyclical fluctuations. Even at the regional level, factor mixes were not quite satisfactory. For instance, Alsace had water-power, a cheap skilled labour force, a weberian group of first-class Protestant entrepreneurs; but she was far from

[50]Personally, I am tempted to exhaust all *economic* explanations before resorting to socio-cultural factors.

[51]M. Lévy-Leboyer, *op. cit.*, pp. 157, 706; also 116–17, on the position of Paris, the largest manufacturing centre in the country, which had no water-power, where coal was imported from Belgium at high prices, and where labour, owing to the high cost of living, demanded high wages.

any coal-field and from the sea-board. But it would be useless to look for some dominating factor of backwardness, in order to build a model around it: in fact it is the complex, the combination of factors which is less favourably oriented than in Britain. Likewise, the progressive erosion of obstacles and loosening of bottlenecks seem to explain the acceleration of growth and change in the later part of the period.

It is, however, rewarding to push the analysis somewhat more in depth, as the main achievements of Continental countries were in particular sectors of industry, where they were obtained by a successful adaptation to the available factor mix. As I stressed earlier, the only relative advantage the Continent enjoyed over Britain was in the cheapness of labour. This was not of much use in the field of common or low quality articles, which Britain could mass-produce with modern machinery more cheaply than the Continentals could by hand processes.[52] But in the manufacture of high quality or fashionable, luxury or semi-luxury goods, the production of which it was difficult to mechanise, and in the cost of which, anyway, labour remained by far the main component, while machinery and fuel costs were small or nil, the Continentals could compete with Britain. Moreover, some groups of workers had a skill and a taste which was up to the British standards, if not better; for instance, in weaving mixed fabrics of cotton, wool or silk; in creating attractive figured designs and brilliant colours patterns. Industrialists who knew how to use these advantages could make goods which were more attractive and cheaper than their British competitors; they were thus able to penetrate foreign markets and to enjoy a faster expansion than those who had to be satisfied with the home market.[53] Moreover, profit margins per unit on such high-quality goods were larger than on coarse articles; capital accumulation within these branches of industry was faster, so that part of these profits was re-invested to develop and modernise the 'basic' industries which made semi-finished articles.

This is why Maurice Lévy-Leboyer has contrasted the 'up-stream' or 'backwards' industrialisation of the Continent with the 'down-stream' or 'forwards' industrialisation of Britain. The English Industrial Revolution started with the 'basic' industries, making semi-

[52]However, one must keep in mind that, up to the generalisation of the power-loom in Britain, the Continent was not in a bad competitive position as far as weaving was concerned; M. Lévy-Leboyer, *op. cit.*, pp. 114–15.
[53]Inasmuch as, in the 1830s, the demand for luxury goods revived on foreign markets; on French textile exports, cf. M. Lévy-Leboyer, *op. cit.*, pp. 145 ff., 175–6.

finished goods such as cotton yarn or pig-iron, and later progressed downstream to the mechanisation of the consumption goods industries, such as weaving. The typical example is Lancashire, which, because of its superiority in cotton-spinning, 'integrated' progressively a whole range of more differentiated manufactures, such as cotton-printing, silk, engineering, etc. On the Continent, the successful industrial centres were those which took advantage of the cheapness and skill of labour to develop first the making of specialised and labour-intensive quality consumption goods, and then, later on, were able to move 'upstream' towards mechanised spinning or the primary iron industry.[54]

This attractive thesis seems to hold good in many cases. In cotton, the backward and relatively stagnant centres were those, like Normandy or Saxony, which made coarse articles which only high tariff walls and/or wretched conditions for labour could save from British competition, but which could not be exported, and left narrow profit margins for reinvestment. Whereas the typical successful district was Alsace, from which quality printed-cottons were massively exported, and which progressed by upstream integration from printing to weaving, spinning, machine-building and chemicals, and which, in the technical field, was the most progressive centre on the Continent. North-eastern Switzerland played also the card of quality goods, and specialised in articles with high labour inputs, which were not amenable to mechanisation: embroideries and light hand-printed cottons, with bright colours and attractive designs, which were varied indefinitely to suit the tastes of different markets. Their output increased enormously and they penetrated many overseas markets, but mechanisation was restricted to the spinning branch.[55] In the wool industry the great French success was the invention, from 1825 onwards, of the *nouveautés*, light fabrics, woven on Jacquard looms, of mixed woollen and worsted yarns, or wool and silk, with a great variety and a constant change of design. The most dynamic centres were those like Reims, Roubaix or Elbeuf, which specialised in these new products and were thus enabled later to establish a 'modern' spinning industry, especially for worsted yarn. One might also mention the artistic industries of Paris, or the silk industry of Lyon, which, despite higher labour costs than its

[54]M. Lévy-Leboyer, *op. cit.*, pp. 49, 65–6, 95, 169–71, 288–92, 410. One might object that in England also, in the late eighteenth century, the 'primary' industries developed on the basis of prosperous consumption goods manufactures, and were partly financed by merchant-manufacturers' capital.

[55]Béatrice Veyrassat-Herren, 'Les centres de gravité de l'industrialisation en Suisse au XIXe siècle (Aspects géographiques et sectoriels): Le rôle du coton', paper presented to the Lyon conference.

competitors, re-established its leadership by the repeated imaginative creation of new fashionable goods, which rival centres had to
imitate.[56] In the iron industry some undertakings, like Cockerill,
started in machine-building and later on extended to the primary
sector; others, like Le Creusot under the Schneiders, became
profitable only when they had diversified towards engineering; or
more frequently, especially in Germany and in *le Nord*, iron-works
started by puddling imported pig-iron and later set up coke-burning
blast furnaces, In Germany, anyhow, the most flourishing sector
was the secondary metal industries, such as the hardware and cutlery
of the Sauerland; and the greatest advance was made in the manufacture of those finished goods – steel and steel products – that demanded special skills and high inputs of labour.[57]

It appears therefore that Continental industrialisation was different, in its pattern and process, from the British, and moreover
that, broadly speaking, it was successful to the extent that it was
different. An interesting remark in that respect can be made about
the tariff policy of Prussia, which was extended after 1834 to the
whole Zollverein. Duties were high on finished articles, but low on
raw materials and semi-finished goods, such as yarn or pig-iron;
this system encouraged the 'upstream' industrialisation process,
which was especially well-marked in Germany. For instance, the
making of iron by puddling developed a great deal in the 1830s and
1840s, using imported British or Belgian pig-iron, and it was only
after the duties on pig-iron and wrought-iron had been raised in 1844
that coke-smelting progressed in a big way. This differential customs
policy seems to have been much better conceived than the French
system, which prohibited or taxed heavily any kind of imports and
encouraged therefore the development of high-cost and inefficient
basic industries. The industrialisation of Germany was delayed,
limited at first to consumption goods industries, based on cheap
labour and imported semi-finished goods,[58] but she started to
integrate backwards and to become less dependent on imports in
the 1840s; and a strong basis for the big jump forwards after 1850
had been laid.

It is clear also that the strategic decisions of manufacturers were
dictated much more by the objective conditions which prevailed in

[56]M. Lévy-Leboyer, *op. cit.*, pp. 121 ff., 130, 137 ff.
[57]*Ibid.*, pp. 291, 375; D. S. Landes, *op. cit.*, pp. 178–9. The Germans, with the
inventions of Lohage and Bremme, and of Krupp, were in the vanguard of
progress, as far as steel was concerned.
[58]Because of these conditions, it relied much less than France on quality
articles, except for a few specialities.

each country or each district, by the market opportunities and the available factor mix, to which they tried, more or less successfully, to adapt their initiatives, than by 'social values' or 'national' aptitudes for entrepreneurship and innovation. Moreover, these conditions, much more than an innate conservatism or the structure of the family firm, explain the low level of concentration in most Continental industries, the dispersion of manufacturing activities. In the making of quality and fashion goods, where short runs of production were the rule, flexibility was indispensable; work had to be divided.[59] In addition, mechanisation had to be progressive and limited, especially in weaving, where for a long time the power-loom was unsuitable for fine fabrics. And growth was restricted by the smaller demand for luxury goods, both on the home and foreign markets. But these handicaps were more or less inescapable, owing to the initial lag behind England. One could perhaps say that Continental manufacturers made the best of a bad job, and after all, they were also innovators – especially the French, but in a different way from the British, because they depended upon a different constellation of factors: they invented new products and new fashions, rather than new machinery. The achievements of Continental industry may have been more creditable than was suggested earlier.[60]

I must now try to draw from this too-long analysis some lessons which could be applied to the industrialisation of the underdeveloped countries of today; but I am afraid that they will be trite and commonplace. A first point might be the necessity of widening the market, which in most underdeveloped countries, except those with very large populations, is far too narrow for absorbing the mass production of contemporary advanced industry and for achieving specialisation and economies of scale. This can be obtained by increasing rural purchasing power through higher agricultural productivity, which at present, thanks to various items of scientific and technical progress, seems more feasible than some years ago, despite the functional resistance to change of traditional agrarian systems. But a short cut might be the formation of regional customs unions, on the pattern of the Zollverein, with a reasonable level of protection – although I wonder if it is politically a practical proposition.

[59] An original character of French industrialisation was the parallel growth of 'small' and 'large-scale' industry.

[60] Owing to the importance of quality goods in French production, the differences in the *volume* of output between England and France are reduced when one considers the *values* – for instance in the cotton industry.

On the other hand, the obvious conclusion to be drawn from Western Europe's nineteenth-century history is that a successful industrialisation is not a slavish imitation of the more advanced countries and possibly that it is the most successful when it is the most original. It has to adapt to the configuration of the national or regional economies, to fit closely to the circumstances of time and place, to the available constellation of factors and especially to existing traditional skills of the labour force. More precisely, it is useful to look for the *créneaux*, the gaps in the range of products, where its factor endowment will enable the developing economy to compete successfully with established producers and to penetrate foreign markets, in order to achieve a fast growth. It is clear that in most cases this would mean, as in early nineteenth-century Western Europe, a concentration on the industries best suited to the relative abundance and cheapness of labour, and to the shortage of capital, on 'light' rather than 'heavy' industries – but keeping in mind that these industries are not inevitably the same as in the last century, and that, for instance, a number of engineering and even electronic industries are today labour-intensive.[61] This seems to be the path which some Asiatic countries, like South Korea, Taiwan, Hong-Kong, Singapore, have entered, with a good deal of success, but I should hesitate to assert that it is open also, let us say, to Mauretania or Paraguay. . . .

[61]M. M. Postan, 'L'expérience de l'industrialisation européenne et les problèmes actuels des pays sous-développés', paper presented to the Lyon conference.

7

Economic Development in India under the British Crown, 1858–1947

W. J. MACPHERSON
University of Cambridge

India under the British has been typified as a dependent country which failed to make long-run economic growth. Adjectives such as stagnant, aborted, arrested and static are applied to it. The aim of this chapter is threefold. First, to demonstrate that the inadequacy of the treated, if not the raw data, the temporal and spatial variations in economic performance, the peculiarities of individual entrepreneurs, landlords, peasants and labourers, and the inconsistency of government policy; that all of these make generalisations about British India of limited value. Secondly, to attempt some sort of estimate, based on quantitative and qualitative evidence, of long-run economic development. And finally to assess the demand-market and factor-supply situation in the major sectors of the economy.

In the enormous historiography of India,[1] one could, by oversimplifying, distinguish between two broad extreme interpretations of the situation under the Raj, one pessimistic, the other optimistic. The first school would include R. C. Dutt, Naoroji, Digby, Jenks, Marx and his disciples Palme Dutt, Komarov and Levkovsky.[2] Some, but not the Marxists, romanticise a pre-British period of wealth, self-sufficiency, absence of famines and landless labourers,

[1] See, for example, M. H. Case, *South Asian History, 1750-1950: A guide to Periodicals, Dissertations and Newspapers* (Princeton, 1968).

[2] R. C. Dutt, *India in the Victorian Age: An Economic History of the People* (7th ed, London, 1950); D. Naoroji, *Poverty and Un-British Rule in India* (London, 1871); W. Digby, *Prosperous British India* (London, 1901); L. H. Jenks, *The Migration of British Capital to 1875* (London, 1927); K. Marx, especially in his despatches to the *New York Daily Tribune* – e.g. No. 3804 (25 June 1853) and No. 3824 (20 July 1853); R. Palme Dutt, *India Today* (London, 1940); E. N. Komarov, 'Survey of Russian Pre-Revolutionary and Soviet Studies on the Economic History of India in the Modern Age', in *Contributions to Indian Economic History*, Vol. I (1961); A. I. Levkovsky, *Capitalism in India* (Bombay, 1966).

and a flourishing manufacturing sector, as described, for example, by European travellers. There is also contrary qualitative evidence. Peter Mundy, who visited India in the early 1630s and saw the building of the Taj Mahal, was not only impressed by the fact that 'gold and silver were esteemed common Mettal [*sic*], and Marble but as ordinarie stones'. He and others were also impressed by *sati*, child marriage and, most of all, by famine and the ensuing cannibalism.[3] One of the greatest historians of India, W. W. Hunter, stressed that 'In the seventeenth century, beneath the extravagance of the few lay the misery of the many'.[4] And, said Marx, 'I share not the opinion of those who believe in a golden age of Hindustan'.[5] The fact is that it is fatuous to generalise about conditions before the accession of the Crown. There were good and bad years, prosperous and impoverished areas. In the absence of reliable data 'it is easy to charge, hard to disprove, that the condition of the people was better in some unspecified past era than in the nineteenth century'.[6]

As common as speculation about Company and pre-Company rule are allegations that the 'standard of living', 'economic conditions' and 'prosperity' deteriorated, or, at best, failed to improve from 1858 until Independence. With some notable exceptions,[7] the bulk of Indian and some other writers until the 1950s took this view. Thus Nehru maintained that 'no statistics, facts or numbers are wanted to convince you of this, that India has suffered terrible economic decline'.[8] Jenks found that 'frequent famine was a painful corollary of the transformation of India by British capital',[9] and Bhatia's study of famines concurs.[10] Thorner, at a much higher level of sophistication, surveyed the whole field of national income estimates. He believed it premature to reject the possibility that *per capita* income was declining in the first half of the twentieth-

[3] *The Travels of Peter Mundy in Europe and Asia, 1608–1667*, Vol. II, *Travels in Asia 1628–1634*, The Hakluyt Society, Second Series, No. 25 (London, 1914).

[4] W. W. Hunter, *England's Work in India* (London, 1881), p. 59.

[5] See, for example, his despatches No. 3840, published in the *New York Daily Tribune*, 8 August 1853, and No. 3804 of 25 June 1853. Reprinted in K. Marx and F. Engels, *On Colonialism* (Moscow, undated).

[6] A. Chatterton, *Industrial Evolution in India* (Madras, 1912), p. 8.

[7] For example, M. G. Ranade in *Essays on Indian Economics* (Madras, 1906); and R. Sharma, 'The Legacy of the British Rule in India', *Journal of Indian History*, Vol. XXXIV, Part III (December 1956).

[8] 'Address to the League against Imperialism', 1927, quoted in *Seminar*, Vol. LIX, 1962–4.

[9] L. H. Jenks, *op. cit.*, p. 288.

[10] B. M. Bhatia, *Famines in India: A Study in Some Aspects of the Economic History of India, 1860–1965* (London, 1967).

century.[11] It will be demonstrated later that the verdict must still be the Scottish legal 'non-proven', but that there are grounds for some optimism.

The alleged causes of the decline are too well known to require elaboration here. Essentially they are in terms of government policy, economic imperialism, free trade, laissez-faire, the transformation of the country into a dumping ground for British goods and a supplier of raw materials, the destruction of indigenous industries, and the economic drain of the home charges.[12] In a nutshell, the reason for India's backwardness was that 'the colonial relationship subordinated India to British political and economic interests'.[13] Or, in the words of Professor Joan Robinson, 'the primitive industry was destroyed and modern industry hampered by rigid insistence on free trade, to the benefit of British exports'.[14] Implicit in many of these writings is a vision of the progress that might have been made under some ideal system.

There is a somewhat different school in the historiography. Mrs Anstey, Hunter, Griffiths, Strachey[15] and a host of British soldiers and administrators place their emphasis on the beneficial aspects of the Imperial connection. This school believe that, on the whole, there was economic progress and that the conditions of the people improved under the Raj. Year after year the Moral and Material Progress Reports to Parliament surveyed all aspects of economic life. One is reminded, occasionally, in their phraseology of Hobson's warning that, in the mouths of Imperialists 'are noble phrases, expressive of their desire to extend the area of cultivation, to establish good government, promote Christianity, extirpate slavery and elevate the lower races'.[16] Be that as it may, the picture the

[11]D. Thorner, 'Long-term Trends in Output in India', in S. Kuznets, W. E. Moore and J. J. Spengler (eds), *Economic Growth: Brazil, India, Japan* (Durham, N. Carolina, 1955), p. 128.

[12]See, for example, B. N. Ganguli, *D. Naoroji and the Drain Theory* (Calcutta, 1965); and B. Chandra, 'Indian Nationalists and the Drain, 1880–1905', *Indian Economic and Social History Review*, Vol. II, No. 2 (April 1965).

[13]H. Lamb in S. Kuznets, *op. cit.*, p. 465.

[14]J. Robinson, *Encounter*, June 1971, p. 5.

[15]V. Anstey, *The Economic Development of India* (London, 1957); W. W. Hunter, *op. cit.;* Sir P. Griffiths, *The British Impact on India* (London, 1952); Sir J. Strachey, *India: Its Administration and Progress* (London, 1911). Not all British commentators were flattering to British rule. James Caird, well known to agrarian historians, wrote a highly critical report to the Government: 'Report by James Caird on the Condition of India', *Parliamentary Papers*, Vol. LIII (1880), Cd. 2732. See also Lytton's reply in a despatch to Lord Hartington: Government of India Despatch No. 38 of 1880.

[16]J. A. Hobson, *Imperialism: A Study* (London, 1938), p. 61.

Reports paint is a far cry from that of the detractors. An even further cry is a 'Memorandum on Some Results of Indian Administration during the past fifty years of British rule in India',[17] presenting, in 1909, an official view. Peace and order, hospitals and sanitation, enormous enhancement of land revenue on 'moderate and equitable principles' with a lighter burden on the ryot than under Akbar, the cheapness of salt in spite of the much abused tax, improved trade and communications; all these and more lead to the conclusion that 'so far as ordinary tests can be applied the average Indian . . . is better off than he was fifty years ago'. In the words of the King-Emperor's Proclamation of 1908, 'We can survey our labours of the past half-century with clear gaze and good conscience'. Some obstacles to advance were found, not in government economic policy or lack of it, but in demographic and socio-religious factors, ranging from inferior civilisation to the backward-bending supply curve of labour. To quote an American view, 'caste, joint family, rural village, Hinduism' have exercised 'a negative influence on economic development'.[18] Anticipating later neo-malthusian fears, *The Economist* was declaring of India as early as 1874 that 'the true accusation against the English government is not that it has lessened the safety of the precarious population, but that it has brought that population into existence'.[19]

Since Independence, and increasingly since Morris and Stein reviewed the field in their notable bibliographic essay in 1961,[20] a new, more sophisticated and analytical approach to Indian economic history is evident. Morris himself in his study of Bombay has thrown a fresh light on labour supply,[21] and Mrs Kumar on landless labourers.[22] Davis and Chandrasekar on population, Blyn and Neale

---

[17]Cd. 4956 (1909), pp. 26 and 33.

[18]K. Davis, 'Social and Demographic Aspects: India', in S. Kuznets, *op. cit.*, p. 314. There is a vast literature on the socio-religious problem, notable among which are G. Myrdal, *Asian Drama: An Inquiry into the Poverty of Nations* (London, 1968); L. I. Rudolph, *The Modernity of Tradition* (Chicago, 1967); B. S. Cohn, 'Society and Social Change under the Raj', *South Asian Review*, Vol. IV, No. 1 (October 1970).

[19]*The Economist*, 28 March 1874. For similar fears of overpopulation long before the inter-war upsurge, see also Lord Lytton in 1878 quoted in Sir J. Strachey, *The Finances and Public Works of India* (London, 1882), p. 72; and J. Caird in 'A Report on the Condition of India', *Parliamentary Papers*, Vol. LII (1880).

[20]M. D. Morris and B. Stein, 'The Economic History of India: A Bibliographic Essay', *Journal of Economic History*, Vol. XXI, No. 2 (June 1961).

[21]M. D. Morris, *The Emergence of an Industrial Labor Force in India: A Study of the Bombay Cotton Mills, 1854–1947* (Berkeley and Los Angeles, 1965).

[22]D. Kumar, *Land and Caste in South India* (Cambridge, 1965).

on agriculture, Malenbaum on general problems, Narain on peasant responses, Rungta on business corporations, Misra on the middle classes, Rosen on industrial change, Leach and Srinivas on caste, K. N. Chaudhuri on exports and the 'drain' – these and many more show a new style and expertise and less emotional involvement with the pro- and anti-British argument than do some of their predecessors.[23] Nor should it be forgotten that, working with defective data, serious attempts have been and are being made to quantify Indian history by, *inter al.*, V. K. R. V. Rao, T. Shukla, K. M. Mukerji, M. Mukherjee, S. J. Patel, N. S. R. Sastry, K. Iyengar, and S. Sivasubramonian.[24] The scholar is now, therefore, in a much better position than ever before to illuminate the British period.

He is faced, however, with problems of time, region, people and data. The 'changeless Orient' is a common phrase, but India was no different from other countries in that it was subject to severe and short-period economic fluctuations. In a largely non-industrial state these did not take the regular cyclical pattern which some observers have dubiously found in the West. The prime determinant was the vagaries of the monsoon. This is clear by the check to growth and the misery of the people in severe famines, especially in the 1890s, when half to three-quarters of the crop may have been

[23]K. Davis, *The Population of India and Pakistan* (Princeton, 1951); S. Chandrasekar (ed.), *Asia's Population Problems* (London, 1967); G. Blyn, *Agricultural Trends in India, 1891–1947: Output, Availability and Productivity* (Philadelphia, 1966); W. C. Neale, *Economic Change in Rural India* (New Haven, 1962); W. Malenbaum, *Prospects for Indian Development* (London, 1962); D. Narain, *The Impact of Price Movements on Areas under Selected Crops in India, 1900–39* (Cambridge, 1965); R. S. Rungta, *Rise of Business Corporations in India, 1851–1900* (Cambridge, 1970); B. B. Misra, *The Indian Middle Classes* (London, 1961); G. Rosen, *Some Aspects of Industrial Finance in India* (New York, 1962); E. R. Leach (ed.), *Aspects of Caste in South India, Ceylon and N. W. Pakistan* (Cambridge, 1960); M. N. Srinivas (ed.), *India's Villages* (London, 1960); K. N. Chaudhuri, *The Economic Development of India under the East India Company, 1814–1858* (Cambridge, 1971).

[24]V. K. R. V. Rao, *National Income of British India, 1931–32* (London, 1940); T. Shukla, *Capital Formation in Indian Agriculture* (Bombay, 1965); K. M. Mukerji, *Levels of Economic Activity and Public Expenditure in India* (Bombay, 1962); M. Mukherjee, *National Income of India: Trends and Structure* (Calcutta, 1969); S. J. Patel, Long Term Changes in Output and Income in India', *Indian Economic Journal*, Vol. V, No. 3 (June 1958); N. S. R. Sastry, 'The Present Position of National Income Studies' in *Papers on National Income and Allied Topics*, Vol. III (London, 1965); K. Iyengar and H. C. Arora, 'Long Term Growth of National Income, 1901–56', in V. K. R. V. Rao *et al.* (eds), *Papers on National Income and Allied Topics* Vol. I (London, 1960); S. Sivasubramonian, 'Estimates of the Gross Value of Agricultural Output in undivided India, 1900–1 to 1946–7', in V. K. R. V. Rao *et al.* (eds), *Papers on National Income and Allied Topics*, Vol. I (London, 1960).

lost.[25] International impulses, notably the American Civil War and the inter-war slump, were of some, but less importance. The general wholesale price index (1952–3 = 100), for example, rose from 20 to 32·6 between 1861 and 1866.[26] The value of raw cotton exports rose from £5½ millions in 1860 to 37½ millions in 1865,[27] and there was a company flotation boom facilitated by the coming of general limited liability.[28] Reaction and depression ensued, as it did in the inter-war slump when the price index fell from 59 to 29 between 1928 and 1933.

Regional variations also make all-India generalisations difficult. The native states, of which there were nearly six hundred in 1858, were themselves not homogeneous. Underpopulated, rice-exporting Burma was part of India until 1937. Within British India proper there were diversities in economic conditions. The Punjab was widely regarded as one of the most progressive agricultural regions but it evinced 'striking lack of uniformity' according to a Government Report.[29] The State Statistical Bureau shows *per capita* incomes at 1948–9 prices in 1958–9 ranging from Rs. 337 in Bombay and Rs. 323 in the Punjab, to only Rs. 225 in Kerala and Rs. 186 in Bihar, the poorest region even in the British period.[30] The high Bombay figure is a reminder of urban-rural contrasts in occupations, incomes and consumption, particularly evident in India where half the factory workers were concentrated in two cities. Even Boeke's concept of dualism is of little service in this complex context. The religious, racial and linguistic dissimilarities have been the subject of comment since Pliny maintained that *'gentes ei urbesque innumerae, si quis omnes persequi velit'*.[31] There is a view that the British introduced a policy of 'divide and rule', as if there had ever been any unity. In fact one of the results of improved communications, limited education and the very existence of an alien ruler was, until Partition, a movement towards greater unification. Even so, there were fifteen major languages in 1941, if one distinguishes

[25]See, for example, *Parliamentary Papers*, Vol. LII (1880), 'Report of the Indian Famine Commission', Part I, p. 27; and B. M. Bhatia, *Famines in India* (London, 1967).

[26]N. K. Thingalaya, 'A Century of Prices in India', *Economic and Political Weekly*, 25 January 1969.

[27]Compiled from 'Statistical Abstracts Relating to British India' in *Parliamentary Papers*.

[28]See, for example, *Parliamentary Papers*, Vol. LXIV, 1867–8, 'Returns of Joint Stock Companies'; and D. E. Wacha, *A Financial Chapter in the History of Bombay City* (Bombay, 1900).

[29]*Report of the Punjab Land Revenue Committee* (Lahore, 1938), p. 163.

[30]M. Mukherjee, *op. cit.*, p. 501.

[31]*Naturalis Historia*, Book VI, Part XXI, 58.

between Hindi and Urdu; there were the subdivisions of caste, perhaps exaggerated by Census requirements before 1947; and there were wide cultural heterogeneities.[32] It is easy to overstress these factors as impediments to development but in no sense was India as homogeneous as Britain or Japan. More important is to avoid generalising about the attitudes and responses of classes of society. Many landlords were absentee and non-entrepreneurial landowners, but there are examples of progressive zamindars who farmed well and established industries.[33] The response of peasants and industrial workers to economic inducements was not uniform but it will be shown later that the attitudes and aspirations of most did not differ markedly from those of the British or Japanese. The traditional view of scarcity of industrial entrepreneurship[34] will also require drastic qualification, as will superficial theses about government free trade and laissez-faire, and the oft mentioned shyness and scarcity of Indian capital.

The greatest problem facing the Indian, as indeed other historians, is the quality of the evidence. Marx in 1853 complained that 'there exists no government by which so much is written and so little done, as the Government of India'.[35] From the Censuses, beginning in 1871, from annual railway reports, and from masses of figures on agriculture and trade, a vast accumulation of data is available. But official reports are sometimes contradictory and misleading. Omissions, changes in method of collection and definition prevent adequate comparison of figures over time. In agriculture, lack of information on livestock, by far the largest capital component excluding land, the frequent failure of provinces and districts to report, the unreliability of 'chowkidars' in permanently settled areas, and the crop-cutting experimental way of estimating yields, are among the problems enumerated by the Royal Commission of 1928.[36]

[32]See, for example, A. J. Appasamy, 'The Cultural Problem', *Oxford Pamphlets on Indian Affairs*, No. 1, (1942); and, on languages, S. K. Chatterji, 'Languages and the Linguistic Problem', *ibid.*, No. 11 (1943); B. R. Nayar, 'Hindi as a Link Language', *Economic and Political Weekly*, 10 February 1968. The 1961 Census showed that only 30 per cent of the population spoke Hindi.

[33]For examples see the *Report of the Indian Industrial Commission, 1916–18, Minutes of Evidence*, Vol. I, Cd. 234, (1919), p. 365; and *Minutes of Evidence*, Vol. III, Cd. 236, p. 333.

[34]See, for example, H. J. Habakkuk, 'Historical Experience on the Basic Conditions of Economic Progress', in L. H. Dupriez (ed.), *Economic Progress* (Louvain, 1955).

[35]K. Marx, despatch No. 3824 to the *New York Daily Tribune*, 20 July 1853, in Marx and Engels, *op. cit.*

[36]*Report of the Royal Commission on Agriculture in India*, Cd. 3132 (1928), Ch. XVIII.

Joint-stock companies and large-scale factory industry, if one remembers the changing definitions of factory, are easier to handle; but the vital small-scale and rural manufacture, the subject of so much pontification, eludes quantification. Thorner and others have warned about occupational categories, and national income estimates are still very tentative. In sum, one cannot give, for the British era, definitive answers to the significant questions, such as the long-run trend of real *per capita* output, the relation between farm output and population growth, the extent of the decay, if any, of the 'native arts and crafts', the savings-investment and capital-output ratios, and aggregate time-series of employment, money and real wages. This is hardly surprising when the producer consumed much of his own output and a high proportion of activity was in the non-monetised sector. Nearly half of India's national income as late as the 1950s was the income of unincorporated enterprises, 37 per cent of rural consumption transactions were non-monetised, and between 27 per cent and 40 per cent of rural household industries' input was 'home' supplied. An estimate of domestic savings by sectors in 1960 shows that 74·8 per cent came from households (16·2 per cent rural and 58·6 per cent urban, although the rural population was at least four times bigger), 17·4 per cent from Government and only 7·8 per cent from the corporate sector.[37] Monetisation and real income are not, of course, necessarily positively related, at least in the short run. There is some evidence that an increase in peasant prosperity reduced money transactions, and that farm labourers were more monetised than better-off farmers who did not need the market for their essentials.[38] The point here is, however, that only after Independence were serious attempts made by, for example, sample surveys, to estimate the output and savings of large sectors of the Indian economy, and that these attempts are liable to wide margins of error.

Bearing in mind the above reservations, some indication of the extent of 'economic growth' in India from 1858 to 1947 will now be essayed. The meaning and measurement of 'economic growth', its costs and purpose, are the subject of controversy.[39] No quantitative record that can embrace all the aspects of material, far less psychic, progress in British India, is yet, and probably ever will be, feasible.

[37]R. K. Diwan, 'Are We Saving Enough for Our Plans?', *Economic and Political Weekly*, annual number, February 1967.

[38]This important point is discussed by W. Malenbaum, *Prospects for Indian Development* (London, 1962), pp. 139–41.

[39]See, for example, S. Kuznets, 'Problems in Comparisons of Economic Trends' in *Economic Growth: Brazil, India, Japan, op. cit.*, Part I, Ch. I.

There is, however, some information on, *inter alia*, national product, population, agricultural production, occupational structure, industrialisation, trade and social overhead capital which might provide indicators.

In the nineteenth century, with the exception of Baring and Barbour in 1882 and Lord Curzon in 1901, British administrators generally avoided measurement of national product. Since then many estimates have been made by scholars, including S. J. Patel,[40] G. S. Raychaudhuri,[41] and Thorner and Mukherjee in their already-cited works. All stress the uncertainty of the figures. Patel's indices of real net *per capita* income are 100 in 1896–1905, 105 in 1916–25 and only 92 in 1936–45. Arora and Iyengar find differently. At 1948-9 prices they present two estimates of average *per capita* income for each of the quinquennia 1901–2 to 1905–6 and 1941–2 to 1945–6. These are Rs. 181 and Rs. 165 for the first period, and Rs. 283 and Rs. 278 for the second, indicating considerable growth.[42] Mukherjee's treatment of the subject, although not definitive, is more comprehensive.[43] He finds that from 1860 to 1900 total real national income grew by about 40 per cent and real *per capita* income by 18 per cent. This growth rate accelerated in the next thirty years, a *per capita* increase of about 30 per cent being noted. Rapid population growth affects the *per capita* figures after 1930. For the next twenty years they fail to show a rise, although total national income grew 30 per cent from 1930 to 1950. Over about ninety years from 1860, the rate of growth of *per capita* real income averages about 0·5 per cent per annum; that of total real national income about 1·15 per cent per annum. By Japanese and British standards, even the relatively optimistic evidence of Mukherjee shows very low rates of growth in India. But his conclusions and those of some others are not consistent with generalisations of decline and hardly consistent, when population is considered, with stagnation. From the national income data, then, to alter Thorner's phrase, it would be premature to reject the view that India experienced slow, but sustained economic development in the long run under the British.

The demographic data are open to discussion, but it is clear that British rule was accompanied by a large growth in popula-

[40]'Long-Term Changes in Output and Income in India, 1896–1960', *Indian Economic Journal*, Vol. V (January 1958).

[41]*Economic and Political Weekly*, 3 December 1966.

[42]H. C. Arora and K. R. R. Iyengar, 'Long Term Growth in National Income, 1901–56', in V. K. R. V. Rao *et al.* (eds), *Papers on National Income and Allied Topics*, Vol. I (London, 1960).

[43]M. Mukherjee, *National Income of India, op. cit.*

tion.[44] Starting from a comparatively high figure of around 255 millions in 1871 (excluding Burma), the average rate of increase to 1941 was approximately 0·60 per cent per annum, giving a population of 389 millions in 1941, and a 52 per cent increase. Not rapid by Japanese and other standards, the Indian increase was sporadic and, until 1921, checked by famines and the influenza epidemic of 1918. From 1921 to 1941 the rate of growth at 1·2 per cent per annum was more rapid and sustained, and total numbers increased by 83 millions. This evidence does not fit easily with theories which postulate a decline from an already 'subsistence' standard of living in 1858. Still less does Davis's 'unmistakeable downward trend' in the death-rate, the main factor of India's population growth, or the modest but marked upward trend in the life expectation of males and females.

Changes in the occupational composition of the labour force, especially a move from the primary to the secondary sectors, are often taken as indicative of economic progress. In India the Censuses are purported to show an increasing proportion of the working force in agriculture, and thus to indicate de-industrialisation and 'backwardness'. The dangers of generalising in this field were pointed out long ago by Bauer and Yamey.[45] Indian farmers were also house-builders, carriers and manufacturers. Railway workers divided their time between the fields and the tracks.[46] There was a large category in the Censuses (around twelve millions in 1881) classified as 'general' or 'unskilled' labourers. Nor does a distinction between urban and rural areas clarify the problem. The Rural Credit Survey maintained that, as late as 1951–2, 12 per cent of self-supporting persons living in urban areas were 'agriculturalists'.[47] What is certain is that there was a large increase in numbers employed in mines, railways, plantations and factories. Before Partition in 1947 there were over two million workers in factories, about 413,000 in coal-mines, over one million in the tea plantations and another million on the railways.[48] Whether this was more than offset by a fall in employment in the non-factory sector is a matter of conjecture. In a careful analysis of the 'de-industrialisation' argument, Thorner could only conclude that 'the industrial distribution of the

[44]The data are from the adjusted figures of K. Davis, *The Population of India and Pakistan* (Princeton, 1951).
[45]P. T. Bauer and B. S. Yamey, 'Economic Progress and Occupational Distribution', *Economic Journal*, Vol. LXI (December 1951).
[46]'Report of the Select Committee on East India (Finance), *Parliamentary Papers*, Vol. VII (1871), 1, App. IV.
[47]*All India Rural Credit Survey*, Vol. II, *General Report* (Bombay, 1954), p. 13.
[48]Government of India, *Indian Labour Year Book* (Delhi, 1949), pp. 2–20.

Indian working force from 1881 to 1931 stood still'.[49] Occupational categories in any case leave unanswered questions of worker productivity and capital-labour ratios. And, of course, as New Zealand shows, there remains the wider and more complex question of the relation between industrialisation and economic growth. Having said all this, no one would deny that the bulk of the Indian working force was in, and the bulk of national product was generated by, the agrarian sector. A rough estimate for 1951 would be seven out of ten persons dependent on agriculture as a principal means of livelihood, and about half the net national product contributed by agriculture, animal husbandry and allied activities.[50]

The absence of adequate data makes agriculture a peculiarly unreliable indicator of economic development. Even for Japan, Nakamura has challenged the dogma for the Meiji period and has himself been criticised by later scholars.[51] For India, an authority finds the output figures, as late as the early plans, 'elusive'.[52] One may assume from the extension of acreage, especially in irrigated areas and from such inadequate statistics as can be culled from Government papers, that agricultural production increased in the nineteenth century.[53] By how much is not known. There is a number of studies covering the present century. One of the most recent demonstrates large fluctuations in food grain and pulse output in the inter-war period, and a lower output at the end than at the beginning.[54] In 1958 the Indian Society of Agricultural Economics showed stagnant food-crop output and a 17 per cent decline in *per capita* food crop output between the early 1900s and the early 1940s.[55] Most influential is Blyn's work for 1891 to 1947.[56] While enumerating the prob-

[49]D. Thorner, 'De-industrialisation in India, 1881–1931', in *Contributions to the First International Conference of Economic History* (Stockholm, 1960), p. 223. His wife has queried the usefulness of the 'tertiary sector' category as a sign of growth. A. Thorner, 'How to use the 1961 Census Working Force Data', *Economic Weekly*, 5 November 1966.

[50]*All India Rural Credit Survey*, Vol. II, *General Report* (Bombay, 1954), p. 14.

[51]J. I. Nakamura, *Agricultural Production and the Economic Development of Japan, 1873–1922* (Princeton, 1966); K. Ohkawa, B. F. Johnston and H. Kaneda, *Agriculture and Economic Growth: Japan's Experience* (Princeton, 1970).

[52]D. Thorner, 'India's Elusive Agricultural Output Figures', *Economic Weekly*, January 1960, p. 199.

[53]See, for example, annual reports on the Indian railways, e.g. *Parliamentary Papers*, Vol. LI, (1871), p. 49; the *Moral and Material Progress Reports and Memorandum on Some Results of Indian Administration, op. cit.*, p. 25.

[54]R. M. Chakrabarti, 'Production Estimates of Food Grains and Pulses 1920–21 to 1964–65', *Artha-Vijnana*, Vol. XII (September 1970).

[55]J. P. Bhattacharjee, (ed.), *Studies in Indian Agricultural Economics* (Bombay, 1958), p. 24.

[56]G. Blyn, *Agricultural Trends in India, op. cit.*

lems, he estimated that total foodgrain output increased slightly from 1891 to 1911 and thereafter showed a secular decline. Over the whole period 1891–1947 the average per annum increase was no more than 0·11 per cent. As in the recent so-called 'green revolution', wheat did much better than rice, and, therefore, the Punjab better than Bengal. Non-food grains show a much more rapid rate of growth, averaging 1·31 per cent per annum for British India. Tea and groundnuts did particularly well. All-crop output figures may mislead because of the heavy weight of backward Bengal and the difference between the relatively successful pre-1911 and post-1911 periods. But the all-crop average per annum increase of only 0·37 per cent failed to keep pace with population growth. The conclusion is a decline in *per capita* all-crop production, of the order of 0·72 per cent per annum in British India after 1911–12. According to Blyn, therefore, the rate of growth of agricultural output in the British period was negligible, and certainly considerably lower than even Nakamura's corrected low figures for Meiji Japan. The unresolved problem is to reconcile Blyn's findings, especially in the inter-war years, with falling mortality, the relative absence of famines until the Bengal, war-complicated disaster of 1943, and rapid population growth at a time when food-grain output was allegedly actually falling. It does not appear that people were multiplying less fast in the worst areas, Bengal, Bihar and Orissa. Nor can the answer lie substantially in less waste or less grain devoted to seed, although more research is needed on these topics. British India imported little food, and, indeed, exported wheat to Britain. Even excluding rice-exporting Burma, India was a net exporter of grains until about 1920 and the net imports thereafter were negligible.[57] Food exports were discussed frequently, for example, in the House of Lords in 1874, in the context of the Bengal famine. The Duke of Argyll supported Governor-General Lord Northbrook's refusal to prohibit them.[58] A similar view was expressed by the Famine Commission of 1880.[59] Apart from ideological arguments, the main justification for non-interference was the likely disincentive effect of an embargo and, in any case, the small percentage of exports to total output.

Blyn fails to cover the important livestock sector. Yet undivided India had 150 million cattle in 1928, and the Indian Union 155

[57]As late as 1939–40 India exported 8,000 tons of wheat and 50,000 tons of flour. 'Statistical Abstract for British India'. Cd. 6441, 1943.

[58]*Hansard's Parliamentary Debates*, Third Series, Vol. CCXVIII, 24 April 1874, col. 1076.

[59]*Parliamentary Papers*, Vol. LII, 'Report of the Indian Famine Commission', 1880, Part I, p. 49.

million cattle and 43 million buffaloes in 1951–2.[60] The 'sacred cow', the ban on its slaughter in several states since Independence, and the marginal productivity of cattle, have stimulated a learned controversy in recent years.[61] It is unlikely, however, that Muslims, and less likely that mainly Hindu Indians, were able or willing to compensate for food grain deficiency with animal products. Allowing for the inaccurate data, and excepting some regions, farmers and cash crops, the agrarian sector does seem to substantiate the view, if not of stagnation, at least of very limited long-run development between 1858 and 1947.

Agriculture, forestry and fishing comprised only about half of the national income at the time of Independence. Mining and manufacturing contributed around 17 per cent, with under 11 per cent of the labour force. There is plenty of evidence of a big absolute increase in the output of mines and large-scale industries.[62] Coal output was about 200,000 tons in 1858, 6 million tons in 1900, 16 million in 1914, and 30 million tons in 1947. Iron ore production was just under $2\frac{1}{2}$ million tons in 1947 and Meek's famous article on 'measures of economic activity' showed an 89 per cent increase in all-mineral production between 1909–13 and 1935.[63] The absolute secular increase in factory manufacturing output, especially in cotton and jute, is too well known to need elaboration. Even finished steel, sometimes regarded as a symbol of 'progress', reached a peak production figure for the British period of around one million tons in 1941. By 1939 India was producing three-quarters of her steel consumption, although this might imply a limited market, rather than spectacular advance. The foreign trade statistics provide a further rough guide to industrial development. In the days of the East India Company manufactures figured prominently in exports. In the nineteenth century, India's exports were dominated by primary commodities and her imports by consumer manufactures. From the First World War the export share of articles mainly or wholly

[60]Royal Commission on Agriculture, *op. cit.*, p. 191, and Rural Credit Survey, *op. cit.*, Vol. II, p. 112.

[61]See, for example, V. M. Dandekar, 'Sacred Cattle and More Sacred Production Functions', *Economic and Political Weekly*, 21 March 1970; C. H. Rao, 'India's Surplus Cattle', *ibid.*, 27 December 1969; 'The Cow, a Symposium', *Seminar*, Vol. XCIII (May 1967).

[62]Descriptions of industrial growth are to be found in many books, e.g. V. Anstey, *The Economic Development of India* (London, 1957); D. R. Gadgil, *The Industrial Evolution of India in Recent Times* (Oxford, 1944); N. S. R. Sastry, *A Statistical Study of India's Industrial Development* (Bombay, 1947).

[63]D. B. Meek, 'Some Measures of Economic Activity in India', *Journal of the Royal Statistical Society*, Part III, 1937, Vol. C, pp. 363 ff.

manufactured rose to as much as 43 per cent of the value of exports in 1940–1.[64]

The evidence of growth in mining and large-scale manufacturing contradicts generalisations about stagnation and decline. Whether it satisfies the second Rostowian condition for 'take-off' or whether it could be described as 'an industrial revolution' is much more doubtful, although Malenbaum surely took too gloomy a view when he wrote that 'India was not an appreciably more industrialised nation in 1951 than in the first decade of the century'.[65] There were, however, signs of relative backwardness. Only a small proportion, probably less than 2 per cent, of the 11 per cent of workers in mining and manufacturing industry at Independence was in the 'modern' large-scale sector. It contributed only about 7 per cent of national income. Spatial and product diversification was limited. Half of the factory workers in the early 1930s were in and around Calcutta and Bombay. Ahmedabad and to a much lesser extent, Cawnpore, Madras and, in iron and steel, Jamshedpur, were the only other large centres of industry. Cotton and jute spinning and weaving employed the bulk of factory workers, some one third to one half towards the end of the period; minerals and metals only one twenty-fifth.[66] Although in absolute terms the engineering industry had grown to employ 350,000 workers by 1947, most of these were in railway workshops. Even the long-established textile industry relied largely on imported machines until the Second World War. Ring-spinning, pioneered in America and only introduced widely in Britain in the 1890s[67] was adopted by Tata at the Empress Mills as early as 1883;[68] but the manufacture of the machines in India had to wait another sixty years. The ruler of Mysore established the first hydro-electric works, supplying, *inter alia*, the Kolar gold-fields, in 1903.[69] With a market guaranteed by David Sassoon's Bombay mills, and with Indian capital, Dorabji fulfilled a dream of his more famous father by launching the Tata Hydro-Electric Supply Company in 1910.[70] Thirteen years after Independence, however, the Government estimated that only 4 per cent of the energy consumed in India came

[64]K. Davis, *The Population of India and Pakistan, op. cit.*, p. 213. These figures beg questions of definition and data.

[65]W. Malenbaum, *op. cit.*, p. 31.

[66]*Indian Labour Year Book* (New Delhi, 1949), p. 2.

[67]J. H. Clapham, *An Economic History of Modern Britain*, Vol. II, Book III (Cambridge, 1932), p. 80.

[68]Indian Industrial Commission, *Minutes of Evidence*, Vol. II, Cd. 235, 1919: Note on the Empress Cotton Mills, Nagpur, p. 516. See also F. Harris, *J. N. Tata: A Chronicle of His Life* (London, 1958), p. 30.

[69]*Report of the Indian Industrial Commission*, p. 67.

[70]F. Harris, *op. cit.*, p. 229.

from hydro-electricity as against 19 per cent from oil, 22 per cent from coal and 55 per cent from firewood, farm-waste and dung.[71] British India, as far as categorisation is possible, even in the factory sector exemplifies Hoffman's first and second industrial stages.[72] A report of the Sample Survey of Manufacturing Industries estimated that in 1953, textiles, food and tobacco comprised no less than 52 per cent of value added by manufacturing in the Indian Union. Metals, engineering and electricity accounted for less than 22 per cent.[73]

This predominance is most striking in small-scale industry, a sector which defies precise analysis, covering as it does a wide range of urban and rural, traditional and modern, hand and machine operated and local and export-oriented crafts. All that can be said with certainty, as Mark Twain once said of himself, is that its death has been greatly exaggerated. There are no long-run aggregate series of small-industry output, employment or contribution to G.N.P. Some small industries declined, some declined to rise again (hand-spinning), some were born, and a large number persisted, throughout the British period. One estimate roughly puts cottage and small-industry contribution to net national income at 11 per cent in 1896–1905 and 9·8 per cent in 1936–45.[74] Another puts their share in the Indian Union in 1948–9, before active State support was effective, at about 10 per cent.[75] Of course, under the influence of foreign competition, indigenous factory competition, changes in taste and habit, loss of princely patronage and other factors, in India as in most other countries, many native trades decayed. High marketing and raw material expenses, dear credit and poor quality made some industries uncompetitive unless protected by market imperfections.[76] These imperfections were reduced by improved

[71]Ministry of Labour, *Report of the Central Wages Board for the Coal Mining Industry*, (Delhi, 1968), p. 8.

[72]W. G. Hoffman, *The Growth of Industrial Economies*, (Manchester, 1958).

[73]See M. Mukherjee, *National Income of India, op. cit.*, p. 184.

[74]K. Prasad, *Technological Choice under Development Planning: A Case Study of the Small Industries of India* (Bombay, 1963), p. 15.

[75]M. Mukherjee, *op. cit.*, p. 176.

[76]There is a large literature on the subject, including P. N. Dhar, *Small Scale Industries in Delhi* (Delhi, 1958); S. Nanjundan, H. E. Robison and Eugene Staley, *Economic Research for Small Industry Development Illustrated by India's Experience* (London, 1962, for the Stanford Research Institute); Society for Social and Economic Studies, *Capital for Medium and Small Scale Industries* (Bombay, 1959). A detailed account can be found in the various district Reports on the Survey of Cottage Industries in Madras, (e.g. Madras, 1929), and in the Government of India, *Report of the Fact Finding Committee (Handloom and Mills)* (Calcutta, 1942).

communications, especially railways.[77] Thus cottage tanning in Madras was virtually dead in the 1920s.[78] Swedish and British imports and, in the mid-nineteenth century, Mr Mackay's short-lived iron-works, killed off the old Birbhum iron industry.[79] Loss of courtly patronage hit gold and silver lace, and cheap glass imports from Austria, Germany and Japan undercut lac bangles in Madura and elsewhere.[80] More important was the well-known decline of hand-spinning, at first due to Manchester imports and later mainly to mill competition in India.

The picture of decay and decline is prominent in the literature. That 'the bones of the cotton weavers are bleaching the plains of India' is still a common quotation.[81] On the other hand, the Royal Commission on Agriculture was impressed by the 'remarkable vitality' of the handloom cotton industry.[82] Mr Chatterton of Madras queried the Census figures and found, in 1916, 'no general falling off in the employment of hand-weavers . . . in the last forty years'. Indeed, output per head was rising and there were growing exports in hand-produced handkerchiefs and shawls.[83] Prasad found hand-loom cloth output greater than mill output up to the First World War; thereafter there was a relative but no absolute decline in the quantity produced.[84] Of 6,000 million yards of cloth consumed in India in 1929–30, 2,420 millions were produced by Indian mills, 1,910 millions imported and 1,670 millions supplied by handlooms.[85] As a percentage of total Indian cotton cloth production, handloom output was, in the 1930s, about 30 per cent according to Meek, and 25 to 30 per cent according to Myers.[86] In 1950–1, again before State support was active, the Indian Union alone had 10 million

[77]Cf. *Third Report of the Select Committee on the Finance and Financial Administration of India* (1873) XII, question 4980, where the inhabitants of Ahmedabad complained of 'the rapid decline and decay of the indigenous industrial arts'.

[78]Report on Madras, *op. cit.*, p. 199.

[79]H. Sanyal, 'The Indigenous Iron Industry of Birbhum', *Indian Economic and Social History Review*, Vol. V, No. I (March 1968).

[80]*Report on Madura District* (Madras, 1928), p. 72.

[81]Cf. K. C. Shukla, 'A Note on Economic Changes and Policy in India during 1800–1947', *Indian Journal of Economics*, June 1968.

[82]Report, p. 569.

[83]*Report of the Indian Industrial Commission, 1916–18*, Cd. 51, App. I, 'Statistics on Hand-loom weaving', p. 388.

[84]K. Prasad, *op. cit.* He provides admittedly dubious data on output and employment. For example, see p. 26.

[85]P. S. Lokanathan, *Industrial Organisation in India* (London, 1935), p. 89.

[86]D. B. Meek, *op. cit.*, p. 372; C. A. Myers, *Labor Problems in the Industrialisation of India* (Harvard, 1958), p. 16.

persons dependent for employment on hand-weaving of cotton.[87] Statistics of hand-pounding of rice, oil, gur, leatherware and many other trades demonstrate a surviving large output and employment.

Many of these industries were traditional in product and method and it is perhaps true that they adapted less readily to twentieth-century technology than did some of their Japanese counterparts. But new products, techniques and inputs were not altogether absent. In Madras in the 1920s changes in taste and incomes created a new demand for hand-made shoes.[88] At the end of the British period 90 per cent of foot-wear output was hand-processed and 95 per cent of foot-wear employment was cottage and small-scale.[89] Calicut, of ancient textile fame, had a growing umbrella industry after the First World War; but it relied on imports for iron-ribs and even water-proof cloth, producing locally only bamboo sticks and handles.[90] Transport improvements and the Western 'demonstration effect' were said to have stimulated the demand for cottage cheroots, cigarettes and toys. As in many other countries, the sewing machine revolutionised tailoring.[91] But the most important technical change was the adoption of the fly-shuttle. New material inputs also improved quality and output between the wars. Coal-tar dyes may have harmed indigenous indigo but they ensured cheaper and more regular supplies for weavers.[92] Imports of brass-sheets reduced the demand for the services of the brass-founder but extended the business of the makers of brass hollow-ware.[93] But the input of greatest significance was yarn. The Glasgow Chamber of Commerce complained, not altogether altruistically, in 1860 that recent increases in Indian tariffs on yarn imports were 'totally at variance, not only with the free trade principle, but with the material interests of the natives of India'.[94] In retrospect, later free trade in yarn benefited Indian hand-loom weavers, especially those who required higher counts for finer goods. Hand-spinners suffered from British and later from Indian and Japanese competition, although resuscitated by the Ghandhi-inspired All-India Spinner's Association. Hand-spun yarn was dearer and of poorer quality than mill yarn of equivalent counts,

[87] *All India Rural Credit Survey, General Report*, Vol. II (Bombay, 1954), p. 116.
[88] *Report on Cottage Industries, op. cit.* (Madras), p. 199.
[89] K. Prasad, *op. cit.*, p. 49.
[90] *Report on Cottage Industries, op. cit.*, p. 211.
[91] *Report of the Indian Industrial Commission*, Ch. XVII, 'Cottage Industries', p. 193.
[92] *Report on Cottage Industries: Salem District*, p. 18.
[93] *Report of Industrial Commission*, Ch. I, p. 6.
[94] *Minutes of the Glasgow Chamber of Commerce*, Vol. VIII, p. 308, 'Petition to the House of Commons, 21 June 1860'.

and the surveyors of cottage industries in Madras found little case for encouraging it.[95] It was regarded as a sign of progress that in Kurnool, in the 1920s, farmers, profiting by a switch from raw cotton to ground-nuts were relieved of the tedious drudgery of the spinning wheel.[96]

The evidence presented here on the small industries is no substitute for long-run aggregate series of output, employment and investment. Nor is this the place to indulge in the theoretical case for artificially stimulating this sector. That there was a great deal of under-utilised capacity in both equipment and skills is clear from the documents. But that all had a low capital-output ratio is an over-simplification. So is the belief that farmers could easily transfer to rural industries in slack seasons.[97] The Royal Commission on Agriculture found no solution for pressure on the land in supporting country handicrafts whose products, in the long run, could not compete with those of the factory.[98] The declining importance of the small-scale, at least the traditional sector, is usually indicative of economic progress.[99] That it was not so regarded in India was partly due to political sentimentality and more to the failure of the expanding modern sector to provide adequate employment.

Although the precise contribution of railways to economic development is now a matter of debate, few would deny the positive benefits of improved communications. The outline history of ports and harbours, canals, roads, railways, and telegraphs in India has oft been told. Roads were a labour-intensive sector utilising abundant local materials and slack-season workers, but in 1928 the Agricultural Commission found that most villages had no proper roads.[100] In 1951–2 there were only 0·22 miles of road per square mile in the Indian Union.[101] Where the tangible wealth of transport animals was much greater than that of vehicles, even in 1950, the absence of 'pakka' roads was not serious in the dry season; during the monsoon, however, it meant the virtual isolation of thousands of villages.

Railways at once provide a major exception to laissez-faire, and

[95]See, for example, report on the Nellore district, p. 3 and the general report, p. 63. Gandhi's case, the provision of work for the underemployed, is now justified by some on sophisticated economic terms.

[96]*Report on the Kurnool District* (Madras, 1927), p. 1.

[97]The Royal Commission on Agriculture stressed the difficulty of training peasants for many rural industries. *Report*, Cd. 3132, (1928), p. 564.

[98]*Ibid.*, p. 575.

[99]Small industry, however, survives in all countries and was remarkably persistent in Japan for peculiar organisational reasons.

[100]*Report*, Cd. 3132 (1928), p. 369.

[101]Rural Credit Survey, Vol. II, *op. cit.*, p. 23.

a major potential implement of socio-economic transformation. Started by guaranteed British companies in the 1850s, later built and managed by a mixture of private and State enterprise, rail mileage open for traffic increased to 4,800 in 1870, 25,000 in 1900 and 40,500 at the end of British rule. There has been controversy over the motives behind Government support for railways, and over their results. On the former one may decide against mono-causalism and find a complex interaction of socio-political, military and economic reasons, ranging from fear of Russian aggression to the carriage of salt and cotton.[102] On the latter Marx[103] and British promoters and administrators were agreed on the likely beneficial effects of railways. Typical was the Court of Directors of the East India Company writing in 1853 of 'the various benefits, political, commercial and social which that great measure of public improvement would unquestionably produce'.[104] One hundred years later Thorner could complain that 'they had surprisingly few constructive results' and Kidron that they 'had little spread effect'.[105] There was much to criticise in Indian railway policy and organisation. In an early, crude Fogel-type analysis, General Sir Arthur Cotton wanted less outlay on railways and more on dual-purpose canals, at once satisfying the needs of transport and irrigation and saving foreign exchange.[106] With Britain's early-nineteenth-century experience of the two modes of transport, and forty-four railway directors in the Lords and 112 in the Commons in 1860,[107] it is hardly surprising that many echoed Lord Bentinck's sentiment that 'the day has gone by when anybody would dream of encouraging the construction of [transport] canals'.[108] Irrigation canals were another matter. Irrigation and agriculture, in which the former predominated, accounted for

[102]See, for example, W. J. Macpherson, 'Investment in Indian Railways, 1845–75', *Economic History Review*, Vol. VIII, No. 2 (December 1955), and a criticism of this by F. Lehmann, 'Great Britain and the Supply of Locomotives ... A Case of Economic Imperialism', *Indian Social and Economic History Review*, October 1965.

[103]Despatch No. 3840 to the *New York Daily Tribune*, 8 August 1853; in Marx and Engels, *op. cit.*

[104]*Railway Letters from Bengal and India*, Vol. I, No. 4, of 4 May 1853. (Manuscripts in London, India Office Library.)

[105]D. Thorner, *Journal of Economic History*, Vol. XI, No. 4, 1951; M. Kidron, *Foreign Investments in India* (London, 1965), p. 14.

[106]A. Cotton, *Public Works in India* (London, 1854), *passim*; and Lady Hope, *General Sir Arthur Cotton: His Life and Work* (London, 1900). Florence Nightingale lent support to Cotton, but Henry Fawcett shrewdly queried the reluctance of British capitalists to invest if the expected profits of canals were as enormous as Cotton maintained, *ibid.*, pp. 504 and 257.

[107]*Herapath's Railway and Commercial Journal*, Vol. XXII, (1860), p. 39.

[108]*Hansard*, Third Series, Vol. XCII, 6 May 1847, Col. 487.

between 12 and 16 per cent of net public investment in 'asset-creating activities' in the first half of this century.[109] The percentage of cultivated area in 1938–9 irrigated by private and public works was estimated at 26, and by public works alone at 15.[110] In the Punjab, Government works irrigated 43 per cent and in dry Sind 86 per cent of the cultivated area. Canals were not without their complications. The neediest could not afford the charges. Channels were sometimes blocked by weeds. Waterlogging, salinity and malaria were problems. But then, as now, few alterations more improved yields than adequate water-supply.

Railways were both more expensive and were allocated more resources than irrigation. Total State investment in 'creative' assets ranged from under 3 to over 5 per cent of national income from the 1890s to 1947. The share of railways fell in the inter-war period, but from about 1898 to 1914 it was over half of gross public 'creative investment'. That this investment had considerably greater impact on the economy than many would allow will be shown below. And, post-Fogel, we would not anticipate the revolutionary results envisaged by Marx and the early British officials. True, there were multiplier leakages to Britain, where the backward linkages were most felt, but the small mileage in proportion to area and population also limited the railways' overall fillip. The highly-critical 1921 Railway Committee said as much when it bemoaned the inadequacy of the existing system, an inadequacy exacerbated by the conditions of the First World War. As railways were by then bringing net revenue to the State, it urged more borrowing for more mileage.[111] Among the greatest legacies of Britain to India was one of the biggest railway networks in the world. But in 1947, per square mile and even more, per head, the mileage open was smaller than that of most developed countries.[112]

[109]M. J. K. Thavaraj, 'Capital Formation in the Public Sector, 1898–1935', in V. K. R. V. Rao et al., (eds), *Papers on National Income and Allied Topics*, Vol. I (London, 1960), p. 216. See also his article, 'Public Investment in India, 1898–1914', *Indian Economic Review*, August 1955. 'Asset-creating activities', included transport and communications, public buildings, irrigation and agriculture, State trading companies, but not education, social services or the biggest field of Government outlay – 'defence'.

[110]V. Anstey, *op. cit.*, p. 616. See also Reports of the Indian Irrigation Commission, e.g. Cd. 1851, Vol. LXVI, (1904).

[111]*Report of the Committee into the Working and Administration of Indian Railways*, Cd. 1512 (1921), pp. 7ff. See also *Report on Indian Railways 1903*, Cd. 1713, Vol. XIVII, and annual reports on the railways, e.g. Cd. 232, Vol. LVIII (1900).

[112]In 1928 India had 2·2 miles of railway, the U.S.A. 8·42, per 100 square miles. Inhabitants per mile were India 7,894; Russia in Europe 3,700; U.S.A. 469; and Canada 222. *Report of the Royal Commission on Agriculture in India*, Cd. 3132 (1928), p. 369.

Irrigation and railways, law and the civil service were the greatest monuments of British rule. But the Government of India also invested absolutely large but *per capita* small sums on public buildings, agricultural services, health, education and other forms of social overhead capital.[113] There was even sporadic aid to industry, expecially in the inter-war period, as will be shown later. Although the State spent a small proportion of its own, and a smaller of national income on obviously creative assets, a limited infrastructure was being laid down. And the burgeoning of foreign-trade, urbanisation and of joint-stock corporations might be taken as further indicators of economic progress. It may be that all these advances were swallowed up, especially after 1920, by the growing population, and that the conditions of the people failed to improve. The vital question then, is what happened to the 'standard of living', and in any definitive sense it must remain an open one.

Standards of living, embracing as they do psychic as well as material concepts, are notoriously difficult to define and measure. The subject has occasioned a large and controversial literature about the industrial revolution period in England, although many would now agree with Hicks that 'industrialism, in the end, has been highly favourable to the real wage of labour'.[114] Indefinite statements about 'poverty' and 'subsistence' abound for India at the beginning and end of our period. Thus, John Bright in 1850 described the lot of the cultivators as one of 'extreme, abject and almost universal poverty'.[115] Ninety years later K. T. Shah pronounced that 'the mass of humanity in India habitually lives below the level of subsistence'.[116] Yet, in between, Davis deduced 'a slight but erratic rise', Mrs Anstey 'a slight but definite improvement' in the general standard of life.[117] With only 27 per cent of income by factor shares going as compensation to employees just after Independence, and wide variations in pay for even similar jobs, quantification is difficult. Kuczynski's pioneering work is now out-dated.[118] Bhattacharya, for the last few decades of the nineteenth century,

[113]See V. Anstey, *op. cit.*, e.g. Table XX, p. 633.
[114]J. Hicks, *A Theory of Economic History* (Oxford, 1969), p. 148.
[115]*Hansard s Parliamentary Debates*, Vol. CXII, 18 June 1850, Col. 16. To improve this situation the allegedly laissez-faire 'Manchester School, saw no inconsistency in urging State intervention in Indian cotton and railways.
[116]*Oxford Pamphlets on Indian Affairs*, No. 3 (1942), 'The Economic Background', p. 13.
[117]K. Davis, *The Population of India and Pakistan, op. cit.*, p. 206; V. Anstey, *op. cit.*, p. 473.
[118]J. Kuczynski, *A Short History of Labour Conditions under Industrial Capitalism* (London, 1947).

adjudged real wages to have fallen. Mukherjee's index of the real wage of industrial workers shows no marked trend from 1882 to 1900.[119] In the textile mills, K. Mukherji thought real wages to be double in 1931–51 what they were in 1900–21.[120] An enormous secular rise in Bombay cotton money wages is shown by Morris, but he warns about the 'frailty and ambiguity of the evidence'.[121] Problems including changes in working hours, bonuses, absenteeism, the job content, not to mention measuring the cost-of-living and unemployment – all these obviate firm welfare judgements based on wage data. Finding employment outlets was and is a crucial difficulty. In India, as elsewhere, real wages of workers who retained their jobs rose in the slump. At the moment, the evidence tentatively suggests a secular rise of real wages for factory workers and, after the First World War, belated legislation on humidification, hours of work, safety and health-care were bringing improvements.

That conditions in factories and towns were deplorable – a reminder of the more emotional passages written about England by the Hammonds and Engels – is seen, *inter alia*, in the pages of the 1931 Royal Commission on Labour in India. An example is quoted of the monthly outgoings of an 'average' factory family of four-and-a-half in 1925–6. Just under half of the expenditure went on food (25 per cent on cereals), 11 per cent on clothing, 9 per cent on fuel and light, 6 per cent on rent, 6·6 per cent on interest on debt, and 7·6 per cent on miscellaneous items. The Commission stressed the prevalence of debt, well known in agrarian circles, even among factory employees. The 'common' rate of interest was one anna in the rupee per month, said to be equivalent to a monthly charge of 25 per cent of the workers' wages.[122] The Industrial Commission judged 80 per cent of Bombay mill-workers to be in debt, half of them paying interest at 75 per cent per annum.[123] As in rural areas, the majority of loans came from money-lenders and 'social-expenditure' was the main cause of debt, especially outlay on

[119]D. Bhattacharya, 'Trend of Wages in India, 1873–1900', *Artha-Vijnana*, Vol. VII (1965); M. Mukherjee, *op. cit.*, p. 90.

[120]See, for example, *Artha-Vijnana*, March 1960, June 1961 and June 1962.

[121]M. D. Morris, *The Emergence of an Industrial Labor Force in India, op. cit.*, p. 223, Table XX.

[122]*Report of the Royal Commission on Labour in India*, 1931, Cd. 3883, pp. 194ff. For earlier periods see 'Report of the Bombay Factory Commission, 6 January 1885', *Parliamentary Papers*, Vol. LXXVII, 399 (1888); and 'Report of the Indian Factory Labour Commission', *Parliamentary Papers*, LXXIV, Cd. 4292 (1908).

[123]Indian Industrial Commission, 1916–18, *Minutes of Evidence*, Vol. IV, Cd. 236, p. 366. See also *Indian Labour Year Book* (Delhi, 1949), p. 185, for evidence that many workers' expenditure exceeded income.

marriages. The mere existence of debt does not necessarily imply abject poverty, and heavy borrowing might refute the backward bending supply curve of labour hypothesis. It was noted that railway workers, with more regular employment and pay, were more indebted than others, simply because money-lenders found they had greater security. The conclusion remains that, although conditions might have been better after the First World War than before, the bulk of factory workers were heavily indebted, had uncertain employment and an income so low that most of it went on what Westerners regard as the bare essentials of life.

Factory workers formed a tiny proportion of the Indian working force. To speculate on conditions in the small-industry sector would be fruitless. The impression from the literature is that, in income and in environmental terms, they were not better than in the factories. The early-nineteenth-century English hand-loom weavers spring to mind. The state of the majority of the people, the peasantry and agricultural labourers, fluctuated according to the weather, and covers a wide range of incomes. For most of the British period we lack quantitative studies such as those of the All-India Rural Credit Survey. Much production and consumption was non-monetised and financial assets, of which 'ornaments' formed a large part, were a small fraction of total assets. It is clear that, as far as one can generalise, rural incomes were, on average, substantially lower than urban incomes. Bansil's estimate, one of many, puts *per capita* urban incomes at more than twice rural in 1948–9.[124] It is clear, also, that there were wide regional disparities. In a superficial survey of five rural classes, the 1909 survey of the past fifty years found all but the landless labourers 'better off'.[125] A Punjab Government Committee of 1939 believed that owner-occupiers, after a set-back in the slump, were enjoying rising incomes and complained of 'the tendency, in the case of the uneducated, for every material blessing to be converted into larger families'. The same Committee, however, generalised that 'tenants were hard put to it to make both ends meet'.[126] And the Census of 1921 enumerated 53 million 'depressed classes', one-sixth of the population.

[124]Quoted by M. Mukherjee, *op. cit.*, p. 434.
[125]Memorandum, *op. cit.*, p. 26.
[126]*Report of the Resources and Retrenchment Committee Appointed by the Punjab Government* (Lahore, 1939), pp. 35 and 88. But see also, for a later date, an econometric analysis which showed no significant relation between the rate of population growth in Rajasthan and the four variables studied: urbanisation, literacy, density of population and *per capita* income. B. C. Mehta, 'Population Growth in Rajasthan, an Econometric Analysis, 1951–61', *Economic and Political Weekly*, 9 May 1970.

Indebtedness is often taken as symptomatic of rural poverty, but it was not peculiar to India, nor was the amount of debt necessarily indicative of low income. The really impoverished classes were unable to borrow. Debt implies lending, and some sections of the rural community had spare resources. The Credit Survey showed that the highest percentage (higher than on purchase of livestock, land or housing) of savings used for investment expenditure of all kinds was on 'lendings'. Close behind in the utilisation of the surplus, however, came repayment of old debts.[127] It is said that in 1951 the all-India proportion of indebted families to total rural families was 63·3 per cent, with a higher percentage among cultivators (land the security) than among non-cultivators. Of total farmers' assets, including land, debt amounted to 5·9 per cent.[128] This tells us little about real incomes. Nor do we know accurately by how much, if at all, indebtedness was increasing under British rule. There were edicts against money-lending in the Code of Manu. The evidence for it waxing after 1800 is more reliable.[129] As reasons, prominence was given to the greater legal rights of money-lenders, the increased alienation of land under the British tenure systems, and the growth of a more widespread cash nexus. Not all saw these as disadvantageous.

What was generally predicted as injurious was the purpose of the borrowing. Darling, in his widely-read book on the Punjab, discussed this long ago.[130] The Credit Survey's break-down of the 'purposes of borrowing' has now become part of the dogma. Admittedly, nearly 28 per cent of borrowing in 1950–1 was for capital expenditure on the farm, a further 9 per cent for current expenditure on the farm, and 6½ per cent for non-farm business expenditure. However, much of the investment was for maintenance rather than for the creation of new assets. In addition, as was frequently discerned of the British period, family expenditure was the main purpose of borrowing (over 50 per cent), and within this category ceremonials such as marriages, funerals and births figured prominently. There is some substantiation of the permanent income hypothesis. Expenditure in many cases was rigidly geared to past incomes and to fixed customary social outlays. It did not fluctuate, in the short run at least, with income. A failure of the monsoon or a marriage, therefore, necessitated borrowing. An unexpected

[127] *All India Rural Credit Survey*, Vol. I, Part I, p. 747.
[128] See, for example, J. P. Bhattacharjee, *op. cit.*, p. 282; and T. Shukla, *op. cit.*, p. 164.
[129] *Indian Central Banking Enquiry Committee*, 1931, Vol. I, Part I, p. 55. See also, United Nations, *Domestic Financing of Economic Development* (New York, 1950), p. 132.
[130] M. L. Darling, *The Punjab Peasant in Prosperity and Debt* (London, 1925).

increase in income, again in the short run, was used to repay debts and to hoard in the form of ornaments and bullion, liquid assets representing future purchasing power. These expenditure habits were criticised frequently as examples of prodigality and extravagance.[131]

Naturally the money-lenders, in the words of the Indian proverb, going 'in like a needle and out like a sword', attracted a great deal of vilification, not least from officials. The State conducted enquiries, passed acts for the scaling down of debts, and tried to curb the creditors' powers by fixing maximum rates of interest and preventing land alienation. Some thought the panacea lay in co-operative credit and, from the 1904 Co-operative Credit Societies' Act, there was considerable absolute progress. By 1938–9 there were over 105,000 agricultural societies with about $3\frac{1}{2}$ million members.[132] But co-operation failed to dominate Indian rural society as it had done in Japan. In progressive Punjab 45 per cent of the villages had no co-operative society in 1938.[133] State-sponsored bodies were not so popular or flexible as money-lenders: they required regular repayments and, most important, they would not make advances for ceremonial outlays. Even in 1951–2 it was estimated that over 70 per cent of borrowings came from money-lenders, only 3 per cent from the Government, 2·9 per cent from co-operatives, and 1 per cent from commercial banks. Rates of interest varied too widely for meaningful generalisation, but 50 per cent was not uncommon. These reflect high risks and uncertainty as well as scarcity of credit and monopoly in supply. In a poor, peasant society, subject to weather fluctuations and conventional expenditure, 'indebtedness was accepted as a settled fact, a natural state of life'.[134] Observation in the field, of widespread disease, bad housing, inadequate medical and educational facilities, and data showing an average intake of only 1,750 calories per day by much of the population, and a *per capita* income of perhaps Rs. 255 per annum in the 1940s – abundant evidence of this sort demonstrates, even to the most avid apologist of the British, a low standard of living. That more and different things could have been done to improve it is axiomatic. But with an inter-war population increase as big as the combined populations of France and Britain, the tasks were massive.

[131]For example in the *Report of the Royal Commission on Agriculture, op. cit.*, p. 435.

[132]V. Anstey, *op. cit.* For a general history of the movement see E. M. Hough, *The Co-operative Movement in India* (London, 1967); D. Thorner, *Agricultural Co-operatives in India* (London, 1965); and H. H. Mann, *The Social Framework of Agriculture* (London, 1968) evaluate the problems critically.

[133]*Report of the Punjab Land Revenue Committee* (Lahore, 1938), p. 90.

[134]*Report of the Royal Commission on Agriculture. op. cit.*, p. 435.

In late-eighteenth-century Britain, a combination of demand
pressures eliciting an elastic supply of factors was sufficient to achieve
a remarkable upsurge of the economy. Pejorative designations such
as stagnation and decay may be unhelpful in the light of considerable
Indian progress, but the British exemplar of growth was manifestly
not experienced. It would be presumptuous in what remains of this
essay to do other than indicate a few of the involved pressures and
factor responses in some sectors of the Indian economy.

Employment-wise and as a generator of G.N.P., agriculture was
the most important sector. The theoretical and historical role of
farming in economic growth is arguable. Its contribution to industrialisation in late-eighteenth-century Britain can no longer be
dogmatically described.[135] Even the once-classic Japanese case is
now open to dispute.[136] Nurkse reasoned that agricultural improvement was not the first prerequisite – that disguised unemployment in
agriculture suggested concentration in other areas and the transfer of
labour from the farms to produce capital goods.[137] Davis postulated
that '200 million might be withdrawn from Indian agriculture with
a net gain in *per capita* production'.[138] The assumptions are that
labour was excess and could be moved. But in early British India, in
the plantations, and in Burma throughout, labour was occasionally
a scarce factor. Seasonal shortages of farm workers were not
unknown, as factory owners and railway managers often complained,
and as often exaggerated.[139] Generalisations of over-all zero
marginal productivity of labour are meaningless when there were
many farms adding hired workers at a positive wage.[140] Fragmentation of holdings, due to the customary law of partibility, reduced the
possibility of removing labour without affecting output. These are
apart from problems of keeping food consumption constant over the
whole population when, at low levels of income, the income elasticity

[135]D. S. Landes, 'Technological Change and Development in Western Europe,
1750–1914', in *The Cambridge Economic History of Europe*, Vol. VI (Cambridge,
1965), p. 307.
[136]J. I. Nakamura, *op. cit.*, K. Ohkawa, B. F. Johnston and H. Kaneda (eds),
op. cit.
[137]R. Nurkse, *Problems of Capital Formation in Underdeveloped Countries*
(Oxford, 1953), p. 36.
[138]K. Davis, *The Population of India and Pakistan, op. cit.*, p. 120.
[139]See, for example, *Railway Letters and Enclosures from India and Bengal*,
Vol. VIII, 1853, No. 6, enclosure No. 5, p. 75; 'Report on Finance and Financial
Administration of India', 1871, *Parliamentary Papers* Vol. VIII, App. IV; Indian
Industrial Commission, *Minutes of Evidence*, Vol. II, Cd. 235, 1919, p. 516.
[140]For an illuminating discussion of this problem, see W. C. Neale, *Economic
Change in Rural India* (New Haven, 1962), p. 166 *et. seq.*

of demand for food may have been high.[141] As the period proceeded and peasants multiplied, unlimited supplies of labour became nearer to reality. But their removal without force was not easy. One may dispute its precise role and argue whether it was a prerequisite for or concurrent with industrialisation, but some agricultural improvement was a significant factor in British and Japanese development, operating through the frequently-quoted demand-market, and food, labour, capital and export supply factors.[142]

In British India there was some farm demand for non-agrarain inputs duch as implements, fertilisers and tractors, but it was small. The Government wrote a great deal about implements,[143] but T. Shukla has quantified their relative insignificance and the persistence of the traditional types. From 1935–6 to 1940–1, implements and machines accounted for 6 per cent, bullocks for 94 per cent of gross investment in implements and bullocks combined. And carts and wooden ploughs comprised over 82 per cent of gross capital formation in implements, tractors and iron ploughs only 0·8 per cent each.[144] As will be seen below, this does not imply a 'wrong' choice of technique. But it does suggest that the growth of an American or British type agricultural machinery industry was not viable. The neglect of natural, far less artificial fertilisers is notorious. Indeed India was a substantial exporter of fertilisers. Thus, more than half of the sulphate of ammonia produced as a by-product in the Tata iron, steel and coal works in 1925 was exported. At Rs. 140 per ton in Calcutta it was too expensive for use in all but the most valuable of sugar-cane and garden crops.[145] More surprising is to find India exporting bone manure in most of the period (52,000 tons in 1939–40).[146] Here religious attitudes rather than price limited internal demand, and it was argued that a prohibition of exports would lead to the extinction of bone-manure manufacture.[147] An artificial fertiliser industry in the modern sense was absent. The rural sector itself satisfied the limited demand for implements, fertilisers and

[141]For an analysis of patterns of consumption, see W. Malenbaum, *op. cit.*, Ch. VIII.

[142]Cf. B. F. Johnston and J. W. Mellor, 'The Role of Agriculture in Economic Development', *American Economic Review*, September 1961, pp. 571–81; and M. Boserup, 'Agrarian Structure and Take-Off', in W. W. Rostow (ed.), *The Economics of Take-Off into Self-Sustained Growth* (London, 1963), p. 202.

[143]See, for example, *Catalogue of Implements and Machines Tried and Found Useful at the Saidapet Experimental Farm* (Madras, 1883).

[144]T. Shukla, *op. cit.*, p. 212. Of course, a large part of G.C.F. was maintenance and repair.

[145]*Report of Royal Commission on Agriculture, op. cit.*, p. 89.

[146]*Statistical Abstract for British India*, Cd. 6441 (1943).

[147]*Report of Royal Commission on Agriculture, op. cit.*, p. 92.

other inputs. There was little spill-over to stimulate urban manu-facture of capital goods. The rural sector was the main market for consumer goods. After food, drink and tobacco, which was esti-mated at 65 per cent of rural consumption expenditure as late as 1957–8, clothing came next with 10 per cent. With rent, water, fuel and light taking another 10 per cent there was little over for luxuries.[148] There was a *potentially* large mass-market for urban industrial goods, but the existence of self-supply and low incomes provided a serious constraint.

The factor supply contribution of Indian agriculture was more significant. India not only fed her growing population, albeit at a low level of nutrition, but was a net exporter of food until the 1920s. The agrarian sector provided the bulk of the raw material for jute and cotton manufacturing, although, in cotton, the poor quality of the short-stapled Indian product necessitated imports for finer counts. It supplied, despite Hinduism, hides and skins for leather work, sugar cane, oil-seeds, rubber and, most important, tea. From the country surplus came much of the industrial labour force. It is more difficult to analyse the contribution to capital supplies. Land revenue or land tax (there was endless controversy over definition) formed a large but declining share of total tax revenue, from over 53 per cent in the early 1880s to 21 per cent in 1923–4. In the same period excise went down from 25 to 22 per cent, customs up from 3 to 24 per cent, and income taxes up from just over 1 to more than 12 per cent.[149] Indirect taxes including land revenue comprised about 95 per cent of tax-take before the first war. After tax, there was still an abso-lutely large rural surplus, much of it in the hands of landlords and money-lenders. Some of this found its way into Government bonds, railways, banks and occasionally manufacturing. Most of it, as will be seen, remained in the rural sector, in purchasing and leasing small land parcels, in lending, hoarding and ceremonials. A large surplus above self-consumption existed, as it always had done in historic times, and was arguably utilised more effectively than in the pre-British era. That ideally it *could* have been used more productively is pleonastic. The verdict remains, however, that the small *per capita* size of the rural residue inhibited the outflow of capital for any purpose.

Finally, until the very end of the period when jute manufactures became dominant, the agrarian sector was by far the largest export earner. From 1868–9 until the slump of 1928–9 the value of mer-chandise exports increased about seven-fold. This may seem small

[148]M. Mukherjee, *op. cit.*, p. 414.
[149]See, for example, V. Anstey, *op. cit.*, p. 388, for tax-take.

growth by Japanese standards but, apart from a little Dutch and Chinese trade, the 'isolationist' shoguns exported little and their Meiji successors started from near scratch. When the Crown took over in India in 1858, opium accounted for one-third, raw cotton about one-seventh of export earnings. Apart from a small quantity of cotton twist and yarn, manufactures were insignificant.[150] Opium declined steadily in importance, especially after the Chinese embargo of 1907, but raw cotton remained the chief export until 1938, when overtaken by tea, and these enabled, until about 1930, a persistent surplus of exports on the visible account.

The dangers of relying heavily on primary commodity exports and their failure to stimulate rapid development in some countries has been much discussed.[151] In India, for example, if the production possibility boundary were fixed, export crops might have been grown only at the expense of food crops for the home market. In some cases opium was competing for scarce food land.[152] A major export crop, tea, however, was grown mainly in hilly, previously jungle areas. Irrigation and reclamation of waste extended the production boundary. Blyn found that 'expanded cultivation of non-food grains did not curtail food grain acreage'.[153] On the whole export crops had higher yields per acre and per man, especially sugar, cotton and tea which, in the 1920s, accounted for half of so-called non-food crop output. In fact, although they comprised only 20 per cent of total crop output in 1940, the export-oriented crops were the most progressive sector in Indian agriculture. Berrill and others have emphasised the existence of enclaves as explaining the lack of spread effects. In British India tea was the only substantial instance of a high degree of enclavity. Even here not all the profits were leaked to Britain; Indian capital was entering the field in large amounts in the present century, and in 1947 one million plantation workers were spending most of their wages in the domestic market. Lesser degrees of enclavity could be demonstrated where, as in the dying indigo industry, British merchants advanced credit and remitted home some of the profits. But, compared with the West Indies and parts of Africa and Malaya, India is a poor example of an enclave economy. Between 1900 and

[150]Compiled from Statistical Abstracts Relating to British India.

[151]See, for example, K. Berrill, 'International Trade and the Rate of Economic Growth', *Economic History Review*, Second Series, Vol. XII, No. 3 (1960); H. Myint, 'The Gains from International Trade and the Backward Countries', *Review of Economic Studies*, Vol. XXII, No. 2 (1954–5); and 'The Classical Theory of International Trade and the Underdeveloped Countries', *Economic Journal*, Vol. LXVII, No. 270 (June 1958), pp. 317ff.

[152]Committee on Finance, *op. cit.*, 1871, question 9694.

[153]G. Blyn, *op. cit.*, p. 233.

1940 the proportion of plantation to total crop acreage was only 0·3 per cent.[154]

In the absence of stabilisation schemes before the 1930s, India's primary commodity exports were subject to considerable price fluctuations. The value of total merchandise exports more than doubled (in sterling at 2 shillings to the rupee) from just under £28 millions in 1860 to £68 millions in 1865. The reaction to the end of the American Civil War saw a fall to £45 millions in 1867.[155] Again export values fell drastically from 1928–9 to 1933–4. These externally inspired price fluctuations introduced an element of instability into the Indian economy. But the vast majority of peasants were affected more by internal weather fluctuations than by changes in world demand. Much more serious is the possibility that, over the long run, income was transferred from India to Britain through a deterioration of the former's terms of trade. As yet we have no definitive index of India's trade terms for the period 1858 to 1947. During the inter-war slump her export prices clearly fell more than her import prices. Majumdar deduced some deterioration from 1919 to 1939, but no pronounced secular movement.[156] For perhaps exceptional Burma, Maung Shein found a favourable movement in the barter terms of trade from 1885 to 1914.[157] Both theoretical and empirical objections could be and have been levelled against generalisations based on Prebisch.[158] More research is required if they are to be validated in the case of British India.

Among other explanations for the alleged failure of India's primary commodity exports to generate faster development was one stating that the imports they financed were largely consumer goods

[154]For tables of crop distribution by acreage see J. P. Bhattacharjee, *op. cit.*, pp. 13–14.

[155]Compiled from 'Statistical Abstracts'.

[156]N. Majumdar, 'Industrial Development and the Terms of Trade, 1919–39', *Arthaniti*, Vol. VI, No. 2 (July 1963), p. 27.

[157]Maung Shein, *Burma's Transport and Foreign Trade, 1885–1914* (Rangoon, 1964), p. 122. See also U. Aye Hlaing, 'A Study of Economic Development of Burma, 1870–1940' (mimeograph), University of Rangoon, 1964, App. B.

[158]R. Prebisch, 'The Economic Development of Latin America and its Principal Problems', *U.N. Economic Bulletin for Latin America*, February 1962, pp. 4–6. Cf. also, J. Bhagwati, 'A Sceptical Note on the Adverse Secular Trend of the Terms of Trade of Underdeveloped Countries', *Pakistan Economic Journal*, December 1960; and T. Morgan, 'The Long-run terms of Trade between Agriculture and Manufacturing', *Economic Development and Cultural Change*, October 1959; F. Mehta, 'Changes in the Terms of Trade as an Income Factor in World Trade, 1929–38', *Indian Economic Review*, February 1957; B. D. Sumitra, 'Terms of Trade and Economic Development . . . , the Indian Case', *International Studies*, October 1960.

which destroyed traditional industries and retarded the growth of new industries. Some imports, however, were complementary rather than competing, and there was, as will be seen later, some transmission of technological know-how. Finally, many scholars found a solution to the problem in the 'drain' thesis, namely that India's export surplus was manipulated to pay the 'home charges' – 'a net loss to India without any corresponding return'.[159] The pros and cons of the drain have been discussed too often to need reiteration here.[160] It could be argued that the part of the home charges which came under the heading of defence services (about 15 per cent in 1870–1 and over 20 per cent in 1934), were 'unproductive'.[161] Similarly with pensions, allowances and some of the 'civil' expenses. The British apologist would claim that in return for these India received a civil service, law, order and defence. Interest on social overhead capital, such as railways and irrigation, was the largest single item, and these had more obviously constructive effects. Whatever the conclusion, the fact is that British administrators were much concerned throughout with the budgetary and transfer problems involved, especially at periods when, in the words of a *Times* leader on the subject, 'our Manchester friends would never hear of increasing the duties on imports'.[162]

The transfer problem was seriously exacerbated in the late nineteenth century by the depreciation of silver, although, parenthetically, this also encouraged exports and 'protected' Indian industries during a period of virtual free trade. Many other reasons were given, but the revaluation, and perhaps over-valuation, of the rupee in 1927 was not unconnected with the need to make remittances from India. Nor does one need to agree with Sir George Wingate, when he wrote in 1859 that 'when taxes are raised and spent in a country . . . the money in one shape or another reaches the mass of the people, but when the taxes . . . are remitted out of it, the money is lost to the country for ever',[163] to accept that the

[159]K. T. Shah, *Sixty years of Indian Finance* (Bombay, 1921), pp. 167ff. This is one of many similar statements.

[160]See, *inter alia*, H. Lamb, 'The State and Economic Development in India', in S. Kuznets, *op. cit.*, p. 492; B. N. Ganguli, *D. Naoroji and the Drain Theory* (Calcutta, 1965). For a bibliography and summary of the two sides of the argument, see B. Chandra, 'Indian Nationalists and the Drain', *Indian Economic and Social History Review*, Vol. II, No. 2 (April 1965).

[161]For an account of how the ryot in India was taxed to pay for Britain's oriental military adventures see L. H. Jenks, *The Migration of British Capital to 1875* (London, 1927), p. 216.

[162]*The Times*, 29 January 1859.

[163]*A Few Words on Our Financial Relations with India* (London, 1859), p. 58.

revenue problem both for Indian and 'home' outlays was a serious one. Part of Indian development may have been, to use Haberler's concept,[164] induced by trade policy and the need to meet sterling obligations, but this does not preclude substantial linkage effects. The need to create an export surplus, in cash crops, may have generated greater productivity and the use of idle resources in agriculture, whose stimulus to income and activity more than offset any adverse effects of taxation and transfer.[165]

In other words, the need to pay 'home charges' and the railways and irrigation which partly occasioned their payment, forcibly got part of the rural sector moving. When we speak of the 'home charges', or indeed total exports, we are dealing with something quantitatively small in relation to national income. This is not to maintain that foreign trade's contribution to growth is readily measurable by its proportion to G.N.P. In an effort to correct the imbalance in the old drain controversy, some current scholars such as Morris and Chaudhuri, have perhaps underestimated the significance of the 'home charges'.[166] It is clear, however, that although foreign trade occupies a disproportionate amount of the literature, its share in G.N.P. was small. Gurtoo put commodity exports, f.o.b. in 1953–4 at 4·9 per cent of India's national income at factor cost.[167] The share may have been higher in the British period but not so much that changes in exports or the 'drain' were likely to have had any revolutionary impact on overall economic development.

The conclusion remains that such agricultural improvement as took place, and particularly the growth and export of cash crops, made a positive contribution to Indian economic growth in the long run. At the same time the failure of agriculture to improve faster provided a serious, perhaps the most serious hindrance to development. Not only was the rate of growth of output small, but even in

[164]G. Haberler, 'International Trade and Economic Development', in G. M. Meier, *Leading Issues in Development Economics* (New York, 1964), p. 354.

[165]On this complex transfer question see L. A. Metzler, 'The Transfer Problem Reconsidered', *Journal of Political Economy*, Vol. L (June 1942); and P. A. Samuelson, 'The Transfer Problem and Transfer Costs', *Economic Journal*, Vol. LXIII (June 1952).

[166]M. D. Morris, 'Towards a Reinterpretation of Nineteenth-Century Indian Economic History', *Journal of Economic History*, December 1963; K. N. Chaudhuri, 'India's International Economy in the Nineteenth Century', *Modern Asian Studies*, Vol. II, Part I (January 1968), where he refers to the 'insignificance of the drain controversy'.

[167]D. H. N. Gurtoo, *India's Balance of Payments 1920–1960* (New Delhi, 1956), p. vii.

those crops where progress was greatest, India's performance compared ill with that of other countries. Colin Clark, Vakil, Davis and others have produced figures showing comparatively low yields per acre and per head in India. Compared with Japan particularly, productivity in rice and wheat was poor.[168]

Agricultural improvement is a function of incentives and the response to them on the one hand, and the availability of inputs on the other. One may start by modifying the belief that the Indian peasant's religious ethos and value system made him unresponsive to economic inducements.[169] Of course, individuals and specific groups reacted in different ways. Nair and others provide plenty of examples where peasants spent their time contemplating the infinite and dozing in the sun, while the weeds grew around them and their irrigation channels became choked.[170] The Agricultural Commission of 1928 described the lack of 'a will to live better' and maintained that, in improving farming 'the central problem is psychological and not technical'.[171] The economic historians' common failing of too violent a reaction to long-established dogma should be avoided. But there is a great deal of evidence to show that Lewis's will to economise and desire for material goods was not absent in rural India.[172] That 'the Bengal peasant is not slow to learn what is and what is not profitable' was pointed out by the Secretary to the Bengal Government in 1864.[173] Datta, in his famous enquiry into the rise of prices before the First World War, illustrated that both the demand for and supply of food were elastic to price.[174] How elastic is another question. Agricultural output was a function of many factors other than price, especially the monsoon. In recent

---

[168]Colin Clark, *The Conditions of Economic Progress* (London, 1951), Ch. V; C. N. Vakil and S. C. Bose, *Growth of Trade and Industry in Modern India* (Calcutta, 1931), e.g. Ch. III; K. Davis, *Population of India and Pakistan, op. cit.*, p. 209.

[169]For a general description and criticism of this thesis see M. D. Morris, 'Values as an Obstacle to Economic Growth in South Asia: An Historical Survey', *Journal of Economic History*, Vol. XXVII, No. 4, (December 1967).

[170]K. Nair, *Blossoms in the Dust* (New York, 1962), pp. 192 ff.

[171]Report, *op. cit.*, p. 499. For more recent statements on the conservative attitude of the peasantry see A. K. Sen, 'The Problem', in *Seminar*, Vol. 57 (May 1964), and Anonymous, 'Flaws in the H.Y.V. Programme', *Capital*, 30 October 1969.

[172]W. A. Lewis, *The Theory of Economic Growth* (London, 1957), Ch. II.

[173]Quoted in S. Gopal, *British Policy in India, 1858–1905* (Cambridge, 1965), p. 31.

[174]K. L. Datta, *Report on the Enquiry into the Rise of Prices in India* (Calcutta, 1914), Vol. I, pp. 65–6. See also the *Report of the Industrial Commission, 1916–18, op. cit.*, App. C, p. 348, for interchange between sugar and jute.

years a number of analyses has been made of the problem.[175] Most notably Narain for the period 1900–39, found that in the case of food grains rainfall was the dominant factor, in cash crops price, and 'there is ample evidence in support of the hypothesis that the Indian farmer is significantly responsive to price'. In a similar vein Harnetty has verified statistically what was already widely known, namely that the American Civil War inflation stimulated agricultural output, especially of raw cotton.[176]

One should not infer that all peasants had a surplus to market, were acting in a profit-maximising manner, or that responses to last year's prices were rational in the sense that they were a good guide to next years' income. But other than supply-price elasticity, evidence can be quoted to show that the Indian farmer's actions were often appropriate to his factor endowments. For example it was justifiably claimed that the heavy-steel inversion plough put too great a strain on draught oxen, that deep-ploughing exposed the under-soil to the drying rays of the sun, and that some new types of implements could not be maintained and repaired in the village. Again, improved seeds were not always clearly beneficial. Cattle would not eat the chaff of certain types of wheat; some long-stapled cotton had a lower ginning percentage than short ones; certain new varieties could not withstand heavy rain or frost; new Coimbatone sugarcane was better quality but produced less quantity; and, if not combined with water, certain manures did more harm than good. On manure, it is notable that many Indian immigrants to afforested Burma continued to use dung for cooking, not because they were slaves of custom but because its slow-burning made it more efficient.[177]

In addition to all this, such failure to respond as existed was often due to disease, especially enervating malaria, and malnutrition. The

[175]See, e.g., S. S. Madalgi, 'Prices and Production Trends in Indian Agriculture during 1900 and 1953', *Indian Journal of Agricultural Economics*, March 1954; V. M. Jakhade, 'Response of Agricultural Producers to Prices'. *ibid.*, July/December, 1964; D. P. Kamala, 'Response of Acreage to Changes in Price', *Economic Weekly*, September 1964; J. Kaul, 'A Study of Supply Responses to Price of Punjab Crops', *Indian Journal of Economics*, July 1967.

[176]D. Narain, *The Impact of Price Movements on Areas under Selected Crops in India, 1900–39* (Cambridge, 1965), p. 158. For a review of this see M. Lipton in *Modern Asian Studies*, Vol. I, Part I, (January 1967); P. Harnetty, 'Cotton Exports and Indian Agriculture, 1861–1870', *Economic History Review*, Vol. XXIV, No. 3 (August 1971). For a view that price variables are not very important see T. Maitra, 'Farmers' Response to Price Movements', *Economic and Political Weekly*, 21 October 1968.

[177]Royal Commission on Agriculture, *op. cit.*, p. 83.

conclusion is not that the Hindu or Muslim religion and value system was conducive to economic growth, or as conducive to economic growth as Weber's Protestant ethic or Scots Presbyterianism or Japanese State Shintoism or Chinese Communism. Nor is it denied that religious mendicants abounded, that caste and the joint-family impeded mobility and saving, that failure to eat and kill cows hindered livestock improvements, nutritional increases and the tanning industry, or that rats and monkeys ate vast quantities of food. The conclusion is simply that, even in the given Indian socio-religious environment, a large number of farmers were desirous of material progress and would have responded if incentives and suitable inputs had been available.

A widening market and rising prices in some cases provided the inducement. Railways were the most important factor in extending, if not deepening the market – and here was perhaps the major contribution of the State to economic growth.[178] The secular rise in agricultural prices until 1919[179] and the growth of overseas demand until the inter-war slump influenced those peasants whose supply was elastic. But there is perhaps a tendency in Harnetty, following Narain and commendably reacting against the old orthodoxy, to exaggerate the positive role of price. While it is impossible to quantify in the aggregate, an inverse relation between price and marketable surplus was sometimes observed.[180] And, because of pressure to pay tax and a weak bargaining position *vis-à-vis* creditors, some peasants had to accept whatever low price they could get in the village. More important, cash crops were a small proportion of total crops. A rough estimate put the marketable surplus of foodgrains in the 1950s at only one-third of total production, and another, that only 26 per cent of cereals were marketed in 1960–1. In sum, the priority was to satisfy family requirements and then enter the price-influenced market.

A serious disincentive to agrarian improvement was alleged to have been the land tenure system. Few subjects have elicited so voluminous a literature.[181] Land reform is no simple panacea, as the

[178]See, for example, annual reports on railways, e.g. *Parliamentary Papers*, Vol. LI (1871). p. 343.

[179]For this point and details of price movements and agricultural terms of trade see J. P. Bhattacharjee, *op. cit.*, pp. 48 ff.

[180] *Ibid.*, p. 77.

[181]See, e.g., B. H. Baden-Powell, *The Land Systems of British India* (Oxford, 1892), and 'The Permanent Settlement of Bengal', *English Historical Review*, Vol. X (1895); R. E. Frykenberg, 'Studies of Land Control in Indian History: A Review Article', *Economic Development and Cultural Change*, April 1967; and a bibliography in W. C. Neale, *Economic Change in Rural India* (New Haven, 1962).

experience of India since Independence has shown.[182] It is difficult to generalise about its effects in the British period, not only because of its complexity, but because some enterprising, cash-crop producing farmers were to be found under all systems. There is dispute also about the motives of Cornwallis and others although clearly in their minds was the idea of English improving landlords and a Smithian 'natural state' where farming would flourish.[183] There emerged a complex of tenurial arrangements. Some land was cultivated by enterprising peasant owners, some was owned by absentee landlords and money-lenders, some was worked by tenants with good security and Government fixed rents, and some by share-croppers and mere tenants-at-will. It is difficult to provide data of the various proportions. Neale thought that in 1882 most cultivators in Oudh were tenants-at-will and over half in the North-Western Provinces in 1892 were 'proprietors or privileged tenants'.[184] The Report of the Punjab Revenue Committee of 1938 found that half of the cultivated area was held by tenants-at-will.[185] Where land revenue was permanently settled as in Bengal, and subject to re-assessment only every twenty or thirty years in many other areas, those peasants who, retaining ownership of their land, dealt direct with the State, stood to gain in times of inflation. Certainly, until the inter-war deflation, British officials claimed that the real revenue burden was decreasing.[186] But a large and increasing proportion of cultivators, namely tenants, were more concerned about high and rising rents, as was the Government. It intervened, often against Indian nationalist opposition,[187] to limit rents and restrict the alienation of land, in a sense counteracting the 'free' market which it originally postulated. Even the Royal Commission on Agriculture complained that legislation which resulted in greater security of

[182]Cf. W. C. Neale, *op. cit.*, p. 279; Anonymous, *Capital*, 19 February 1970; Anonymous, *All India Congress Committee Economic Review*, 15 February 1969; V. M. Dandekar and G. J. Khundanpur, *The Working of the Bombay Tenancy Act, 1948* (Poona, 1957).
[183]R. H. Baden-Powell, *English Historical Review*, Vol. X (1895).
[184]W. C. Neale, *op. cit.*, p. 99.
[185]*Op. cit.*, p. 7.
[186]Cf., for example, J. S. Mill's, *Memorandum of the Improvements in the Administration of British India during the last thirty years* . . . (London, 1858), pp. 20–9; the 'Memorandum on Some Results of Indian Administration during the Past fifty Years', Cd. 4956 (1909), p. 9, maintained that the Punjab assessment was then one-tenth to one-fourteenth of gross produce compared with one-third under Akbar.
[187]B. B. Misra, *The Indian Middle Classes* (Oxford, 1961), p. 355; and J. R. McLane, 'Peasants, Money-Lenders and Nationalists at the End of the Nineteenth Century', *Indian Economic and Social History Review*, Vol. I, No. 1 (July-September 1963).

tenure discouraged enterprising farmers from acquiring land for expansion.[188]

Social justice and economic efficiency, as has been found since the war, were not necessarily compatible. Most tenants were unaffected by legislation; there remained market rents and land was frequently transferred. How far one agrees with Neale that high rents were merely a symptom of more basic problems, and how far with others that the land revenue system was a cause of backwardness, is a matter for discussion.[189] Nor is it easy to demonstrate that productivity was higher among owners than among insecure tenants. Perhaps most Indian tenants-at-will were unlike Marshall's ideal peasant proprietor, whose 'feeling of ownership gives him self-respect and stability of character and makes him provident and temperate. . . .'[190] Whatever the real and psychological disincentive, many Indian cultivators had little ability after taxes, interest and rent, to invest in improvements.

As for the disposal of the surplus siphoned off by landlords, P. C. Joshi pronounced a prevailing view that 'by and large they existed as functionless intermediaries, interested only in appropriation of rental income which they squandered away in conspicuous consumption and other unproductive pursuits'.[191] The meaning of 'unproductive' could be queried, and exceptions quoted of landlords investing in railways, oil presses, paper and match factories and in large-scale farming.[192] But there is also abundant evidence that they and other middlemen found the most profitable outlet for their funds in renting land, lending money and trading. Had the tenants been left with their surplus they might or might not have invested it more 'productively'. Progress was made in certain areas, but a combination of population pressure, lack of alternative employment opportunities and tenurial arrangements resulted in the market system failing, by and large, to create the hoped-for entrepreneurial landlords and tenants who would revolutionise agriculture.[193] Indian agrarian organizations fell between the various stools of large capital-

[188]*Op. cit.*, p. 12.

[189]W. C. Neale, *op. cit.*, p. 165. See also V. Anstey, *op. cit.*, p. 177.

[190]A. Marshall, *Principles of Economics* (London, 1922), pp. 645–6.

[191]P. C. Joshi in *Seminar*, Vol. 38 (1962).

[192]See Indian Industrial Commission, *op. cit.*, Minutes of Evidence, Vol. I, Cd. 234, p. 365; *ibid.*, Vol. III, Cd. 236, p. 333; *Report on the Survey of Cottage Industries, Vizagapatam District* (Madras, 1929), p. 35; *Annual Report on Railways Parliamentary Papers*, Vol. III (1870) p. 803, para. 12.

[193]Thorner believes that the 'industrial revolution' of the 1960s has for the first time, created, paradoxically in socialist India, a class of capitalist entrepreneurs in agriculture, 'Capitalist Farming in India', *Economic and Political Weekly*, Vol. IV (27 December 1969).

ist holdings, co-operative small holdings, and collectivisation. The demand for, and therefore price of land ensured that renting small plots was more profitable than buying and farming consolidated holdings. The small 'uneconomic' size and fragmented nature of land holdings were widely regarded as at once a disincentive to improvement and an obstacle to higher incomes and saving. Again, this is a large subject, too complex for generalisation. The optimum size of holding may be small in the case of labour-using horticultural crops, or for rice where the soil requires intensive weeding, irrigation and fertilising. The Japanese experience on small plots was and is often quoted to the Indians. Indeed, a controversy has arisen in recent years over the Farm Management Study Reports that output per acre falls as size increases.[194] Apart from the problem of defining the *optimum* size, there were wide variations in the *actual* size in British India over space and time. The Agricultural Commission of 1928 put the average size of holding in the south and east at 5 acres.[195] The U.N. in 1951 found that under 2 acres were held by 56 per cent of families in what had then become Uttar Pradesh, and by only 12 per cent in the Deccan. In the 1930s the average size of holding in the then United Provinces was said to be $5\frac{1}{2}$ acres.[196] It is impossible to construct a long-run, average-size series of holdings, but there is some evidence of a downward trend. Certainly the statistics of cultivated land per head show a large decline from 1891 and especially between 1921 and 1951, when the fall was 25 per cent.[197] Although there is dispute about the cause and the extent,[198] fragmentation of holdings was also widespread, due, *inter alia*, to the partibility inheritance system. The harmful effects of fragmentation, however, should be qualified by the existence of joint family operations, and the general abundance of labour and time.

The persistence of many small holdings was a function, *ceteris paribus*, of population pressure. It resulted in a great deal of underutilisation of resources including labour. Seasonal factors and differences according to size of holding and type of crop reduce the validity of generalisations about under-employment. On one compilation, for example, the average employment on the farm per

[194]See, e.g. A. K. Sen, 'An Aspect of Indian Agriculture', *Economic Weekly*, annual number, February 1962; A. P. Rao, 'Size of Holding and Productivity', *ibid*, 11 November 1967; A. Rudra, 'Farm Size and Yield per Acre', *Economic and Political Weekly*, special number, July 1968.

[195]*Op. cit.*, p. 2

[196]W. C. Neale, *op. cit.*, pp. 151 ff.

[197]Census of 1951, Vol. I, Part IA, Report, p. 141.

[198]D. Pandit, 'Myths around Subdivision and Fragmentation of Holdings', *Indian Economic and Social History Review*, Vol. VI, No. 2 (June 1969).

farm worker in 1955–6 was only 68·6 days in West Bengal and 278 days in Nasik (Bombay).[199] The Royal Commission on Agriculture maintained that small plots occupied only half of the cultivators' time and the 1931 Banking Committee that 'most cultivators have at least two to three months absolute leisure'.[200] Underemployment is amply if not precisely verifiable, and in it Nurkse and others saw a potential source of real capital formation.[201] With suitable qualifications it can be concluded that small and fragmented holdings exercised a serious constraint on even enterprising and responsive peasants. But there was room for considerable improvement with the existing factor endowments. In particular the best use was often not made of the avialable capital supplies.

The strategic role in development accorded by some economists to capital has been queried by J. H. Adler, Bauer, Frankel and especially Cairncross. Youngson sums up many views in the phrase, 'innovation, not capital accumulation, is the key to economic development'.[202] It will be shown later that innovating entrepreneurs with sound, profitable schemes had little difficulty in raising funds in India for their industries. For railways, the India Office Records and other sources illustrate occasional problems in floating loans even in Britain, as in 1847–8, in 1854 when the Crimean War made money tight in London, and during the 1866 crisis.[203] Generally a guarantee from the State was sufficient to attract ample private funds. Indians, with some notable exceptions, such as the Nizam of Hyderabad and the Maharajas Holker and Patiala, invested little in

[199] J. P. Bhattacharjee, op. cit., p. 233. He and others give many other figures. See, e.g. J. S. Uppal, 'Measurement of Disguised Unemployment in Punjab Agriculture', Canadian Journal of Economics and Political Science, November 1967; J. L. Price, 'The Paradox of Surplus Agricultural Labour and Positive Marginal Productivity of Labour', Indian Economic Journal, April-June 1966; S. Mehra, 'Surplus Labour in Indian Agriculture', Indian Economic Review, April 1966; M. V. S. Rao, 'Estimates of the Idle Time for the Working Population in Rural Areas', Indian Labour Journal, March 1965.

[200] Royal Commission on Agriculture, op. cit., p. 3; Indian Central Banking Committee, 1931, Vol. 1, Majority Report, Part 1, p. 239.

[201] For criticisms of Nurkse, see, e.g., N. V. Sovani, 'Unemployment, Removable Surplus and the saving fund', Artha-Vijnana, Vol. I, (1959); J. Viner, 'Some Reflections on the Concept of Disguised Unemployment', Indian Journal of Economics, July 1957; A. K. Sen, 'Unemployment, Relative Prices and the Saving Potential', Indian Economic Review, August 1957.

[202] A. J. Youngson, Overhead Capital: A Study in Development Economics (Edinburgh, 1967), p. 71.

[203] See, for example, The Times, 14 January 1848, p. 7, and 19 April, 1848, p. 6. Also Railway Home Correspondence (A), Vol. I, East Indian Railway to Court of Directors, 18 October 1847; ibid., Vol. VI, No. 418, 7 April 1854; The Economist, 10 August 1857.

the early railways, subscribing only one per cent of the share capital up to 1875.[204] But there were many reasons connected with registration and payment of interest in London which would explain this, besides 'shyness' of indigenous capital.[205] Dobb and Reddaway have notably criticised, in an Indian context, over-emphasis on capital scarcity and on the capital-output ratio.[206] There is a danger of the pendulum swinging too far against the older views. The British-Indian Government continually complained that lack of funds was hampering its investment in fields regarded as proper for intervention.[207] Nor, as experience under the plans has shown, would Keynesian prescriptions appropriate to Western slump conditions have necessarily provided a simple panacea for growth. Capital in India *was* scarce, but less scarce than was often supposed. Considerable progress could have been achieved with a better choice of technique.

While difficult to define and measure, and lacking studies such as Rosovsky's for Japan, there is some qualitative and statistical evidence particularly for the plan periods, of capital accumulation. For example, a large number of estimates agree that net domestic capital formation as a percentage of net national income in 1950–1 was between 5 and 6 per cent.[208] This does not tell us much except that the Indian figure was well below Rostow's mythical breakthrough percentage and well below the Japanese savings-investment rate. For the British period the ground is more unreliable. Nineteenth-century administrators avoided the problem except in vague terms. Twentieth-century economists have produced some conjectures. Colin Clark suggested a net investment rate of 3·3 per cent in

[204]Calculated from tables giving the number of proprietors of Indian railway stocks and shares in *Parliamentary Papers*: annual reports on Indian railways.

[205]See, e.g. *Railway Home Correspondence (A)*, Vol. VII, No. 215, of 2 September 1854.

[206]M. H. Dobb, 'Thinking about Economic Development', *Economic Weekly*, January 1960; W. B. Reddaway, 'Self Help and External Assistance', *Economic Weekly*, annual number, February 1963, and *The Development of the Indian Economy*. (London, 1962), Ch. 4.

[207]One could quote many references but see, e.g. *Parliamentary Papers*, LVIII, 1884–5, 'Copy of Correspondence in 1883 between the Government of India and the Secretary of State . . . on the steps to be taken for the reduction of the expenditure of India.'

[208]H. Rosovsky, *Capital Formation in Japan, 1868–1940* (Glencoe, 1961). For India, M. Mukherjee, *op. cit.*, table of various estimates on p. 383; A. K. Bagchi, 'Long-term Constraints on India's Industrial Growth', in E. A. G. Robinson and M. Kidron (eds), *Economic Development in South Asia* (London, 1970), p. 180; Anonymous, *Seminar*, Vol. CXIV (February 1969), p. 39. W. Malenbaum, *op. cit.*, p. 65, gives a savings ratio of 4 to 5 per cent from 1931 to 1951, and a capital coefficient of between 3·0 and 3·5.

1919–23 and 5·9 per cent in 1934–8.[209] The *net* figures were beyond another authority, but gross capital formation as a percentage of net national income was given as 6·4 per cent in 1900–1 and 10 per cent in 1947–8[210] Few would argue that the savings rate was significantly higher before than after Independence.

Most capital formation was in agriculture. Agricultural and allied activities, even excluding land, accounted for about one-third of the reproducible tangible wealth of India in 1950.[211] Information on aggregate *working* capital, such as seeds, fertilisers and pesticides is confined for the British period to qualitative remarks.[212] There is better but still dubious data on 'durable' physical assets.[213] The stock of capital in these increased at about one per cent per annum from 1920 to 1960, with a marked check in the growth rate in the slump and war years. There appears to have been little fall in the capital-labour ratio but a slight rise in both capital-output and capital-land ratios. Financial assets were a very small proportion of total assets. Excluding land and housing, livestock dominated investment, accounting for from half to three-quarters of gross agricultural capital formation from 1920 to 1960. Irrigation was next, and implements, especially modern implements, relatively unimportant. Leaving aside its indirect contribution via co-operatives and taccavi and other loans, the Government's share in total fixed investment in agriculture was measured at about 2·6 per cent net and 10·3 per cent gross in the late 1930s.[214] The clear picture is of rather more fixed investment than is often realised. Most significant, however, is that the statistics reveal some, but comparatively little technological change or *new* investment. Most capital formation was merely to maintain existing stocks of housing, implements, wells, and especially to replace bullocks. After depreciation, and excluding many individual cases, there was comparatively little savings for improving peasant assets. Those who had a surplus, in so far as they invested it at all, tended to lend it or, notoriously, hoard it.

India's capacity to absorb specie has been the subject of comment since Pliny estimated the drain from the Roman Empire to have

[209]He gives much higher rates in the *Eastern Economist*, Vol. XI, No. 14, (October 1948).

[210] B. Roy, 'Capital formation in India, 1901–51', *Economic Weekly*, 29 April 1967.

[211]M. Mukherjee, *op. cit.*, p. 392.

[212]The 1928 Royal Commission has a Chapter XII on the finance of agriculture.

[213]One of the most detailed recent studies on which the generalisations in this paragraph are based is T. Shukla's *Capital Formation in Indian Agriculture* (Bombay, 1965). Unfortunately it excludes working capital.

[214]T. Shukla, *op. cit.*, p. 158.

been 50 million sesterces per annum.[215] From 1858 and before, there was invariably a net import of treasure until the inter-war slump. How much of it was 'hoarded' in the form of ornaments, jewels and coins is hard to assess. But the External Capital Committee of 1924, the Royal Commission on Indian Currency and Finance of 1926, and most writers, official and otherwise refer to 'vast sums lying idle in hoards'.[216] One estimate reckons that 75 per cent of the financial assets of rural families consisted of 'ornaments'.[217] Given the poverty and indebtedness of many peasants, there has probably been a tendency to exaggerate hoarding. So, in any case, thought the Banking Enquiry Committee of 1931. Its Provincial Committees believed that hoarding was declining, especially where institutional outlets, such as co-operatives and banks, were developing.[218] V. Prakash has tried quantification.[219] He estimated gold stocks at one-quarter and silver stocks at one-sixth of national income in 1957. 'Hoarding' amounting to Rs. 60 crores per annum in the 1860s, and Rs. 150 crores per annum from 1910 to 1930 is suggested, but these figures must contain large margins of error. In absolute terms very large sums were hoarded, perhaps enough to reduce the 'effective' savings rate by one or two per cent.

Hoarding is common in all peasant societies. It fluctuated in amount in good and bad years and no thorough analysis has been made of its effects on Indian economic development. It might, for example, be regarded as stabilising consumption over the long period. And many believed that India's ability, as a result of earlier hoards, to export gold in the Depression mitigated the latter's evil effects.[220] Generally, however, in a country which produced little gold and silver locally,[221] hoarding was rightly considered a misuse of scarce foreign exchange and a potential source of funds for productive investments. High interest rates were partly offset by factors contributing to high liquidity preference, notably distrust of

[215]*Natural History*, Book VI, Ch. XXVI, 101. Two counter-flowing 'drains' appear in Indian literature; one the flow of specie to the East, the other the flow of profits, interest and 'home charges' to the West.

[216]See, e.g., Royal Commission on Indian Currency and Finance, *Report* Vol. I, Cd. 2687 (1926), pp. 10 and 25; B. R. Shenoy, *Problems of Indian Economic Development* (Madras, 1958), Ch. VII.

[217]T. Shukla, *op. cit.*, p. 102.

[218]*Indian Central Banking Enquiry Committee, 1931*, Vol. I, pp. 434 ff.

[219]V. Prakash, 'Estimate of Stock of Precious metals in India', in V. K. R. V. Rao et al. (eds), *Papers on National Income and Allied Topics*, Vol. I (London, 1960), pp. 273 ff.

[220]V. Anstey, *op. cit.*, p. 499.

[221]321,000 oz. of gold in 1938 valued at Rs. 3 crores, *Statistical Abstract for British India*, Cd. 6441 (1943).

Government, monsoon, custom, ignorance of other outlets, and inadequate financial institutions. There were in rural India some post office savings banks, co-operative credit societies, other Government loan agencies and indigenous banks; but adequate suitable institutional outlets for funds in many areas were absent. Conversely, in their absence the peasant mainly relied for his working capital on landlords, merchants and money-lenders. The Imperial Bank of India financed some big farmers on the security of produce and gold, and there were sporadic atetmpts at land mortgage banks.[222] But the formal banking system had a negligible role to play in the financing of Indian agriculture. A more efficient market for rural credit would have had benefits but, as the Banking Committee pointed out, inadequate credit and high interest rates were merely the symptom of a more basic malaise.

Fixed capital was relatively scarce in rural India. More land, and more investment in irrigation, roads, railways and suitable implements would have, *ceteris paribus*, stimulated output. But one must beware of talking of scarce physical assets when rotation was unscientific and even available ploughs, wells and livestock were under-utilised for much of the year. Working capital was scarce in the sense that many peasants had to borrow seeds at high rates of interest in kind, and that, in spite of some Government experimental farms and research centres, very little progress was made in disseminating new crop varieties, insecticides or fertilisers. But there was also much under-utilisation of potential fertilisers. Composting of village waste and night-soil was neglected and, even allowing for its use as fuel, a great deal of livestock dung was wasted. One lesson from Japan for India is that moderate investment in the right kind of human capital in a receptive peasantry can achieve much, albeit though plots are small and material capital in short supply.

The slow rate of agricultural growth, itself a function of complex interacting variables, limited the growth of other sectors. In turn, especially with respect to employment opportunities, rural advance was checked by languid industrial expansion. Although, as Meier has pointed out,[223] 'industrial development versus agriculture has become a false issue', and although undue emphasis was placed on certain kinds of industry in the heady days of early Independence, industrialisation played a crucial role in the economic development of many countries. In particular it can be argued that India's lack of industrialisation excluded Marshallian and other external econo-

[222]Banking Committee, *op. cit.*, p. 191.
[223]G. M. Meier, *Leading Issues in Development Economics* (New York, 1964), p. 285.

mies. Long before Nurkse and the controversy about balanced sectoral growth, the Famine Commission of 1880 believed that, to cure rural poverty and famine, 'the complete remedy lies only in the development of industries not affected by the weather'.[224] Such industrialisation as took place in India was clearly not large enough, given population growth, to provide adequate employment off the land or to increase the average size of holding. There is no single, simple explanation of Indian industrial development. Free trade, laissez-faire, the monopolistic power of British managing agents, 'shyness' of capital, inadequate financial institutions, especially of the much admired and even more misunderstood German and Japanese industrial bank type, railway alignment and policy, the caste system, and immobile and inefficient labour, scarcity of entrepreneurs – these and many other factors have been discussed. In essence the problem compresses to an analysis of market or other incentives and the response to them.

Under a 'market' system, strong incentives are needed to induce entrepreneurs to move from the traditional channels of trade and land. In industrial revolution Britain rising population and rising real incomes ensured a strong pressure from internal demand, especially for basic commodities such as cotton. In addition, the export market had a prominent, although often exaggerated role to play. Incentives existed for entrepreneurs willing and able to respond to them. In India, effective demand for indigenous factory products was limited, to the extent that the rural area was self-sufficient and had low *per capita* incomes, by manufactured imports and, until late in the period, by an evanescent export market for all but primary commodities and semi-processed goods. Where adequate inducements existed, the Tatas, Birlas and other entrepreneurs were not slow to respond.

One can dismiss the market for manufactured exports as having played a significant role in overall Indian industrial development, although in particular cases it was important. Thus tea, if it could be classed as a semi-manufactured product, exported over 90 per cent of its output before the First World War, and still over 70 per cent in the late 1930s.[225] In cotton yarn, the Chinese market, until reduced by Japanese competition towards the end of the nineteenth century, was a stimulus to Tata enterprise.[226] But mill yarn exports

---

[224]*Report of the Famine Commission, op. cit.*, p. 34.
[225]V. Anstey, *op. cit.*, p. 340.
[226]S. D. Mehta, *The Cotton Mills of India* (Bombay, 1954), p. 76; F. Harris, *J. N. Tata: A Chronicle of His Life* (London, 1958), p. 6. It is interesting, also, that the local hand-loom industry in Nagpur was the major early market for the yarn of the Empress Mills.

were down to less than 5 per cent of total production by 1925.[227] There was some compensation in the growth of piece-goods cotton exports which overtook twist and yarn in value in the mid-1920s, but the large Indian cotton-weaving industry relied heavily on the home market. The same could not be said of jute. While Dundee effectively reduced the traditional handloom exports of gunny bags from Bengal in the nineteenth century, the exports of the modern Indian jute industry rose to become India's biggest single foreign-exchange earner by the outbreak of the Second World War. About 90 per cent of output was exported. In the case of jute gunnies and cloth, then, the export market was the dominant generator of Scots and later Indian enterprise and capital. By 1940, 60 per cent of Calcutta jute mill shares were Indian-held.[228] India exported other manufactures such as woollens, leather-work and even metals, but in these, as in cotton, the urban market problem was often lack of demand and competing imports.

Because market incentives in India mainly existed at home, the spectre of British imports and free trade immediately raises its head. Much studied, particularly by the many inter-war Tariff Board Reports, this is a field in which superficial generalisations often masquerade as scholarship. India under the British, because of revenue needs, was rarely without some import duties. But, avoiding the complexities of tariff history, it may be said broadly that until 1917, when a discrepancy was introduced between the import duty and the excise on cotton, India did not have a policy of protection. An official report summed up the Government's attitude when it described how an excise duty countervailing an import duty was imposed in 1896 'in order to deprive the tax of any protective character'.[229] How far 'free trade' was imposed under Manchester pressure and how it related to Imperialism are much-discussed problems.[230] And the theoretical arguments about the relevance for underdeveloped countries of comparative cost advantages, the basic British doctrine until the First World War, need not be reiterated here. Nor is it easy to assess by how much, even if desirable, Indian

[227]C. N. Vakil and S. C. Bose, *Growth of Trade and Industry in Modern India* (Calcutta, 1931), p. 144.
[228]The process of Indianisation had speeded up in the 1930s. S. K. Basu *Industrial Finance in India* (Calcutta, 1961), p. 161.
[229]*Memorandum on Some Results of British Administration, op. cit.*, p. 17.
[230]See, for example, P. Harnetty, 'The Imperialism of Free Trade: Lancashire and the Indian Cotton Duties, 1859–62', *Economic History Review*, Second Series, Vol. XVIII, No. 2 (August 1965); P. Harnetty, 'The English Cotton Duties Controversy, 1894–96', *English Historical Review*, Vol. LXXVII, No. CCCV (October 1962).

imports from, say, low-cost Britain would have been reduced by various degrees of protection. What is clear is that imports were a small proportion of G.N.P. (about 6 per cent in 1939); that the share of manufactured articles was dominant but declining (of non-treasure imports, 75 per cent in the first decade of this century, and 57 per cent in 1940); that there was a large secular increase in imports until 1929–30; and that in some instances imports were a disincentive to enterprise. Before the First World War provided its own protection in 1914 the potentially-important cement industry could produce only 1,000 tons to 166,000 tons of imports.[231] Lack of external economies are seen by the difficulties of an Ahmedabad match manufacturer who, in 1900, had to import gum, printed paper and sulphur.[232] All non-traditional agricultural machinery in India was imported because the limited market made a local industry unviable.[233] Attempts to establish a glass factory in 1909 failed in the face of competition from Austria and Japan. Other examples were given by the 1916–18 Industrial Commission of imports of soap, paints and pencils.[234]

After the First World War there was a rapid growth of import-substitutes. By 1930 India, with nine factories and excess capacity, was producing 80 per cent of her cement requirements. In matches, Indian production, or Swedish-Indian production with the aid of the 1921 and 1922 duties, soon exceeded imports. Import-substitution in cotton, despite free trade and aided in the late nineteenth century by silver-depreciation, began earlier, and was more significant than in most other industries. By 1921–2 when there was still no effective statutory protection, cotton imports comprised only 26 per cent of Indian demand, compared with 64 per cent in 1900.[235] Where India relied most heavily on imports was in technically-sophisticated, capital-intensive iron and steel, railway materials and machinery. While mainly British, imports from other countries also expanded until Imperial Preference was imposed. Thus Belgium supplied 24 per cent of India's imports of railway plant and rolling stock in 1927–8 and Germany 31 per cent of hardware imports. Long before, by the 1890s, Belgium was competing seriously with Britain for the Indian steel market. A. K. Sen and others have suggested that this competition rather than altruism lay behind Curzon's concern over industrial problems, the establishment of the Industrial

[231] *Report of the Indian Industrial Commission, op. cit.,* p. 39.
[232] *Ibid., Minutes of Evidence,* Vol. II, Cd. 235 (1919), p. 440.
[233] *Report, ibid.,* p. 49.
[234] *Report,* pp. 54 and 418.
[235] *Report of the Cotton Tariff Board, 1927,* p. 12.

Commission and inter-war discriminating Protection.[236] Be that as it may, the same Commission demonstrated clearly the war-time difficulties caused by India's heavy reliance on imports for metals and machines, and Tata did not look in vain for State aid for his iron and steel.

The illustrations of yarn, brass, chemical dyes and other inputs, show that some imports had benefits to the entrepreneur. Cotton, for example, covered a wide variety of counts and specialist pieces, not all of which were competing with local products. There were plenty of complaints from Indians when imports were restricted. The manager of a chemical works at Cawnpore opined that the expansion of his industry was checked by an import duty on Sicilian and Japanese sulphur.[237] And, of course, Government apologists, and sometimes the usually-inarticulate working classes, found a ready identity of interests between welfare aims and cheap imports.[238] Undoubtedly, however, protection for steel and paper in the late 1920s and for cotton in the 1930s was a great incentive to entrepreneurs at a time when industry was suffering from world-wide depression. But protection had serious disadvantages. Notably it discouraged rationalisation and reorganisation, and in cotton delayed the introduction of more efficient machinery. Bhogendranath, in his study of Madras, believed that the failure of the Government to insist on reform and reorganisation in cotton meant that 'the granting of protection to a badly organised industry was so much waste of public funds'.[239] Free trade and imports were a barrier to Indian enterprise in some fields, but they were a barrier which the most aggressive surmounted. Protection inter-war enabled Indian industry to expand at a difficult period, but not without substantial costs in efficiency.

The Japanese experience, so appealing and appealed to by Indian observers, did not provide support before the First World War for the advocates of protection, but the Japanese State's internal initiation of and aid for industry, much exaggerated, was often compared favourably with the Indian Government's policy of laissez-faire. Laissez-faire is a vague term, and many instances of State

[236]A. K. Sen, 'Sociological and Economic Explanations. An Illustration from the Iron and Steel Industry', *Economic Weekly*, annual number, February 1963.

[237]*Report of the Indian Industrial Commission, Minutes of Evidence*, Vol. I, Cd. 234 (1919), p. 84.

[238]B. B. Misra, *The Indian Middle Classes* (Oxford, 1961), p. 263.

[239]N. C. Bhogendranath, *Development of the Textile Industry in Madras* (Madras, 1957), p. 63. See also A. K. Bagchi, 'Protection and Rationalisation', *Arthaniti*, Vol. VII, No. 1 (January 1964).

intervention in the economic sector could be quoted from India.[240]
The railways, irrigation and other public works might be examples,
but they were held not to conflict with the general principle. Tea
provides a case where the State, as in the later Japanese pattern,
established the industry and then handed over 'to the enterprise of
individuals to pursue the business as an object of speculation'.[241]
Even between 1858 and the First World War, the Government
occasionally intervened in the iron industry, as when Lord Ripon
in 1880 bought out the Bengal Iron Works against the advice of the
Secretary of State. Later, after it was sold to the Bengal Iron and
Steel Company, the State guaranteed a market for rails.[242] The first
short-lived steel works in India, erected by the same company in
1904, had both a subsidy and guaranteed market from Curzon's
Government.[243] The more successful Tata Iron and Steel Company
in 1906 was aided by a State railway for carrying raw materials, by
reduced rates for iron ore, and, most important, by a guaranteed
market for steel rails of 20,000 tons per annum for ten years.[244]
Notorious was Morley's despatch disbanding the 1906 Madras
Department of Industries – a department later transformed into the
Pumping and Boring Department.[245] There were other Government
experiments in industry at the beginning of the twentieth century;
for example, loans to a sugar factory and oil mill in the United
Provinces. And, after the First World War, the State was much more
active through the Provincial Departments of Industries, although
not always successfully.[246] Laissez-faire is an inappropriate description of Government policy under the East India Company and after
the First World War. It may even be too sweeping for the period
1858 to 1914. Nevertheless, there were frequent conflicts between the
generally more interventionist Government in India and the Secretary of State nearer the London Indian lobby; financial requirements

[240]S. Bhattacharya, 'Laissez-faire in India', *Indian Economic and Social History
Review*, Vol. II, No. 1 (January 1965).

[241]*Parliamentary Papers*, Vol. XXXIX (1839): copy of papers on the introduction of the tea plant to India, p. 239.

[242]For this and other details of Government 'stores policy' see S. K. Sen,
Studies in Industrial Policy and Development of India, 1858–1914 (Calcutta, 1964),
passim.

[243]This company was eventually absorbed by the still-extant Indian Iron and
Steel Company in 1936. W. A. Johnson, *The Steel Industry of India* (Harvard
University Press, 1966), p. 9.

[244]See F. Harris, *op. cit.*, Ch. XVIII, and *Report of the Indian Industrial
Commission*, pp. 20 and 21.

[245]This despatch is mentioned in most Indian economic history books. But see
also, *Report of the Industrial Commission*, pp. 78–81.

[246]See, for example, V. Anstey, *op. cit.*, pp. 221 ff.

dictated pragmatism, and a long-term consistent and positive policy of State intervention in industry was absent.

Whether the State should have created a bigger market for import substitutes in India is a matter for discussion but is often taken as axiomatic. And indeed the direct and indirect incentives generated by Government demand are often underestimated. Thus Myers refers to 'the government policy of buying *all* Government Stores in England' before the First World War, when, in fact, there was a gradual relaxing of the Stores Rules from the time of Lord Salisbury's Financial Despatch in December 1876.[247] In the words of Jenks, railways 'did not call to life in India a vigorous industry to provide structural materials'.[248] The bulk of railway materials *was* imported throughout the period, but the declared policy of the companies and Government from the early days was that purchases were to be made in the cheapest markets, regardless of country.[249] As early as 1867 'vehicles of all kinds are constructed in India from pattern carriages sent from the United Kingdom'[250] and the railway engineering workshops were one of the few sources of technical training.[251] By the inter-war period the railways were the main market for steel. They were also the major factor in the growth of the coal industry. The colliery-owning East Indian Railway in particular was closely associated with the development of the Bengal coal-field, and the routing of its early lines had this object partly in view.[252] In 1916 the railways were taking $33\frac{1}{2}$ per cent of Indian coal output.[253] There were large Government purchases of many other industrial commodities, including woollens, paper, leather-work, engineering products and printing materials.

It remains true, however, that India, especially before 1930, not uniquely, was heavily dependent on imports for metals, machinery and railway materials. It is in this sense that one can talk of lack of

[247]My italics. C. A. Myers, *op. cit.*, p. 16.
[248]L. H. Jenks, *op. cit.*, p. 227.
[249]See, e.g., *Railway Home Correspondence, (C,)* Register 1, No. 187, of 18 October 1960, and *Railway Letters and Enclosures from India and Bengal*, Vol. III, *Government of India to Court of Directors*, No. 30 of 31 July 1856. The India Office railway correspondence provides many instructions to the guaranteed companies to buy in India wherever possible.
[250]*Parliamentary Papers*, Vol. L (1867), Letter from the East Indian Railway to the Secretary of State, 21 March 1867. Cf. A. O. Hirschman's 'final touches' stage, *The Strategy of Economic Development* (New Haven, 1958), p. 112.
[251]For examples, see *Report of the Industrial Commission, op. cit.*, p. 25.
[252]*Draft Railway Despatches to India*, Vol. III, No. 18 (16 May 1863), and *Railway Letters and Enclosures from India and Bengal*, Vol. IV (1851), No. 19, enclosure no. 18.
[253]*Report of Industrial Commission, op. cit.*, p. 18.

linkage effects and the transferring of many of the benefits of railway and other Government outlays to the British and other economies. The 'stores rules' were relaxed only slowly and piecemeal, and then against considerable opposition from British interests. Counter-factually one may speculate on what an ideal government might have done. Factually Government market incentives and other support played an underestimated, although small, direct role in stimulating industrial enterprise in British India.

A great deal more could be said about the market. Interesting, for example, is the story of the Swadeshi movement, a political attempt at import substitution.[254] Important also, were market imperfections, particularly the inadequacy of transport in many areas. The freight charge on a case of tinned fruit was as much from an up-country factory 350 miles to Calcutta as it was from Calcutta to London. The freight rate on an oil-engine from Liverpool to Calcutta was less than half what it was from Calcutta to Muzzaffarpur.[255] There were often justified allegations that railway alignment and rates policy favoured the import-export rather than cross-country trade, and the ports rather than inland centres.[256] Mr Vansittart complained in the House of Commons in 1861 that the Madras line was designed to run straight from point to point 'and so cleverly had that been done that the railway continued to avoid every town and village of importance'.[257] Long hauls and large consignments enabled reduced rates for imports and exports, but the Annual Railway Reports demonstrate also a large quantity of short-distance traffic. The 1921 Railway Committee maintained that the charging of 'block-rates' to stifle competition was dead, and that raw cotton from the cotton-fields to Bombay paid the same rate whether it was consigned to the Indian mills or to British ships.[258]

The main conclusion on the Indian market for manufactures is that it was growing, but circumscribed by imperfections including lack of roads, inadequate warehousing, monopolistic local traders and, of course, the limited rural surplus. Imports provided many consumer goods and capital equipment at lower cost than India, in the short run, could achieve. Certainly they made difficulties for

[254]The Industrial Commission described the rise and fall of many Swadeshi industries. *Op. cit.*, pp. 73–4.

[255]*Industrial Commission, Minutes of Evidence*, Vol. I, Cd. 294, p. 428.

[256]See, e.g., D. R. Gadgil, *The Industrial Evolution of India* (Oxford, 1942), p. 135; and R. D. Tiwari, *Railway Rates in Relation to Trade and Industry in India* (London, 1937), p. 326.

[257]*Hansard*, Vol. CLXIV, 25 July 1861, col. 1531.

[258]*Report of the Committee into the Working and Administration of Indian Railways*, Cd. 1512 (1921), pp. 49–51.

some infant industries, but their demonstration effect also challenged some entrepreneurs to imitation. It was, after all, the sight of Manchester cotton goods in Bombay which encouraged Tata to visit Lancashire, learn the business, buy machinery, and set up textile factories in India – all without Government help. Neither market incentives nor State aid, however, will achieve industrialisation unless they call forth latent supplies of raw materials, labour, capital and enterprise.

India superficially appeared to have an advantage in raw materials compared with Japan. Her main textile industries were largely supplied locally, whereas Japan, after the Tokugawa period, found her comparative advantage in importing cotton and specialising in rice and silk. As Jenks stated in an oft-quoted remark, 'India had coal and she had iron. But enterprise and Empire could not wait upon their development.'[259] A positive contribution of the Government was to survey the raw material resources, and they uncovered iron ore, lead, zinc, bauxite and other minerals.[260] However, the existence of raw materials and their cost and suitability are different matters. There were frequent complaints about the quality and cost of transport of Indian raw cotton in the mid-nineteenth century, and railway motivation was partly to improve this situation.[261] The unsuitability of some Indian cotton for finer yarn and, occasionally, world prices differentials. led to India importing significant quantities of raw cotton, (over 1 million cwt. in exceptional 1927-8). Good-quality coking coal with a low ash content was limited to a narrow area of West Bengal, Bihar and Orissa.[262] In Madras, as late as 1871, the railways burned mainly timber at one-third the price of seaborne coal.[263] Before hydro-electricity, many Bombay manufacturers found foreign coal less costly than Indian. Of course, the supply of raw materials is both a cause and an effect of industrial development. India, for example, exported about one million tons of ores per annum in the late 1930s, and even exported pig-iron to Japan. There were difficulties in the location and quality of some

[259]L. H. Jenks, op. cit., p. 227.

[260]Report of the Indian Industrial Commission, op. cit., Ch. IV.

[261]Cf., for example, Glasgow Chamber of Commerce, Minute Books, Vol. VII, p. 155, 'Memorial to the Court of Directors', 1 July 1847.

[262]Report of the Indian Industrial Commission, op. cit., p. 64; Government of India, Report of the Central Wages Board for the Coal Mining Industry (Delhi, 1968), p. 10.

[263]Report of 1871 Finance Committee, op. cit., questions 2589–2605. For outline coal problems see A. B. Ghosh, 'Coal Industry in the Pre-Plan Period', Economic Weekly, 25 October 1969; K. V. Subrahmanyam, 'Shades of Darkness: The Annals of the Coal Industry', ibid., 5 October 1968.

natural resources, but a scarcity of raw materials was not a major impediment to industrialisation.

Labour supply and quality for industry provides a field in which views have radically changed since Morris's Bombay study. Mrs Anstey Mehta, the Labour Commission and many others painted a picture of difficult recruitment, at best partial commitment to the factory, of the restraining pull of the village, of low material aspirations and backward-bending supply curves, of high absentee and turnover rates, and of low productivity and efficiency. Employers, in spite of large profits and queues of potential workers at their gates, readily blamed their troubles on labour problems. In recent years, Myers, Moore, Lambert, Sharma, Papola and Morris,[264] *inter alia*, have substantially modified the traditional thesis. In particular Morris's first systematic quantitative study concluded that 'it was not difficult to create an industrial labour force in India'.[265]

If raw labour generally was in scarce supply, it was only before the 1920s, before population growth became rapid and the pressure on the land severe. Rangoon may provide an exception in that throughout the British period the Burmese were said to be reluctant to work in factories. However, the shortage in Burma was adequately met, if at slightly higher cost, by immigrants from India, especially Telegu-speaking Madrassis.[266] The tea plantations, often remote and lacking transport, were notorious both for recruiting difficulties and the indenture system which was used to overcome them. Even here, these problems were eventually solved and one million workers were employed on the plantations by the end of the British period.[267] During outbursts of plague, especially the bubonic plague of 1896, there were temporary shortages of workers. Harris, in his study of Tata, and Mehta, both adjudged a chronic shortage of labour for the cotton industry before the First World War. Indeed, early in the nineteenth century, a short-lived Calcutta mill imported Glasgow girls as workers, most of whom appear to have died.[268] Witnesses

[264]C. A. Myers, *Labor Problems in the Industrialisation of India* (Harvard University Press), 1958; W. E. Moore and A. S. Feldman (eds), *Labor Commitment and Social Change in Developing Areas* (New York, 1960); R. D. Lambert, *Workers, Factories and Social Change in India* (Princeton, 1963); B. R. Sharma, 'The Industrial Worker, Myth and Realities', *Economic and Political Weekly*, 30 May 1970; T. S. Papola, 'The Indian Labour Market', *ibid.*, 27 July 1968.

[265]M. D. Morris, *op. cit.*, p. 208. His bibliography lists a number of important articles by himself and others.

[266]*Report of the Royal Commission on Labour in India*, Cd. 3883 (1931), p. 10.

[267]*Ibid.*, p. 359: Government of India, *Report of the Central Board on the Tea Plantation Industry*, 1966, p. 22.

[268]S. D. Mehta, *The Cotton Mills of India, 185419–54* (Bombay, 1954), p. 115.

before the 1916–18 Industrial Commission were not always in agreement on labour supply except that technical expertise and managers were lacking. Some found that 'India has plenty of labour and the workers are docile and skilful'.[269] But the majority stressed the scarcity of labour. The Royal Commission of 1931 summed up when it wrote that 'throughout the greater part of its history, organised industry has experienced a shortage of labour'.[270] These qualitative statements are no substitute for precise quantitative analysis. They are contradicted, at least for Bombay, by the evidence of wages, even allowing for the fact that these only partly reflect labour-supply conditions. To some extent they are also contradicted by the persistence of labour-intensive methods and by the inefficient under-utilisation of workers. More study is needed for areas other than Bombay, but the hypothesis is that, with some exceptions, at the very least the scarcity of labour before the First World War has been over-stressed. After the war few would look to the inadequate quantity of workers for an explanation of India's industrial problems.

The quality and stability of labour is another question. Specifically, the impermanence and lack of commitment were stressed. Thus the village nexus, or Myer's 'restraining pull' of the village and joint-family are often described.[271] There were allegedly high absentee and turnover rates, and seasonal shortages connected with harvesting and planting. The early East Indian Railway manager, for example, complained of the scarcity of workers during the rice harvest.[272] There is a great deal of evidence from the coal mines of both seasonal and irregular working habits. Coal output was alleged to be 50 per cent greater in February than in the sowing and planting month of July. And mine-workers, at least before legislation on hours of work in 1929, notoriously worked a few days at a stretch and then absented themselves.[273] High absentee and turnover rates are hardly surprising in the mines when, as late as 1928, 27 per cent of underground workers were women.[274] In the Empress Cotton Mills at Nagpur the entire working force of the factory was estimated to turn over every eighteen months. Cash bonuses had to be paid for

[269]*Minutes of Evidence*, Vol. I, Cd. 234, p. 106.
[270]*Op. cit.*, p. 21.
[271]C. A. Myers, *op. cit.*, pp. 38 ff.
[272]*Railway Letters and Enclosures from Ind'a and Bengal*, Vol. VIII (1853), No. 6, enclosure 5, p. 75.
[273]There are many references to these habits. Cf. Royal Commission on Labour, *op. cit.*, pp. 115 ff.; R. Mukherji, *The Indian Working Class* (Bombay, 1951); B. S. Rao, *The Industrial Worker in India* (London, 1939), p. 220.
[274]International Labour Office, *Industrial Labour in India* (Geneva, 1938), p. 53.

regular attendance.[275] In other cases the absence of long-service workers was evinced as a sign of high impermanence and contrasted unfavourably with the Japanese 'commitment for life' experience. In addition there were many references to the low level of workers' material aspirations. The Industrial Commission echoed the views of many employers, and echoed the views of Defoe and Arthur Young in industrialising England, when they maintained that workers were satisfied with a 'low standard of comfort' and that higher wages would lead to less work.[276]

By selecting certain evidence one could establish an impressive case for an unstable and uncommitted work force, still mainly agricultural, frequently voluntarily returning to the village for festivals, funerals and farming. One could invoke caste and the joint-family as effective barriers to mobility for all but the lowest castes and outcastes. But there are also contrary indications, even in the official documents. For example, the Royal Commission on Labour, while agreeing that many workers had village ties, found that few were actually agriculturalists. In the Bengal jute mills, holidays were taken usually in the *slack* agricultural season. Moreover, although they estimated, as Redford has done for England, that a high proportion of workers migrated short distances from the nearby countryside, there was abundant evidence of long-distance movement in addition to the Burma immigration.[277] It was difficult to reconcile a general low level of aspirations with the prevalence of borrowing. To get reliable data on absentee and turnover rates before the Second World War, far less the causes behind them, is virtually impossible. Absentee rates, although perhaps not turnover rates, were high. But this is explicable not so much in any inherent psychological weakness of the worker, as in ill-health, low wages, wretched urban housing, and bad factory conditions. Similarly, many of the abuses of recruiting and turnover were a function of the foremen-jobbers and their "perks".

In India it may have been more difficult, especially before 1920, to create a settled, disciplined work-force entirely divorced from the land, than Morris's Bombay study allows. But his analytical work is the pointer to further research and, by the inter-war period, the supply of factory workers was greatly in excess of the demand. The problem was then to find adequate employment for workers at the factory gates. What all the official reports agree upon is that the

[275]*Report of the Indian Industrial Commission, Minutes of Evidence*, Vol. II, Cd. 235 (1919), note on the Empress Cotton Mills, pp. 516 ff.
[276]*Report of the Indian Industrial Commission, op. cit.*, p. 179.
[277]*Op. cit.*, pp. 10 ff.

labour scarcity was to be found in lack of education, training, mechanical skills and supervisory ability. This was an excuse for the perpetuation of the employment of Europeans in many superior and technical posts. In turn, the ready supply of Europeans, while vitally contributing to industrial progress, reduced the urgency to find means of substituting Indians for them. That the education system, such as it was, had too literary a bias, and that the training provided in industrial schools, by the railway workshops and by occasional entrepreneurs such as Tata, that these were quite inadequate for the country's needs has been the subject of frequent comment.[278] Here, and particularly in inefficient management, lay the real problems of labour. If labour productivity was low, of which there exists plenty of evidence, it was largely because of poor direction from above. In turn 'cheap' labour was a disincentive to managers to organise it efficiently and to install and work at full capacity the machinery which would boost productivity.

The 'shyness' of Indian capital for industry and the scarcity of indigenous entrepreneurs due, *inter alia*, to the socio-religious ethos, are legendary. Again, generalisation is difficult, but the conclusion will be that the existence of considerable excess capacity, the failure to use existing capital efficiently, and the response, at times the over-response, of investors in both the layman's and Keynesian sense, necessitate a substantial qualification of the traditional view.

It should be said at the outset that much of the capital and enterprise for Indian industry came from Britain, and came through the well-known and, to some people, infamous managing agency system.[279] The managing agents undertook three main functions, those of entrepreneur, financier and business manager. For a fixed fee and/or a percentage of profits or sales, managing agents promoted and managed a wide variety of firms. In some cases they were share-holders and virtual owners. They tided over companies in times of slump and provided a channel for both Indian and British investors. In 1914 Europeans controlled virtually all the jute mills, most

[278]There is a large literature on this. But see especially R. I. Crane, 'Technical Education and Economic Development in India before World War I', in C. A. Anderson and M. J. Bowman (eds), *Education and Economic Development* (Chicago, 1965).

[279]For details of this system see R. S. Rungta, *Rise of Business Corporations in India* (Cambridge, 1970), Ch. XII; S. K. Basu, *Industrial Finance in India* (Calcutta, 1961), Ch. VI; A. Brimmer, 'The Setting of Entrepreneurship in India', *Quarterly Journal of Economics*, Vol. LXIX (November 1954); B. B. Kling, 'The Origin of the Managing Agents in India', *Journal of Asian Studies*, Vol. XXVI, No. 1 (November 1966); D. H. Buchanan, *The Development of Capitalist Enterprise in India* (New York, 1934). For a review of foreign investment, see M. Kidron, *Foreign Investments in India* (London, 1965).

of the tea plantations and coal mines, most of the engineering work-shops and paper factories and, of course, the non-State railways. Their share in cotton was much less, but not negligible.[280] At the eve of the Second World War, one managing agent, Andrew Yule (the Scots were disproportionally represented) had eighteen companies in tea, fifteen in coal, eleven in jute, two in jute-pressing, three in shipping, as well as single companies in a variety of other enterprises ranging from soft-drinks to electricity.[281] Although foreign, mostly British capital was attracted more to transport, trade and processing primary commodities, it also dominated large sectors of 'modern' manufacturing. Kidron believes that in 1926–7 companies registered abroad averaged eight times the paid-up capital of companies registered in India.[282] Except in cotton and iron and steel it was not until the inter-war period that Indianisation of large-scale industry became prominent. The managing agents, British and Indian, had many often-described defects. The quasi-monopoly power of foreign-ers was said to have stifled the growth of Indian enterprise, but it clearly did not prevent it altogether. Equally abused was the 'drain' of a proportion of profits to Britain, although how much was re-ploughed *in situ* is a subject for more research. On the other hand, the managing agents played an important pioneering role in es-tablishing and, in British firms, efficiently managing many enter-prises. Capital scarcity was rarely a problem for British managing agents.

In the case of indigenous industrial capital supply the evidence is overwhelming that where sound, well-organised enterprises were proposed or existed, especially when supported by well-known agents, neither fixed nor working capital supply presented a serious problem. The most-quoted Indian example is Tata Iron and Steel, although a British witness told the Industrial Commission that 'the Parsees are foreigners like ourselves'.[283] Four-fifths of the capital for the works was promised in London in 1906 but the promise was not fulfilled, partly due to the alleged tightness of money in London and partly to Tata's unwillingness to give enough control to British investors. Perhaps fortunately coinciding with the upsurge of the Swadeshi movement, Tata was able to raise the rupee equivalent of £1½ million from 8,000 Indians for fixed capital and £400,000 for working capital from the Maharaja Scindia of Gwalior.[284] The

[280]For statistics of European control in 1915, see C. A. Myers, *op. cit.*, p. 20.
[281]M. Kidron, *op. cit.*, p. 6.
[282]*Ibid.*, p. 4.
[283]*Report of the Indian Industrial Commission, Minutes of Evidence*, Vol. II, Cd. 235 (1919), p. 67.
[284]F. Harris, *op. cit.*, pp. 188–90.

same Tata found personal and other Indian funds for his Empress Mills, pioneering a new cotton area at Nagpur in 1877, the year in which Victoria assumed the Imperial title. So profitable were they that he was able to raise Rs. 50 lakhs in 1912 at only 5 per cent.[285] Once the Lahore Electric Supply Company had 'demonstrated its value' and the competence of its manager, it had no problem in raising funds.[286] Coal-mines readily attracted capital, gold excited bonanzas, but not other untried types of mining.[287]

As in Britain at the time of the Industrial Revolution, many Indian enterprises started with small amounts of fixed capital, supplied by the entrepreneur and his relations and friends, and expanded through the reploughing of profits.[288] Profits are notoriously difficult to define and measure. They fell drastically in the inter-war depression. But there is plenty of evidence of very high profit rates in Indian manufacturing. Harris maintained that the rate of 'profit' on the original investment of the Empress Mills for the first eighteen years averaged 18 per cent per annum, or 43 per cent with bonus.[289] Mehta refers to large profits in the Oriental mill[290] and other instances are quoted by the Industrial Commission.[291] In Madras textiles profits were fluctuating but high, and a large proportion was reploughed.[292] An estimate, admittedly very rough, of the average rate of profit (dividends as a percentage of ordinary capital or common stock outstanding) in all organised industries, was 25 per cent in 1918–22, 12·6 per cent in 1922–29 and 8·6 in 1930–9.[293] The absence of the word 'profits' in the indices of nearly all books on Indian economic history reflects at once the neglect and complexity of the subject. Yet, when one reads, for example, Boyson's recent book on the English Ashworths, one is impressed by the comparative profitability of many Indian companies.[294] Not all industries could start small and grow large through self-finance. Iron and

[285]*Report of the Indian Industrial Commission, Minutes of Evidence*, Vol. II, *op. cit.*, p. 516.

[286]*Minutes of Evidence*, Vol. I, p. 1.

[287]*Minutes of Evidence*, Vol. III, p. 19.

[288]See, for example, *Minutes of Evidence*, Vol. IV, p. 123; H. Spodek, 'Traditional Culture and Entrepreneurship: A Case Study of Ahmedabad', *Economic and Political Weekly*, 22 February 1969.

[289]F. Harris, *op. cit.*, p. 35. He provides other rather dubious statistics.

[290]S. D. Mehta, *op. cit.*, p. 20.

[291]*Minutes of Evidence*, Vol. II, pp. 516 ff.

[292]N. C. Bhogendranath, *op. cit.*, Part II, Ch. I, *passim*.

[293]Quoted by D. L. Spencer, *Indian Mixed Enterprise and Western Business* (The Hague, 1959), p. 35.

[294]One is impressed also by the comparative literacy of the workers. R. Boyson, *The Ashworth Cotton Enterprise* (London, 1970), e.g. p. 29.

steel, as has been seen, went outside. Railways, with a long gestation period and a large proportion of fixed capital, required guarantees of interest. Tea, with a four to six years' gestation, showed a short-period price – inelastic output and needed large funds – hence its early dominance by the British.[295]

However, many firms made profits; these were not siphoned off by taxes before the First World War, and labour's share of output was low. In these cases entrepreneurs complained little, or if they did, with little justification, about capital shortage. Plenty of other entrepreneurs did. Unestablished, little-known entrepreneurs found fixed and working capital a serious obstacle. An interesting case was a Bengal tannery, anxious to expand in the First World War. The Calcutta branch of the Delhi and London Bank refused credit. Hindu money-lenders declined directly to invest in cow-hides. But non-Hindu money-lenders borrowed from Hindus and provided the working capital.[296] Initial fixed capital was often a problem.[297] S. N. Dutt, for example, was inspired to start a galvanising works in Bengal by a visit to the Paris Exhibition of 1900. He went to England and taught himself the trade in Staffordshire. But he had to work several years in commerce for Rs. 2,000 to provide the intial funds for his Bengal Galvanising Works, which soon made profits and attracted Marwari money-lenders.[298] This was one of many examples of enterprise leading and finance following.

Among the reasons given for difficulties in raising funds were the bad management of the business, the example of failed firms, the competition for funds elsewhere and the inadequacy of financial institutions. The first needs little comment except the reminder that some Indian entrepreneurs established badly-run, technically-inefficient, and even fraudulent companies. Under-capitalisation at the start was common. Later, more prominent was surplus capacity and idle machines, although this was due to market demand factors as well as to organisational incompetence. The managing agency system throughout and protection in the 1930s often prevented the translation of inefficiency into bankruptcy. But the failure rate was high. In turn, these failures frightened off investors. Indeed if one catalogues the record of industrial and banking failures one is surprised with Lokanathan 'how optimistic the investor continues to

[295]G. K. Sarkar, 'A Note on the Supply Function of Tea', *Arthaniti,* VII, No. 2 (July 1964).
[296]*Report of the Indian Industrial Commission, Minutes of Evidence,* Vol. II, p. 764.
[297]*Minutes of Evidence,* Vol. IV, p. 19. One of the question headings used by the Commission was 'capital'.
[298]*Minutes of Evidence,* Vol. II, p. 63.

be in India'. War years 1913–17 saw enormous bank failures through unsound finance and over-optimism.[299] Many nationalist Swadeshi entrepreneurs rushed in to produce import-substitutes, but their poor record of success scared capital suppliers.[300] Underlying all this were the competing outlets for funds in Government loans, trade, money-lending and land.

One of the most serious problems in expanding the industrial capital supply was the existence of lucrative opportunities elsewhere. Those who wanted steady, safe income found Government securities increasingly attractive. A continual complaint was that merchants and money-lenders and landlords with savings chose, in preference to manufacturing, the booming export-import trade or advancing loans to peasants or buying and leasing land. It was simpler and more profitable, for example, to import textile machines from Britain than to contemplate their construction in India. It was here that the British emphasis on commerce and agriculture, the market in land and the high rural and urban interest rates on personal loans, impinged on industrial finance. With the notable exception of the Ahmedabad cotton mills, the Marawaris in the 1930s, and some provision of working capital elsewhere, money-lenders eschewed industry. Even the relatively high industrial profits cited above were not, by and large, a sufficient inducement to entice enterprise and funds on a wide front away from the traditional and more profitable channels. The Indian here was not avoiding industry for the eso-teric reasons suggested by some sociologists. He was content with his known business, and this business was often more lucrative than the best-run new manufactures.

Finally there was the inadequacy of financial institutions, of banks and of bank credit, not to mention finance corporations and stock exchanges. 'Bank credit', according to Landes, 'became a pillar of the industrial edifice' in Britain.[301] In India the grumble was that the joint-stock banks practised British, or at least English, rather than German and Japanese ways. In a splendid but cumbrous metaphor, the Banking Enquiry Committee bemoaned the lack of financial insti-tutions as 'an impenetrable barrier intercepting the overflow of wealth and barring the channels of communication between the reservoirs of capital and the parched fields of industry, dried up for the want of the wealth-bearing and fertilising moisture'.[302] There was no central

[299]For details, see P. S. Lokanathan, *op. cit.*, pp. 146–7.
[300]*Report of the Indian Industrial Commission*, p. 73. See also *Minutes of Evi-dence*, Vol. III, pp. 78 and 88.
[301]D. Landes, *op. cit.*, p. 307.
[302]*Indian Central Banking Enquiry Committee*, 1931, Vol. I, p. 1.

bank in most of the period. The Imperial Bank was legally restricted in its powers to finance industry. British exchange banks confined themselves to trade and exchange. British and Indian joint-stock banks were too security-conscious to provide fixed capital for manufacturing concerns. The Swadeshi banks which did, showed an alarming failure rate. Even Tata's attempt at an industrial bank in 1922 ended in disaster.

The story, of course, is not all gloom. As was mentioned before, the managing agency system channelled funds into the agents' companies. Money-lenders and banks were prominent in the financing of Ahmedabad cotton mills. Perhaps peculiar to India, although there was something similar in Lancashire, was the public deposits system. Taken from the public direct, or from indigenous bankers at six or twelve months' notice, these deposits provided a major source of working capital for the Bombay and especially the Ahmedabad cotton mills. Rates of interest were low but the danger of sudden withdrawal was a disadvantage in hard times.[303] Financial institutions were clearly inadequate. A more highly-organised banking system might, as in Britain, have reduced hoarding and channelled some of the agrarian surplus into towns and industry. But aggressive, innovating entrepreneurs could and did, perhaps with difficulty, overcome these obstacles.

The last generalisation to consider, therefore, is that India lacked indigenous entrepreneurs, that the low position of business in the caste hierarchy and the spiritual ethos restricted this essential ingredient of capitalism. It is obvious from what has been said about trade and money-lending and small industrialists, and what could be said about Indians in Burma, East Africa and Malaya, that the enterprising spirit was not altogether absent. But these were mainly in traditional fields. For branching out into manufacturing, where the British may at once have provided an example to follow and an obstacle to entry, a different degree of enterprise was needed. The industrial revolution in Britain was essentially one of technological change and invention. Although they had done in the past, Indians in the British period did not and did not need to invent or pioneer technological change. Of the 548 annual average applications for patents between 1893 and 1915, only fifty-three were from Indians, and these unimportant.[304] Late starters could borrow foreign technology, as the Japanese (with the exception of the Toyoda loom) had shown. They could also adapt it to suit their factor endowments, and here, compared with Japan, India was sometimes inept. There

[303]*Ibid.*, p. 269.
[304]*Report of the Indian Industrial Commission, op. cit.*, p. 175.

are, for example, instances of imported sophisticated machines lying in packing cases for months because they were quite unsuitable for local power and skills. It is arguable, also, that the demonstration effect of the British connection foisted onto India an unduly expensive and elaborate railway system with castellated bridges, and with stations a mixture of St Pancras gothic and Taj Mahal oriental. Counteracting this was the ability, because of the Imperial link, to raise capital in London for railways at comparatively low rates of interest. The Western technology was there to be imitated and adapted by Indian entrepreneurs. The question is what was their response.

Industrial entrepreneurship in a capitalist society is a function of, on the one hand, incentives, profits and a generally stimulating environment; and, on the other, of access to capital and labour, of lack of obstacles to entry, of an education and business acumen sufficient to make men aware of and able to grasp opportunities, and, more vaguely, of an 'open society' or a socio-religious structure and value-system conducive to change. As has been shown, in some cases the profit incentive was sufficient to attract Indian entrepreneurs. And in India, as in Japan, the ability to replough existing profits, if not in the long-run to increase profits, was favoured by the lag between real wages and productivity and by a fiscal system which, at least before the First World War, lacked a progressive element and profits taxes. Thus, where the environment was conducive, as during the First World War, there was a rapid spurt in industrialisation. Indeed the Industrial Commission complained of over-reaction. After a few successes, there was a 'phenomenal expansion' of Indian-owned rice mills and a plethora of oil mills. In the United Provinces, ninety-two ginning factories were established, 'far in excess of requirements'.[305] Domestic production of manufactures rose from 23 to 29 per cent of enhanced off-take between 1913 and 1921–2; and in this Indians were taking an increasing share.[306] The inter-war depression presented a serious obstacle. But its effects were mitigated by increased State support for industry and by protection. And the Second World War provided a further stimulus to enterprise. It was in the 1930s and 1940s that the Indianisation of industry proceeded most rapidly, particularly through the Marwaris. By 1943–4, three-fifths of the off-take of manufactures came from local plants.[307]

As already discussed, access to raw labour did not, in general,

[305]*Minutes of Evidence*, Vol. III, p. 78; Vol. II, p. 43.
[306]M. Kidron, *op. cit.*, p. 20.
[307]*Ibid.*, p. 21.

provide a deterrent to entrepreneurship. But it should be reiterated that there was a continued scarcity of skills, technically-trained personnel, and efficient managers.[308] It was shown that access to capital was not difficult for well-established, sound firms. Most of them started off with wealth accumulated in trade. The Parsis, for example, had a long history of links with the British, of banking, shipping and merchanding in the West of India. Jamsetji, the famous Tata, was the son of a general merchant and contractor. China's demand for opium and cotton provided him with early wealth. So did his contract for the Abysinnian expedition commissariat of 1867. This enabled him to turn a derelict oil mill into the Alexandra Cotton Factory, named after the Princess of Wales, and later sold to K. Naik, a Bhatia cotton merchant.[309] Cowasjee Davar, the 'Tata of the 1850s', was the son of a wealthy merchant.[310] Cursetji Wadia, who was the first Indian F.R.S., and lit his house with gas, and built a steamboat in 1893, acquired funds in shipping.[311] Gujerati merchants and bankers were prominent in Ahmedabad cotton. The biggest mill to date was founded in 1878 by two brothers of the Jain 'bania' community.[312] Trade and money-lending also formed the background of Marwaris such as Agarwal, Birla and the Dalmia-Jain group. By the 1930s they and the Gujeratis had overtaken the Parsis in the cotton industry.

That barriers to entry were a disincentive to budding entrepreneurs is often stated and occasionally substantiated. Here, of course, the quasi-monopolistic position of the British managing agents is most cited. Thus, it is alleged, the financiers of Bengal hand-woven jute in the first half of the nineteenth century failed to make an impact on the modern jute industry, because of the monopoly of the Scots. The British dominated Bengal industry in a way they never did in Bombay, but even in Bengal, Parsis, Katchees, Gujeratis, Jews, Armenians and, later, Marwaris were to be found.[313] Less-known is the effective barrier even the enterprising Tata found in shipping. One of the most striking contrasts between

[308]This was the subject of much comment in, for example, the Industrial Commission. See *Report*, p. 71. Also, A Basu, 'Technical Education in India, 1900–20', *Indian Economic and Social History Review*, Vol. IV (December 1967).
[309]For biographical details, F. Harris, *op. cit.*: D. E. Wacha, *The Life of J. N. Tata* (Bombay, 1915). See also A. V. Desai, 'The Origins of Parsi enterprise', *Indian Economic and Social History Review*, Vol. V, No. 4 (December 1968).
[310]S. D. Mehta, *op. cit.*, p. 113.
[311]A. Guha, 'Parsi Seths as Entrepreneurs, 1750–1850', *Economic and Political Weekly*, 29 August 1970.
[312]H. Spodek, *op. cit.*
[313]R. S. Rungta, *op. cit.*, pp. 165 ff.

India and Japan is found in this field. Navigation laws, tariff policy, and lack of contracts under the East India Company led to the decline of the ancient Indian shipping and ship-building industry. By the time of the accession of the Crown, Indian ship-builders could no longer compete with the British, and the P. and O. soon finished off the Parsis in the carrying trade.[314] Nearly all India's foreign trade and much of her coastal and inland navigation trade were carried in British bottoms, a fact which at once confused the trade figures and used scarce foreign exchange.

Tata tried to break the P. and O. stranglehold of the China trade in the 1890s and, with the Nippon Usen Kaisha, to undercut the British company. Vessels were bought second-hand in Britain and Japan, and promises given by Indian cotton merchants. Freight-rates were lowered below those of P. and O. But the reaction was immediate. A freight war started. P. and O. gave rebates to merchants if they agreed not to use Tata's or the Japanese company. Money was more important than sentiment to the Bombay traders and Tata's effort in shipping collapsed within a year.[315] Barriers to entry were not exclusively British. The Indian managing agency system was notoriously nepotistic and caste- and family-dominated. This prevented in many cases efficient management and free entry. Ahmedabad cotton mills became a virtual closed shop of the small bania community. Barriers to entry are found in all countries, but the dominance of the British managing agency system made them particularly powerful in India.

Many Indian entrepreneurs failed to get off the ground because they lacked business acumen, managerial skill and technical competence. This was stated time and time again to the Industrial Commission of 1916–18. Thus, a lac trader failed in shellac manufacture because he was ignorant of the techniques and because other manufacturers maintained secrecy.[316] Mr Sinha of the Bengal Preserving Company tried the Californian process of canning and found it wanting in the case of delicate mangoes.[317] Second-hand equipment, bought for cheapness and now advocated in some sophisticated circles as a cure for capital shortage in developing countries, was a continual problem because it frequently broke

[314]D. Thorner, *Investment in Empire* (Philadelphia, 1950), Ch. 2. See also R. S. Rungta, *op. cit.*, App. 15; A. Guha, *op. cit.*; A. C. Staples, 'Indian Maritime Transport in 1840', *Indian Economic and Social History Review*, March 1970.

[315]See F. Harris, *op. cit.*, pp. 92 ff. and *Report of the Indian Industrial Commission, Minutes of Evidence*, Vol. II, p. 508.

[316]*Minutes of Evidence*, Vol. I, p. 367.

[317]*Ibid.*, p. 427.

down, spare parts were lacking and maintenance difficult. The most enterprising overcame these difficulties. Tata and others visited Lancashire and thoroughly versed themselves in cotton processes. Babu Ghose went to Japan in 1909 to learn the trade for his Jessore Comb, Button and Mat Manufacturing Company.[318] Lack of scientific and formal training, far more the lack of general education, can easily be over-stressed as a hindrance to labour and managerial efficiency. And if these were an obstacle to private enterprise, were they not equally so to the establishment of an enlightened non-British government, which by setting up industries and instituting planning at an unspecified cost to the tax-payer, would revolutionise the economy? All that one can say is that, compared with Japan, the Indian educational outlay and policy and the ease of importing know-how or, at least the lack of urgency to substitute home-produced for imported know-how, resulted in problems at the technical and supervisory level. That was the reality. The vision of what might have been can be left to the soothsayers.

The socio-religious impediments to enterprise, as to the responses of workers and peasants, are considered by many scholars as the key to Indian problems under the Raj. The best known Indian entrepreneurs were, after all, non-Hindu Parsis, highly literate, socially at ease with the British, closely-knit, not of the established society, and unable to ascend traditional ladders. Superficially one likens them to low-ranking Tokuguwa merchants, Scots and non-conformists in Britiain, Chinese in south-east Asia, and Jews everywhere including India. The Marwaris, a generic term not amenable to precise definition, were also an exceptional group, separated from others by dietary and marital habits. Indian society has been described as 'particularistic' rather than 'universalistic', with a strong establishment of caste, undivided family, property in land, inheritance customs, religious and ceremonial requirements, and other symbols of a pre-industrial age.

Socio-religious factors can be shown to impinge directly on economic life. The spending and hoarding habits of peasants, the veneration of the cow, the inability of outcastes to ascend the economic ladder, the reluctance of higher castes to work in factories, the disincentive to saving of the joint family, the proclivity of the educated for the law and nationalist politics, all these are the subject of endless comment. So is the explicit British policy of non-intervention in all but the worst abuses of *sati*, *thagee* and infanticide. Some Hindus broke the constraints of their environment. Thus high-caste

[318]*Ibid.*, Vol. II, p. 88.

Brahmin Ranchhodal pioneered the first modern cotton mill in Ahmedabad.[319]

There were numerous other examples of Muslim and Hindu entrepreneurship, and it has been argued above that the societal constraints on responses to economic incentives have generally been exaggerated. The society was far from stagnant. Caste taboos of pollution by low-caste 'fall-out' were hard to maintain in the intimacy of railway carriages and buses. Morris's study of Bombay found that 'there seems little basis for arguing that any of the traditional features of the caste system as it may have functioned in the countryside affected the employer's ability to recruit labour as he saw fit'.[320] The belief that the supply of labour was a function of the 'cultural inadequacy' of the traditional society, and that those who found it least adequate (for example untouchables) were the ones to migrate, has to be modified by the wide spectrum of class and caste evident in factory workers.[321] Lambert's Poona survey for 1957 showed that nearly 20 per cent of factory workers were Brahmins, admittedly in the higher posts.[322] Hindus would not slaughter cows, but when there was no legal ban in the British period, they were willing to sell them to others to kill. Indeed, Brahmins were found among shareholders of Bombay slaughter-houses. The non-economic nexus is both a condition of and conditioned by economic growth. Where the possibility of material gain existed, plenty of Indians were able to rationalise their behaviour, to circumvent the shibboleths of religion and to act as economic men. British apologists found, as do some modern observers, too ready an explanation of Indian problems in the structure of society and the ethos of religion.

The conclusion is a reiteration of a truism, that Indian economic development was a function of a large number of interacting economic and non-economic variables ranging from Government policy to, in the inter-war period, the demographic upsurge. Regional, social and individual heterogeneities preclude meaningful all-India generalisations. Such evidence as exists, for example from National Income data, must now cast doubts on the relevance of adjectives such as 'stagnant' and 'decline'. India may once have been high in the economic league. That, in comparison with many Western

[319]S. D. Mehta, *op. cit.*, p. 23.

[320]M. D. Morris, *op. cit.*, p. 82.

[321]See R. D. Lambert, *Workers, Factories and Social Change in India* (Princeton, 1963), p. 4. For an analysis of caste and untouchables in Bombay mills, see M. D. Morris, *op, cit.*, pp. 71 ff.

[322]R. D. Lambert, *op. cit.*, p. 34.

countries and Japan, she lagged under the British is obvious. But some long-run economic progress was experienced between 1858 and 1947.

Gladstone, speaking of India, told the Commons in 1879 that 'the administration of that Empire, in the final judgement of history, will bring no advantage or glory to us, except in the exact and precise proportion that that administration confers benefits upon that Empire and renders India prosperous and happy'.[323] Nearly one hundred years later, and a quarter of a century after Independence, neither India nor Pakistan are prosperous or happy. But in their struggle to elevate the standards of life of the mass of their people, they inherited from the British some limited but basic prerequisites for development: rudimentary education, Western technology, some of the appropriate concepts of law and order, the foundations of a civil service, irrigation and railways. Their governments, with massive foreign aid and all the accumulated experience of economic thinkers and planners, are finding, as did the British before them, that the problems of maintaining existing levels, far less of accelerating long-run economic growth, are not easily resolved.

[323] *Hansard*, Third Series, Vol. CCXLVI, 12 June 1879, col. 1741.

8

The Irish Experience in Relation to the Theory and Policy of Economic Development

R. D. COLLISON BLACK
Queen's University Belfast

I. INTRODUCTION

Insofar as it is fashionable nowadays to study the problems of economic development quantitatively and with reference to present and future conditions, this is a decidedly unfashionable paper. Not only is it concerned with past rather than present problems; it is also concerned more with ideas than with quantities, more with the philosophy than the measurement of economic development.

What is the justification for such an approach? How far can a non-quantitative study of certain aspects of Irish economic development, mainly in the nineteenth century, be of any value or interest in relation to present-day problems? Clearly only to the extent that it provides lessons which may be relevant to the study and solution of those problems.

That 'A study of the past is surely not irrelevant to a consideration of the problems of the present', and further that 'Of all the problems with which economists have wrestled over the last two hundred years, that of the economic development of nations is undoubtedly the most susceptible of historical analysis',[1] are propositions which have been ably defended and widely accepted within the last decade. Hence, especially in this company, there seems no necessity to justify the use of a historical approach as such. It may perhaps be pointed out that in addition to the arguments which have been generally put forward for studying the historical experience of economic growth, there is a special interest in examining the Irish experience. 'A good deal of our thinking about industrialisation of backward countries

[1]Barry E. Supple, 'Economic History and Economic Underdevelopment', *Canadian Journal of Economics and Political Science*, Vol. XXVII (1961), 478; idem, *The Experience of Economic Growth* (New York, 1963) 'Preface', p. vii.

is dominated – consciously or unconsciously – by the grand Marxian generalisation according to which it is the history of advanced or established industrial countries which traces out the road of development for the more backward countries';[2] but the Irish case does not provide such an instance. Instead it provides one of the first and most important instances[3] of an advanced (or rapidly advancing) industrial nation becoming involved in promoting the development of a backward agricultural country. As such it affords a closer parallel to many present-day situations of economic development, and may provide new insights into these.

To concentrate in this context on the history of ideas rather than the history of events or processes may require rather more in the way of explanation and justification.[4] The first point to be made here is that the more one is concerned with policies, the more important ideas become – since policies are sometimes the result of ideas, and sometimes justified by reference to ideas, or ideologies. Economic development today is, for the most part, a matter of deliberate policy rather than spontaneous events, and the Irish experience in the nineteenth century contained much that was the result of deliberate policy, as I shall later try to show.

It might therefore be interesting to look at the ideas which were involved in the debates on economic development and development policies in Ireland a century or so ago; but would the interest be anything more than antiquarian? Do the ideas used then bear any resemblance or relationship to the ideas used now, and can we learn anything of value at the present time from a re-examination of them? These are the central questions which this paper will seek to answer. About the means towards economic development there is no dearth of ideas today, but equally no set of agreed principles. However, these two points can be made without much fear of contradiction. First, just as economic growth has been a particular preoccupation of economists for the last twenty-five years, so was it also a particular preoccupation of the classical economists. Second, when the present-day economist writes a sentence like: 'Consider the familiar ratio of gross national product (G.N.P.) to total population (P). This ratio,

[2]Alexander Gerschenkron, *Economic Backwardness in Historical Perspective*, (Cambridge, Mass., 1962), p. 6.

[3]It could be argued that the experience of Britain and India in the nineteenth century is of the same period, and certainly of no less importance.

[4]But cf. Hla Myint's comment: 'I have always maintained that a good development economist should also be something of an applied historian of economic thought' – H. Myint, 'Economic Theory and Development Policy' *Economica*, Vol. XXXIV (May 1967), p. 120.

G.N.P./P, is the measure usually employed to distinguish rich from poor countries'[5], he is essentially echoing, in less elegant language, the words of Adam Smith: 'According, therefore, as this produce, or what is purchased with it, bears a greater or smaller proportion to the number of those who are to consume it, the nation will be better or worse supplied with all the necessaries and conveniences for which it has occasion'.[6] When the basic concepts of economic development display such durability, we may reasonably expect that historical study of ideas on the subject will not be without some current relevance.

II. THE IRISH ECONOMY IN THE NINETEENTH CENTURY:
A SUMMARY REVIEW

Ireland in the half century before the Great Famine presented the phenomena of economic underdevelopment in almost classic form. In modern terminology it could be described as a labour-surplus dual economy with a very small amount of industrial development, and at least two-thirds of all families deriving what was, on the whole, a very low standard of living from agriculture – mainly the one-crop agriculture of the potato. The dominating features of the economy were a rapidly-growing population and a defective land system, which interacted perniciously upon each other. Nominally the English system of land law prevailed, but instead of the landlords investing in the soil and leasing well-equipped farms to substantial tenants who would not pay rents which would not leave them a fair return on their own capital, they leased the bare soil initially to tenants who then sub-let it to very small farmers. These had little or no capital and no incentive to carry out improvements when they could, at any time, be evicted without compensation. Lacking working capital as much as fixed, these small farmers often secured labour by giving the labourers a plot of ground sufficient to grow a crop of potatoes in lieu of wages; and as population increased the distinction between these cottier-labourers and the small farmers tended to become increasingly indistinct. With few possible sources of wage-paid employment, the only guarantee of subsistence lay in getting hold of a piece of land; and tenants were prepared to bid against each other and offer unrealistic rents for a plot.

The resultant rural economy was a curious hybrid – not a pure

[5]Herman E. Daly, 'Toward a Stationary State Economy' *in* Harte and Socolow (eds.) *The Patient Earth* (New York, 1971).
[6]Adam Smith, *The Wealth of Nations*, Introduction and Plan of the Work.

subsistence economy but certainly not a fully-developed money one.[7] High money rents were paid, the tenant obtaining the cash sometimes from the sale of crops or livestock, sometimes from labouring on the roads, or going across to Scotland or England to help with the harvest; but this was almost the only money transaction in which he would be involved, he and his family living entirely on the potatoes produced from their holding.

From this miserable pattern there were regional variations. The excellent grazing lands in eastern counties like Meath and Kildare were not broken up, but held in larger units. The most striking difference, however, was between Ulster and the rest of Ireland. In Ulster a customary 'tenant right' was recognised – by which a tenant willing to pay a fair rent could not be evicted from the land without being paid the market value of his interest in the land. The effect of this was to provide a measure of security of tenure which farmers in the rest of Ireland lacked, and contemporary observers were unanimous in attributing the greater relative prosperity of Ulster to this cause.

Ulster and parts of Leinster, where agriculture was more prosperous and there were opportunities for employment outside it, escaped the worst effects of the Famine, because their inhabitants had not become dependent on a single crop. For the rest of Ireland, however, the potato blight was an inescapable disaster, sweeping away the one foundation on which the whole wretched economy had rested so precariously.

There is no necessity here to go over the dreadful story of the Famine years again;[8] but no account of the Irish experience in economic development can omit the fact that it was a turning point in the process. The shaky structure of the old Irish economy was destroyed, and both landlords and tenants were overwhelmed in its collapse. Many tenants gave up their holdings in order to obtain poor relief; many others were evicted. In either event the landlord's rents went unpaid, and many of them were unable to meet the sharply-rising cost of poor rates.

From 1850 onwards, the tenants in increasing numbers found a solution to their problem in voluntary emigration; the Incumbered Estates Act of 1849 offered a prompt but harsh solution to the

[7]For a different view, characterising the rural economy of pre-Famine Ireland as a pure subsistence one, virtually distinct from the 'commercial-exchange economy' of the eastern part of the country, see Lynch and Vaizey, *Guinness's Brewery in the Irish Economy, 1759-1876* (1960).
[8]See Edwards and Williams *The Great Famine: Studies in Irish History 1845-52* (Dublin, 1956); Woodham-Smith, *The Great Hunger* (1962).

problems of the insolvent landlord by making possible the rapid disposal of his property. Whatever the cost in human terms, it seemed possible at the time to think that the way had been cleared for genuine advances in economic development. With reduced pressure of population, an increase in the average size of holding was possible, and more varied cultivation could be introduced. The new proprietors of the land were more substantial men than the old, with a better grasp of the requirements of estate management – could not Irish agriculture become as prosperous and stable as English?

For a time it seemed as if this prospect might be realised. Until a series of poor harvests in the early 1860s brought renewed distress, Irish agriculture did improve and share to some extent in the prosperity of the mid-century. However for the majority of the Irish rural population there was little satisfaction in what one writer described as 'the present and future of Ireland as the cattle farm of England'.[9] The new landowners looked on their estates primarily as a source of profit, and were less inclined to be lenient with their smaller tenants about arrears of rent than their more slipshod predecessors had been. The new substantial tenants gave little employment to the 'landless men' who now depended upon them, because they were mostly livestock farmers with small labour requirements. Non-agricultural employment was not growing fast enough, so that emigration or the workhouse were the only alternatives left to those who could not find work on the land.

The land, indeed, remained the source of livelihood for the majority of the population and just as they had no security of employment off it, so they had no security of tenure on it. The last three decades of the century were largely taken up by agitation and legislation for land reform – reform which was at first sought and carried out within the framework of the landlord-and-tenant system, by legal recognition of tenant rights to compensation for improvements and security. Depression in world agriculture accompanied by bad harvests in the late 1870s and early 1880s led to further distress and evictions, which the tenants countered by the invention of the boycott and the withholding of rents. After this 'Land War' it became clear that no solution was possible short of the elimination of the landlord-and-tenant system and its replacement by peasant proprietorship.

It would be a distortion of facts to represent all this as merely an economic phenomenon, part of a none-too-successful search for economic development. It was also an important facet of a growing

[9]Francis M. Jennings, *The Present and Future of Ireland as the Cattle Farm of England, and Her Probable Population*, (Dublin, 1865).

nationalism: in the words of one of Ireland's most distinguished historians, 'the two aspects of the national fight, Land and Home Rule, were to be the national passion from 1870 onwards'.[10] By 1914 the land question could be regarded as having been settled, although the Home Rule question was not. Throughout the period from 1870 and indeed even up to the present time the political issue of national independence interacted with questions of economic development in a special way, of which an explanation will be attempted in a later section of this paper.[11]

Looking over the whole of the nineteenth century, Ireland could certainly be said to have experienced economic development, in the sense of an increase in income per head, although not to anything like the extent which England had. While some part of this development was the consequence of improved techniques in agriculture, of railways and public works, and of a measure of industrial development largely confined to the north-eastern part of the country, much of it could also be attributed to the reduction of population in rural areas from pre-Famine levels.

III. POLICIES FOR ECONOMIC DEVELOPMENT IN NINETEENTH-CENTURY IRELAND: THE CLASSICAL VIEW

Let us turn now to consider the ideas about Irish economic development which were evolved, both outside and inside Ireland, in the nineteenth century, and the policies which were put into effect in the course of attempts to promote it.

At the outset the question arises: was the problem recognised and viewed in a manner comparable to that in which a problem of economic development would be viewed at the present day? To this, the brief answer is: comparable though certainly not identical. Obviously it would be naive and unhistorical to think that any of those who made policy or sought to influence it thought specifically in terms of a co-ordinated plan or programme for economic development; yet it would be equally wide of the mark to think that they were hidebound by the doctrine of laissez-faire, and precommitted to non-intervention. In a recent stimulating discussion of the question of laissez-faire and government policy in the hey-day of Classical Political Economy,[12] H. Scott Gordon confesses himself

[10]Edmund Curtis, *A History of Ireland* (6th edn, 1950), p. 373.
[11]See below, Section IV.
[12]H. Scott Gordon, 'The Ideology of Laissez-faire', in A. W. Coats (ed.) *The Classical Economists and Economic Policy*, (1971), pp. 180–205.

'tempted to locate the seat of laissez-faire ideology in the bureaucracy' because of the evidence of their doctrinaire inaction during the Irish Famine. 'But it will not work,' he goes on to say. 'I cannot believe that the great myth of a pervasive laissez-faire ideology in Victorian England is founded on the rock of Ireland, though one must grant that the Irish policy was a notable instance.'[13]

In fact while Irish policy undoubtedly affords striking instances of the influence of a doctrinaire laissez-faire approach, it also supplies equally striking instances of deliberate state intervention, sometimes to an extent which would not have been countenanced in England[14]. More broadly, it can be said that, certainly from about 1830 onwards, all those concerned with government policy recognised clearly enough that no 'solution of the Irish question' would be achieved without considerable economic reforms – in effect, that economic development would be required and that government would have to play some part in promoting it.

It must be remembered, however, that the mechanism of government, within which policy had to be evolved and operated, was a somewhat special one. By the Act of Union of 1800, the United Kingdom of Great Britain and Ireland was ruled by one parliament, but Ireland did have a largely separate executive. For successive ministries the essential task was the good government of the United Kingdom, and to the extent that economic development in Ireland seemed appropriate to that task, they were prepared to encourage it. Although it was possible to argue that Ireland was a special case, and the existence of the Irish executive made it possible to implement special policies for it, what could be done was always limited by the parliamentary situation in Britain, and the problems of Ireland were only some amongst many with which Victorian governments had to cope. In other words, Irish economic development in the nineteenth century was more analogous to a regional than a national development problem of the present day.

In dealing with Ireland's economic problems, ministers and their officials in the nineteenth century had no lack of advice, commissioned and gratuitous. I have attempted elsewhere[15] to survey in detail the views which were put forward by the classical economists and the influence which they had on policy, but it seems necessary to the argument here to summarise again what seems to me to have

[13]H. Scott Gordon, op. cit, p. 200.

[14]A case in point is the operations of the Board of Works in Ireland from 1831 onwards. In and after 1870, the series of Irish Land Acts provided examples of increasing interference with property rights and freedom of contract.

[15]In my *Economic Thought and the Irish Question, 1817-1870* (Cambridge, 1960).

been the character of their thinking. First of all, then, the classical economists generally considered economic development in Ireland to be not only desirable, but practicable. In terms of the Ricardian model, they did not see Ireland as having reached the stationary state; it was rather a case of stagnation or arrested development which could be cured by appropriate policy. As to what the limits of appropriate policy might be, it should be remembered that all the classical economists took the political situation oulined above for granted and did not consider any modification of it necessary; hence they viewed the improvement of the Irish economy entirely within a free trade context. The possibilities of achieving it by protection, manipulation of exchange rates or major fiscal variations were therefore excluded from debate.

Within these limitations, the classical economists, up to the time of John Stuart Mill, presented a generally-agreed diagnosis of Ireland's ills, and a consistent set of proposals for their treatment. The diagnosis rested essentially on those propositions about the relation of population to capital which were basic to the analysis of wages and profits from the time of Adam Smith onwards. In the light of these, it seemed clear that in Ireland the increase of population had outstripped the growth of capital, and this accounted for low wages and the intense competition for occupation of land. Hence it followed readily that the first condition for any economic development in a genuine sense was an alteration in the ratio of population to capital, whether by an increase of capital, a reduction of population or some well-timed combination of these two.

With agriculture as the source of livelihood for the vast majority of the population, it was here that the adjustment would have to start; most economists considered that a more efficient and productive agriculture could only be secured through replacement of Ireland's cottier system with capitalist leasehold tenancy on the English model – involving an increased investment of capital and the removal of population to allow consolidation of small farms into larger units. For the – inevitably considerable – population thus displaced from the land, what were the possible alternative sources of real income and employment? To this the economists' answer was that some, perhaps a majority, might find employment on the land as wage-paid labourers, earning more than they might previously have been able to grub out from their patches of potato ground. The remainder must either be absorbed into non-agricultural employment promoted by private or public investment, or encouraged to emigrate.

On the whole, the economists were disposed to favour state investment in public works only to the extent necessary to create the basic infrastructure required by private enterprise. Incentives to private investment, in turn, were not commonly thought of as going much beyond ensuring 'security' through a stable political climate. Since this could only have a substantial effect in the long term, with pre-Famine rates of population growth it followed that a quite considerable amount of emigration might be required in the short run if the programme were to be effective.

On the whole, this was a consistent and positive programme, based on a reasoned appraisal of the position in terms of the political economy of the time. To carry it into proper effect would have required a concerted series of measures; this 'package' as a whole was never within the realm of practical politics, although some of its separate ingredients were. Yet even if the obstacles to carrying the whole programme out had been removed it is far from certain that it would have produced the desired result. The economists generally seem to have over-estimated the amount of employment which a capitalist agriculture in Ireland would give and to have under-estimated the problems of finding non-agricultural employment or emigration outlets for the remainder of the working population. Above all, they overlooked the strength of the Irish tenants' belief in their right to the occupation of the soil, which made them deeply reluctant to accept the status of wage labourers as a substitute.

In fact, as John Stuart Mill forcefully pointed out,[16] much of this development programme was based on the premise, explicit or implicit, that English conditions provided a norm towards which Ireland should be adjusted as far and as fast as possible. Mill himself did much to change this attitude by his powerful advocacy of peasant proprietorship as a system which he contended would be more acceptable socially in Ireland and no less productive economically. This, however, was not until the 1860s, and by that time what Mill described as 'the revolt of mere nationality' had begun – and mere nationality had a political economy of its own.

IV. POLICIES FOR ECONOMIC DEVELOPMENT IN NINETEENTH-CENTURY IRELAND: THE NATIONALIST VIEW

The economic ideas associated with nationalism have received comparatively little attention from either contemporary economists

[16]J. S. Mill, *England and Ireland* (1868), p. 8: 'What was not too bad for us, must be good enough for Ireland, or if not, Ireland or the nature of things was alone in fault.'

or historians of economic thought – perhaps because all the main systems of economic ideas of the last two centuries have been essentially international in outlook. Yet in virtually all countries now experiencing or seeking economic development, an intense nationalism is an important feature, and again the historical experience of other countries may have its relevance. So it seems worth while to consider the economic ideas of Irish nationalists, although again with due caution against generalising from special features of the Irish case.

The history of Irish nationalism is long and tangled, and has yet to be fully written,[17] but the appearance within it of a set of economic ideas clearly distinguishable – and sometimes deliberately distinct – from orthodox political economy can be said to date from about 1845, when the leadership of the national movement was passing from Daniel O'Connell and the Loyal National Repeal Association, to Thomas Davis and the Young Ireland group.

No full and reasoned statement of this set of ideas was published by any Irish writer of the nineteenth century, so that to compare them with the more carefully thought-out and presented ideas of the orthodox political economists is not always easy or perhaps altogether fair to either group. Almost all the academic economists in nineteenth-century Ireland remained firmly within the 'internationalist' tradition of classical and neo-classical economics; the one clear exception was Isaac Butt, the leader of the Irish Parliamentary party before Parnell and pioneer of 'Home Rule', who as a young man had held the Whately Chair of Political Economy at Trinity College, Dublin – and held it with distinction. In his professorial capacity, in 1840, Butt had delivered a series of lectures on 'Protection to Home Industry', notable for their originality and independence, particularly on the question of protection in relation to employment.[18]

Apart from this one instance there was no overlap between academic economics and nationalism in the Ireland of last century,[19]

[17]But see L. J. McCaffrey, *The Irish Question 1800–1922* (Lexington, Kentucky, 1968); N. Mansergh, *The Irish Question 1840–1921* (1965); E. Strauss, *Irish Nationalism and British Democracy* (1952); F. S. L. Lyons, *Ireland since the Famine* (1971).

[18]Isaac Butt; *Protection to Home Industry: Some Cases of Its Advantage Considered* (Dublin, 1840). For a fuller account of this work, see R. D. Collison Black, 'Economic Studies at Trinity College, Dublin', *Hermathena*, No. 71 (1948), pp. 54–5.

[19]Some sympathy towards nationalism in economics might have been expected from Irish followers of the Historical School, such as T. E. Cliffe Leslie and John Kells Ingram. None is evident in their writings, although Ingram in his youth earned some fame for a patriotic poem, 'The Memory of the Dead', contributed to the Young Ireland newspaper, *The Nation*.

and the economic ideas of nationalists must be pieced together from speeches, newspaper articles and pamphlets. Two themes recur constantly – the land and protection. On land tenure, all nationalists were agreed as to the necessity of a reform of the landlord-and-tenant system, but this broad agreement nevertheless contained a diverisity of views within it.

In the period from about 1845 to 1875 moderate nationalists like Butt did not urge more than the introduction of fixity of tenure: establishment and legal confirmation of the rights of the tenant, involving limitation but not denial or extinction of the rights of the landlord.[20] Even James Fintan Lalor, one of the first to link the issue of land tenure specifically with the idea of nationality, was prepared to concede that landlords, once national independence had been gained, could retain their estates 'in fee from the Irish nation' so long as they granted security to their tenants.[21]

In later years, particularly after 1879, when the threat of evictions revived and was countered by the tactics of the Land League, Irish nationalist opinion moved more strongly in favour of the establishment of peasant proprietorship through land purchase. Parnell, for example, put forward 'two basic principles – that the solution to the whole problem lay in the tenant's becoming the owner of his farm, and that the government must advance him the money for the purpose'.[22] These principles did not command the respect of Michael Davitt, the organising genius of the Land League, who stated bluntly that 'peasant proprietorship is simply landlordism in another form'[23] and favoured nationalisation of the land. Davitt clearly recognised the conservative character of peasant proprietorship and argued that 'such a system but multiplies the difficulties which are now experienced in regard to the development of the industrial resources of a country'. In this he was an exception to the rule; the majority of nationalists felt that Fintan Lalor's demand for 'the land of Ireland for the people of Ireland' would be adequately met by peasant proprietorship.

Part of the argument in favour of peasant proprietorship was that it would enable a greater number of people to be supported on the land; but the development of additional sources of employment in

[20]Cf. Isaac Butt, *Land Tenure in Ireland: A Plea for the Celtic Race* (Dublin, 1866).
[21]T. P. O Neill, 'The Economic and Political Ideas of James Fintan Lalor', *Irish Ecclesiastical Record*, Vol. LXXIV (1950), 398–409.
[22]F. S. L. Lyons, 'The Economic Ideas of Parnell', *Historical Studies*, Vol. III (1959), 67.
[23]M. Davitt, *Leaves from a Prison Diary* (1885), p. 242.

industry was always a cardinal feature of Irish nationalist thinking. Negatively, 'the decline of manufactures in the south and west after 1800 was blamed on the commercial clauses of the Act of Union rather than on the progress of the industrial revolution which, Union or no Union, would have destroyed manufacturing in an area where capital was even more scarce than coal'.[24] O'Connell and his party vigorously denounced these 'Commercial Injustices'.[25] but were not explicit about the type of trade policy which an Irish parliament might be expected to adopt if repeal of the Act of Union were secured. Nationalists from the time of Davis onwards varied in their definition of what nationalism involved, but as they moved towards Patrick Pearse's uncompromising view that 'national independence involves national sovereignty',[26] they also tended increasingly to adopt the view that independence would bring with it a policy of protection to develop Ireland's native manufactures once more. Thomas Davis had no doubt that an Irish parliament would have the ability 'to create vast manufactures here by protecting duties in the first instance and to maintain them by our general prosperity'.[27] This seems to be a straightforward use of an 'infant industry' type of argument, but Davis's position on this was not always consistent. Essentially a romantic, he was opposed to utilitarian ideas (which he tended to identify with laissez-faire) and attracted to the teachings of Sismondi.[28] Hence he was not always sure that 'vast manufactures' were what Ireland should want or have. He tended to hanker for domestic industry – 'in favour of such a thing, if it be possible, the arguments are numberless. . . . Besides there is the strongest of all reasons in this, that the factory system seems everywhere a poison to virtue and happiness.' Here was a dilemma which Davis never clearly resolved. 'Some invention, which should bring the might of machinery in a wholesome and cheap form to the cabin, seems the only solution of the difficulty,' he concluded lamely.[29]

The more sophisticated arguments for protection developed by Isaac Butt have already been mentioned, but he did not deploy these

[24]James Meenan, *The Irish Economy since 1922* (Liverpool, 1970), p. 272.
[25]John O'Connell, *The Commercial Injustices. Extract from appendix of a report to the Repeal Association, on the general case of Ireland for a repeal of the legislative union* (Dublin, 1843).
[26]Patrick H. Pearse, 'The Sovereign People' (1916), reprinted in MacAonghusa and Ó Reágáin (eds), *The Best of Pearse* (Cork, 1967).
[27]Thomas Davis, *The Nation*, 2 December 1843.
[28]E. Sheehy, 'Davis's Social Doctrines' in M. J. MacManus (ed.), *Thomas Davis and Young Ireland* (Dublin, 1945), pp. 28–31.
[29]'Home Manufactures', in T. W. Rolleston (ed.), *Prose Writings of Thomas Davis* (n.d.), p. 284.

specifically when he became the leader of the Home Rule League, concerning himself more with the broad political implications of his plan for a federal United Kingdom.[30]

Butt's successor, Parnell, also tended to favour protection as necessary to the revival of native manufactures. In 1881 he declared that 'if we had our own parliament with full powers, we should undoubtedly be invited to protect Irish manufactures by import duties'.[31] Parnell, however, was essentially a practical politician rather than an academic thinker, and when he realised that protection was not much desired by the Irish commercial and manufacturing interests of the time, and that Home Rule would have to be carried, if at all, through the support of the English Liberal Party, he dropped protection from his programme.[32]

Here indeed was another dilemma which nationalist thinkers never faced squarely. Protection to them was a means of developing native industries catering primarily for the home market: yet such industries as did exist, mainly in the north-east of Ireland, were principally oriented towards export markets, and those who had developed them were wedded to the doctrine of free trade. This was later to be one of the factors which divided north and south on the Home Rule issue.

With the failure of the Irish party at Westminster to secure Home Rule, the end of the century saw nationalists turning again towards the ideas of complete separation and independence. Not surprisingly, with this came a revival of protectionist thinking. Arthur Griffith, the architect of the policy of Sinn Fein in 1905, derived many of his political ideas from the example of Hungary, but his economic ideas were taken from the work of Friedrich List. Protection was prominent amongst them and, like Davis sixty years before him, he was extremely optimistic about the benefits which it could bring to Irish industry.[33] His contemporary and friend James Connolly did not share these views, being perhaps the only Irish nationalist of that time who derived many of his ideas from Karl Marx. 'With [Sinn Fein's] economic teaching, as expounded by my friend Mr Arthur Griffith in his adoption of the doctrines of Friedrich List, Socialists have no sympathy, as it appeals only to those who measure a nation's prosperity by the volume of wealth produced in a country, instead

[30]Cf. F. S. L. Lyons, *Ireland since the Famine*, pp. 139–47.

[31]Quoted by F. S. L. Lyons, 'The Economic Ideas of Parnell', *Historical Studies*, Vol. III (1959), 70.

[32]*Ibid*, 72.

[33]T. de Vere White, 'Arthur Griffith', in Conor Cruise O'Brien (ed.) *The Shaping of Modern Ireland* (1960), pp. 63–73.

of by the distribution of that wealth among the inhabitants.'[34] Again, this was an exceptional view: most nationalists emphasised the income and employment which protection could give to Irish workers, and were not much concerned about the profits it could give to capitalists so long as these too were Irishmen. Protection, in fact, had become a part of the orthodoxy of Irish nationalism before the Irish Free State was established, perhaps as much by way of reaction against the prevailing British free trade orthodoxy as because of any clear calculation of economic costs and benefits. Yet because such doctrines had been enunciated by past leaders of the national movement, they long continued to command respect and exert considerable influence on policy. The consequences have been shrewdly described by a leading Irish economist of the present day:

'The issues which have confused thought since then [1916] may be traced to a number of assumptions which had acted as a source of inspiration in the national struggle. The origin and purpose of these assumptions must be remembered. Very often, they were first formulated by political writers in the eighteenth and nineteenth centuries. The circumstances in which those writers lived differed as widely as their definitions of legislative independence would have varied. But popular tradition has blended the centuries as fully as it has obliterated divisions of political, social and religious belief. In this manner, claims that originally might have been reasonable enough were reiterated decades after they had lost any relevance to contemporary conditions. . . . A peculiarly arid form of traditionalism may be discerned in this repetition of past claims. It is no wonder that another Irish writer, whose name stands in the succession to Swift, should have remarked that "Ireland is at this moment a regular rag-and-bottle shop of superseded ideas".'[35]

V. THE OUTCOME OF THE POLICIES:
A SUGGESTED INTERPRETATION

We have now considered both the classical and the nationalist interpretations of Ireland's economic problems and policy needs in

[34] James Connolly, 'Sinn Fein, Socialism and the Nation', *Irish Nation*, 23 January 1909. On the cleavage between Sinn Fein and Irish labour, see N. Mansergh, 'The Economic Background to Sinn Fein', *Ireland in the Age of Reform and Revolution* (1940), pp. 187–214. Cf. also F. S. L. Lyons, *Ireland Since the Famine*, pp. 271–3, 278–9.

[35] James Meenan, *The Irish Economy since 1922*, p. 269. The Irish writer referred to in the last sentence was George Bernard Shaw.

the nineteenth century. Let us now examine more specifically their implications with regard to economic development.

The classical economists' interpretation, as has been suggested above, amounted to a consistent and positive programme – but one which unfortunately took too little account of the facts of life in Ireland at the time. The policy prescriptions which followed from it certainly gave high priority to the need for economic development – and were essentially based on the assumption that this objective could, and would, be rationally pursued within the framework of a contract exchange economy – in fact the system with which they were familiar in England and which formed the basis of their theorising. That such an economy was only very imperfectly established in Ireland, and that landlord-tenant relationships on a pure contract basis were unacceptable to the mass of Irish people, was something of which the classical economists took no account.

The nationalist interpretation had almost precisely the opposite set of strengths and weaknesses. It gave all due weight to the character and aspirations of the Irish people – especially, and increasingly, to their aspirations for a national identity and their desire to be rid of landlordism. On the other hand the romantic bias of the early nationalists in particular led them to look on economic analysis with disdain and on economic fact as something which could be manipulated more or less at will. Security of tenure for the existing cultivators was the first and most fundamental principle of their thought, associated with the idea that those not consequently maintained on the land could easily be absorbed in manufactures fostered by protection. At times they tended to suggest that an almost indefinite expansion of large-scale industry could easily be secured in this way; at other times to contend that the Irish would be better to preserve their traditional way of life, combining agriculture with handicrafts, but eschewing industrialism.

In spite of Connolly's strictures against Griffith,[36] this could not be said to be a programme which laid primary emphasis on economic development. Rather the emphasis lay on social stability, with status rather than contract as the basis of the economy.

Here, then, were two sharply-contrasting approaches to Irish economic problems. The one, starting from the premise of the British Isles as one United Kingdom, would have treated those problems much in the manner in which a problem of regional economic backwardness might be treated today. The other, starting from the premise that Ireland must be a sovereign nation, would have treated them more as a question of securing to Irishmen the right to

[36]Cf. above, p. 204.

live on Irish soil – without precisely defining the level at which they could do so. The former approach was better attuned to the needs of the commercial and manufacturing economy which had established itself in Dublin and Belfast and along the north-east coast of Ireland; the latter to the needs of the essentially peasant economy of the south and west.

Eventually the main features of the nationalist approach were adopted – but their adoption began not with the establishment of an independent government in Dublin, but with the passage of the Land Purchase Acts which from 1886 onwards began the conversion of Ireland into a land of peasant proprietors. To speak in terms of a distinction first made familiar by Professor Allan G. B. Fisher,[37] the effect of this was to make the Irish economy one which favoured security rather than progress.

Looking back to the situation in Ireland before the Famine, it is abundantly obvious that it was one in which economic development was lacking, largely because the incentives for it were lacking. In an interesting recent article,[38] Professor Bertram Hutchinson has shown that in this period the Irish people were 'confined within a tradition inappropriate to economic growth', not only through causes externally imposed, such as the character of the land system, but also through causes whose origin can be traced to traditional Irish society, which placed a high value on social activities and encouraged conformity and the retention of status. Now the reorganisation of the land system in the latter part of the nineteenth century certainly removed most of the injustices which had been deterrents to activity under the old land laws, but at the same time it strengthened and preserved the rigid framework of traditional rural society. As Michael Davitt had foreseen, peasant proprietorship was essentially a conservative force, and not a force conducing to rapid economic growth.

This brings up the question of the importance attached to economic development as an end. If the Irish people were content to accept the advice of many of their national thinkers, to eschew industrialism and accept the benefits of a simple life lived in their homeland, then the change was all to the good, and it would be wrong to criticise them for not going the right way about securing economic development if in fact they did not want it. Professor Hutchinson has indeed argued that 'the Irish . . . were blamed for failing to achieve materialist and rationalist goals in which they were only marginally

[37]A. G. B. Fisher, *Economic Progress and Social Security* (1945).
[38]B. Hutchinson, 'The Study of Non-Economic Factors in Irish Economic Development', *Economic and Social Review*, Vol. I (July 1970), 509–29.

interested, thus finding themselves in the position of an author criticised for not having produced a book he had no intention of writing'.[39]

This may have been true of the Irish before the Famine, but it is questionable whether it remained true by the end of the century. Professor Hutchinson has argued that the middle class 'was too few in numbers to suggest to the rest of the Irish people a path to material improvement or social promotion' – and this can be accepted; but by the end of the century the middle-class prosperity of emigrant friends and relatives was an effective substitute. Hence, as I have contended in an earlier paper, 'in the intervening years the Irish people have ceased to be content with a low standard of living, and they have not shown themselves notably more disposed to forgo material comforts for the sake of less tangible values than have other European peoples'.[40] Thus while the remodelling of institutions and policy created a desired security, the fruits of economic progress were also sought – and, in some measure, obtained. That it should have proved possible to pursue two apparently conflicting objectives like this with even limited success was due to a much-deplored feature of the Irish economy – persistent emigration. For most of the twentieth century it has been comparatively easy for Irishmen to transfer their labour to the advanced economies of Great Britain or the United States, so that a proportion of the population in Ireland have been able to maintain themselves in their secure niches at acceptable standards of living. Those for whom there are no such niches, and who are not content to accept lower standards, have always been able to find opportunities in other countries. By this means the Irish reluctance to accept change and surrender traditional values has been reconciled with the equally real Irish desire to enjoy the fruits of economic progress.

Of late years[41] there has been a considerable increase in interest in economic development in the Republic of Ireland and a considerable improvement in the growth performance of the economy, largely as

[39]Hutchinson, *op. cit.*, 529.

[40]R. D. Collison Black, 'Contribution to symposium on "Economic Development" ', *Journal of the Statistical and Social Inquiry Society of Ireland*, Vol. XX, Part II, (1958), 123.

[41]Especially since 1958, when a notable report by the Secretary of the Department of Finance, Dr. T. K. Whitaker, was published under the title *Economic Development* (Pr. 4803, Stationery Office, Dublin).

The ensuing discussion here relates to the Irish Republic because the Government of Northern Ireland, while no less committed to economic development, pursues its policy within the broader U.K. context – i.e. more on the lines described as 'classical' above (pp. 197–200).

a result of deliberate shifts of policy. The continuing commitment to growth policies is exemplified by the recent Buchanan Report on regional development up to 1986,[42] which includes very ambitious estimates, particularly for the expansion of manufacturing employment. Commenting on these, a colleague of mine has recently written that 'growth of this dimension would require not only very good luck but complete dedication by the Irish people to the goals of economic development.'[43] It is very doubtful whether such complete dedication exists, or will emerge. Despite considerable changes, the traditional values still exert a real attraction, and an appeal to them can have considerable political effect. In this connection it is interesting to note that while the two major political parties are agreed on the desirability of Ireland's entry into E.E.C., more markedly nationalist groups, such as Sinn Fein, are opposed to it, partly on the ground of the threat which they see in it to traditional values.

VI. IMPLICATIONS OF THE IRISH EXPERIENCE FOR THE THEORY AND POLICY OF ECONOMIC DEVELOPMENT AT THE PRESENT DAY

Finally we may return to what were posed above[44] as the central questions of this paper: do the ideas used in relation to Ireland in the nineteenth century bear any resemblance to the ideas used now, and can we learn anything of value at the present time from a re-examination of them?

Looking at what has recently begun to be called 'Standard' economics,[45] I have an uncomfortable feeling that the classical ideas used in relation to Ireland in the last century bear all too much resemblance to the 'Standard' ideas used in relation to developing economics at the present day. Clearly I do not mean by this that economic theory itself has not changed or advanced, but that the error which the classical economists made of taking the institutions of the advanced economy in which they lived as typical or normal is too often repeated at the present day by Western economists. Just as there were those in the classical period who recognised the mistake

[42]Regional Development in Ireland. Report prepared by Colin Buchanan and Partners in association with Economic Consultants Ltd and An Foras Forbartha (Dublin, 1968).

[43]W. Black, 'Employment in Ireland' (1971). I am indebted to Dr Black for permission to quote from his paper in advance of publication.

[44]See page 192.

[45]Cf. N. Georgescu-Roegen, 'Economic Theory and Agrarian Economics', *Oxford Economic Papers*, Vol. XII (1960), 1.

and drew attention to it,[46] so there are economists today who rightly condemn 'the widespread practice that authors and lecturers have, of not merely concentrating on the economics of some developed industrial country, but presenting it as universally valid'.[47] Yet in spite of such protests and warnings the practice goes on; reciting the cautionary tale of Ireland may help to curb it. It should also help, if properly interpreted, to guard against the opposite error of thinking that there is nothing in the hard lessons of orthodox economics which the authorities in a developing country need heed, or that repetition of the slogans of past leaders can be a substitute for realistic assessment of current economic problems.

A point which has been particularly stressed in this paper is the clash, half-concealed by the peculiarities of the Irish case, between the desire to retain the social stability of the traditional society, and to obtain the advantages of economic progress. Such a clash is also to be discerned in many of today's developing societies. Clearly the lessons of Ireland could not be applied directly to such cases, but may serve to point the value of combining the study of economic development with cultural change. Here, one suspects, is another precept to which all economists give lip-service, but which most are willing to forget.

More specifically, it is possible to see other ways in which the lessons of the Irish experience might help the science of economics to make a more effective contribution to the practice of economic development. For example, it emphasises the need for a stress on institutional economics in relation to development – no one examining it can fail to be struck time and again by the relativity of economic theories and the consequent value of comparative studies of institutions. Again, within the field of such studies, the Irish experience points towards the importance of an examination and analysis of peasant agrarian economy which, it has been rightly said, 'has to this day remained a reality without a theory'.[48]

[46]J. S. Mill was perhaps the leading example, but the same criticism had been voiced earlier by Richard Jones, in *An Introductory Lecture on Political Economy, Delivered at King's College, London, 27 February 1833*. p. 20.

[47]Dudley Seers, 'The Limitations of the Special Case', *Bulletin of the Oxford Institute*, Vol. XXV (May 1963), 79.

[48]N. Georgescu-Roegen, *loc. cit.*

9

Economic Changes in Africa in Historical Perspective

S. HERBERT FRANKEL
University of Oxford

INTRODUCTION

I shall attempt to examine some of the fundamental factors affecting economic change in Africa. It is a daunting task, and obviously the first question that springs to mind is whether such an attempt is even meaningful.

Until recent times Africa was little more than a term of classification for geographers or cartographers; a goal of explorers and navigators; a foothold for slavers, traders and adventurers; an abstraction for poets and philosophers musing on the good and evil state of man in nature; and, more importantly, a series of outposts for victualling and defending the sea-route to India. Only in the second half of the nineteenth century, and for the most part only at its end, did Africa become of significant concern to the modern world economy – as an area of economic penetration which created those new economic, political, and racial tensions which have drawn taut the bow-string of its brief modern history.

One of the modern economic expressions of the 'idea' of Africa took the form of Cecil Rhodes' dream of the Cape to Cairo railway.[1] It symbolised not only the power of the British Empire, but of the potential economic unification of a continent which was for the most part still veiled in the mists of the age-old past. There are people alive today who knew Cecil Rhodes; little did they realise at the beginning of this century that the European powers which were then

[1] The Cape to Cairo dream had a fascinating origin. Dr Francisca Lacarda, the Brazilian explorer, predicted in 1796, two years before Napoleon's descent upon Egypt, that there would be a British Empire from the Cape to Cairo. For further reference to the development of the idea see my 'The Tyranny of Economic Paternalism in Africa: A Study of Frontier Mentality, 1860–1960', Supplement to *Optima*, (Johannesburg, December 1960).

211

in the process of establishing their sovereignty over most of Africa south of the Sahara would have lost it before the succeeding generation had disappeared, nor did they realise the costs of imperial hegemony, nor the difficulties of developing the resources of Africa from which they could be paid.

Yet in the short period of imperial rule there were vast changes – the full extent of which the present generation finds difficult to grasp. Whatever the extreme critics of European colonisation in Africa may, in their vicarious sense of real, or projected, guilt, wish to overlook, at least one crucial fact cannot be lightly dismissed: from the Cape to Cairo there was established in this century at least that framework of communications, ordered government and the rule of law, under which, with only temporary interruptions of world wars, it was possible for the first time in the history of the continent to move from the location of the tribe through the length and breadth of Africa – and to move in safety.

The men and women of the Western nations responsible for the great feats of exploration, organisation, education and economic change, were imbued, like men and women everywhere, with mixed motives – creditable and discreditable, lofty and debased, avaricious and saintly – but the overriding spur to their achievement was something else: it was to liberate Africa from its age-old isolation and to unloose the bonds of slavery, superstition, and idolatry within which it lay imprisoned. The dream of the Cape to Cairo railway was perhaps its most appropriate symbol. It represented the power of the new forces of industrialism – which it was thought would add yet another continent to the world economy of the West.

The builders of that century were in a hurry (a trait which it ill-behoves our generation to cast in their teeth, insisting as it all too frequently does on rapid economic development at all costs – even sometimes at the cost of millions of lives). Like all those in a hurry, the bearers of industrial civilisation in Africa failed to see what it was easiest to ignore – the effect of their actions on those whose different ways of life were being destroyed or forgotten in the process. But, whatever else they did, they did not deliberately exterminate the indigenous population, as in parts of the New World – and as in our generation in the Old. The moving industrial frontier of money economy simply by-passed much of it, just as it by-passed the game: the steam engine and the derricks moved on. The indigenous subsistence economies were left as tribal areas under paternalistic and unimaginative protection of their age-old ways of life: in the hope that they would one day somehow throw up shoots of modern advance.

By and large, the areas of subsistence economy remained outside the awareness and the preoccupations of the carriers of modern economy. Only the missionaries, the dedicated civil servants, the scientists and social investigators were in some degree acquainted with the thoughts and tribulations of those eking out a living in them, and feeding the metropolitan regions with the labour of their young able-bodied workers.

Perhaps the most significant of all the changes in Africa has been on the psychological and political plane. As I have suggested elsewhere,[2] the history of economic development of new countries can usefully be looked upon as a process of adjustment on three planes: (*a*) political and territorial; (*b*) sociological and economic; and (*c*) psychological. None of these can be separated into hard and fast compartments. They can all be seen as a struggle which is both objective and subjective. In any historical situation the actors not only play a role, but they have ideas and beliefs concerning it which sharpen their perception of reality in some directions but blunt it in others. Neither Cecil Rhodes nor Smuts, neither Churchill nor Roosevelt, and not even de Gaulle until late in his career, realised the rapidity of the emergence of African nation states, seeking to assume responsibility for the fate of their peoples in the modern world.

The achievement of the new political independence may open the way for many of them to overcome at last the psychological and political dilemmas of security, and to transcend local loyalties by the creation of strong national entities. The political stability of these new states is still uncertain, and to the vast mass of the peoples these changes as yet convey relatively little meaning. Indeed, why should we expect them to do so? To how many Europeans can it be said that the idea of European unity has more than an abstract appeal even now? For most of the large number of diverse tribes of Africa the African continent is still a closed book – as indeed it is for all of us. Its real resources lie undiscovered; the latent powers of its peoples are untested; its relatively poor soils and sparse vegetable covering are threatened by unsuitable farming practices; and its political relations among those within and with those outside it are in dangerous flux.

Notwithstanding the efforts of the European Powers to bring Africa into the orbit of the modern world, the basic factors which lie at the root of its problems are – like its treasures – still mainly unexplored. They lie deeper than those who would fain bring deceptively easy expedients to the African people are apt to realise.

[2]*Ibid.*, p. 1.

213

How stable these new states will prove to be will greatly depend on the rate at which they can foster or permit economic change, and only the future will reveal it. But the tasks involved will, I believe, become clearer if we examine some of the fundamental factors which have determined the rate of economic change in Africa south of the Sahara so far.

What therefore I hope to show in this paper is that the answer to the question in my opening paragraph does not lie in attempting generalisations, but rather in examining the processes of change itself in order to throw some light on the very complex, and it must be stressed, often quite accidental factors which have impelled or constrained them.

ENVIRONMENTAL FACTORS

It is necessary first to remind ourselves of some of the environmental factors which for long isolated Africa from the outside world, and which continue to impose high costs and severe constraints on efforts to bring the economic operations of the continent within the orbit of the modern world economy. There is first of all the vast size of the continent: it would, figuratively speaking, not be difficult to pack into it the land areas of China, India and the United States, and still leave room to spare.[3] It covers a great multiplicity of climatically-diverse regions – many of them isolated from each other by deserts, mountains, or forests. Some 91 per cent of the area and 91 per cent of the population south of the Sahara is situated within the tropics.[4] For the most part, the interior of tropical Africa remained isolated from the outside world until the beginning of the century – whereas, penetration of the southern end of the continent had begun three centuries before. There is still much uncertainty concerning the real effect of tropical environments on peoples of different races. Whatever increased scientific knowledge, new technology and greater experience of modern development in tropical areas may hold out for the future, it is clear that man has in the past generally not grappled with the ecological and economic problems of these regions

[3]The total area of Africa is estimated to be about 30·3 million sq. km., compared with 4·9 million sq. km. for Europe, 27 million sq. km. for Asia, 22·4 million sq. km. for the U.S.S.R. and 21·5 and 20·5 million sq. km. for North and South America respectively. The overall density per sq. km. of the population of Africa is as a whole 11 – the same as the U.S.S.R., and comparing with the figure of 12 for America, 13 for Latin America, 72 for Asia, 93 for Europe, and 370 for Japan.

[4]The temperate zone of South Africa covers an area of roughly 2·7 million sq. km; the corresponding figure for Latin America is 4·1 million sq. km.

as successfully as he was able or forced to do in temperate zones.[5]

In tropical Africa ecological disadvantages were intensified by the great distances which had to be spanned in order to establish trade between its large land mass and the outside world. It is, therefore, not surprising that there has been relatively small permanent immigration from outside Africa. It has been estimated that from 1886 to 1929, there was a gross emigration from twelve countries in Europe of just over 28 million people: which figure probably accounts for three-quarters of the whole of the gross emigration from Europe in that period. Yet only 1·7 million (6 per cent) went to Africa, and the net emigration to Africa was only 300,000 (1·6 per cent).[6] Contrast with this the experience of the climatically most temperate country in Latin America – Argentina – which, during the forty years from 1870 to 1910 received a net immigration of over two million.

Broadly speaking, the peoples inhabiting most of sub-Saharan Africa could only survive by very close adaptation to an interdependence with their localised environment. This led to stringent communal and tribal controls on agricultural and pastoral activities. There was in most areas continual pressure of population on available food resources; high infantile death rates and high adult morbidity rates regulated population growth: there was thus little opportunity for 'savings' for economic growth, or to cope with the vicissitudes of drought and other natural catastrophies. In general, African populations had until very recently (and, indeed, mostly still have to) concentrate their efforts on the day-to-day task of survival through minimum standards of consumption. The size of any population unable to benefit from economies of production for wider regional, national and international markets necessarily depends on the food supplies which can be obtained locally. But in Africa the natural ecological environment is not generally favourable in this respect. Areas economically suitable to agricultural production are interspersed between large areas which are for one reason or another unfavourable for these purposes, or require large capital investment to make them so; or to link them with world markets.

[5]For an excellent analysis of the problem, see the article by Professor William O. Jones on 'Environment, Technical Knowledge, and Economic Development in Tropical Africa', *Food Research Institute Studies* Vol. V. No. 2. 1965 (Stanford University, California).

[6]Cf. *The Balance Sheet of Imperialism: Facts and Figures of Colonies* by Grover Clark, published for the Carnegie Endowment for International Peace (Columbia University Press, 1936), p. 49.

TRAUMATIC CONCERN WITH LAND

The close dependence on the environment, in which African peoples were for centuries imprisoned, led inevitably to an almost traumatic concern for tribal rights to land to ensure that limited type of econo- mic security which it could provide.

Let me illustrate this concern from one of many similar experiences when I was a member of the East African Royal Commission in Kenya in 1953. We attended a meeting in Uganda in the open air, and listened for a whole day to representations from the elders of the Bagishu tribe, who placed before us many requests for further financial grants from the United Kingdom for agricultural and other improvements. They constantly implied in their criticisms that such assistance was after all an obvious obligation of His Majesty's Government. Towards evening I ventured, in replying, to point out that we had had similar requests from neighbouring tribal authori- ties, some of whom were much worse off. I asked whether the Bagishu would be prepared to assist their neighbours by making some of their *unutilised* tribal lands available to them. This question was received with unmitigated incredulity and loud ironical laughter: 'Why should we care about them – they are nothing to us. It is not our business', they cried.

This episode illustrates the conflict for land so characteristic of the history of African population movements, and so basic to the relationship between the Bantu and the European peoples in southern Africa. It is probable that the distribution of population in Africa has been as much influenced by wars and the depopulation and migra- tion resulting therefrom, as by differences in ecological conditions. The recent tragedy and devastation in Biafra is nothing new in Africa.[7] As Kimble writes:[8]

'The more it is studied, the more important this military factor is seen to be in West Africa with its troubled pre-European history. More than any other single factor it helps to explain the important agglomerations of population in the relatively stable kingdoms

[7]For example, it has been suggested that nodular clustering of population in the wooded grassland (Savanna) belt, especially in Northern Nigeria, is probably related to the fact that 'civil strife in the nineteenth century depopulated large areas in the marcher zone between the emirates of Katsina and Sokoto and east of Kano, in the old shatter zone between the Fulani and Bornu Empires – Keith Buchanan, 'The Northern Region of Nigeria: The Geographical Background of Its Political Duality', *Geographical Review*, Vol. XLIII (1953), pp. 457–9, quoted by Kimble, (see note 8).

[8]George H. T. Kimble, *Tropical Africa*, Vol. I, (The Twentieth Century Fund, New York, 1960) p. 103.

of Ashanti-Dahomey and Southern Nigeria, and the relative emptiness of the "middle belt" separating the densely populated coastal and interior zones. The lesser nodes of population, such as those of Fouta Djallon in Guinea and the difficult hill country of Northern Togo and those of Central Dahomey, may also owe their existence to the need in earlier times for a place of refuge from the military invader and the no less bloody slave raider. During the three centuries and more that the American slave trade lasted, raiders repeatedly swept over the area, and if they did not always succeed in carrying off the local population, they forced it to retreat to the sanctuary of the densest bush or most difficult terrain. It can be argued that the population of the middle belt has not yet recovered from the havoc wrought in those times.'

The same can be said of much of south-east Tanzania (formerly 'Tanganyika', and, prior to the First World War, 'German East Africa'). There the vast depopulation resulting from the scorched-earth policy adopted by the Germans in putting down the African Maji-Maji rebellion opened the country to the tsetse fly, the carrier of Trypanosomiasis, the cause of sleeping sickness. As a result, even now the depopulation has not been made good. Possibly, as Professor John Phillips, the well-known South African ecologist once remarked, the sole advantage was that, by thus letting in the tsetse fly, the ecology of the region was protected from the ravages of unsuitable agricultural practices by the Bantu themselves.

THE SEARCH FOR SECURITY

The point which I wish to stress in this connection is that the greater part of Africa's population is still very precariously dependent on the meagre returns yielded by primitive agricultural or pastoral techniques. Any appreciable disturbance in the ecological, economic, political or demographic circumstances brings about increased unemployment, and leads to labour migration in search of employment. It is this continuous re-filling of the reservoir of unskilled labour, either by accident, war, or design, which has probably affected the structure and rate of economic change in Africa more than any other single factor.

It is very easy for the outside observers to speak and write concerning change for the sake of 'economic growth', but in doing so, it is often forgotten that the aggregates and averages in which growth is measured hide the costs thereof to the individual participants in the process and, particularly, to those not sheltered against

217

or compensated for the individual or communal adversities and costs which growth involves. Unfortunately, most of the peoples of Africa still continue to live in conditions of age-old insecurity.

The fears resulting from the very great insecurities to which African tribes have always been subjected only served to perpetuate the longing for access to land as a haven from and bulwark against change itself.

One of the main tasks which the Royal Commission on East Africa (1953–5) set itself was to examine the 'dilemma of security' which this land hunger reflected. The Report of the Commission[9] pointed out that: "If the living standards of the people are to rise . . . access to new land merely for subsistence production can no longer form the basis of 'security' for all the indigenous population. . . . The test of land *needs* must be replaced by a test of land *use*." Also, the Commission stressed that tribal units could not revert to a past which offered their members no prospect of material advancement, nor, on the other hand, could they go forward, or even stand still, under their existing customary, legal and economic organisation of land, labour and capital. "To go back to the subsistence economy of the past, or even to stand still in the dawn between the old institutions which are dying and the new which are struggling to be born would be to court economic disaster. To go forward without modifying drastically those features of the tribal system of land tenure which impede progress is impossible. This is the dilemma which confronts the African people in their own areas."

In this connection it is not a little sad to reflect on the efforts – patterned as they unconsciously are on the same paternalistic attitudes as characterised so much of the benevolent efforts of British colonial policy in the rest of Africa – which are now being made by South African officials in some of the so-called Bantu Homelands in the Republic of South Africa. These efforts are still gravely hampered by the failure to grapple with the problems and constraints of communal land ownership and the overcrowding, over-grazing and deterioration of the land associated therewith – and this after more than a hundred years of political discussion as to what might possibly be 'done' in them!

MYTHS OF THE PAST

For an understanding of the legacy of this century of change in Africa, it is worth looking at some of the myths and beliefs which influenced it. Indeed, there are significant parallels with the myths

[9]Cmd 9475, London, Ch. V, p. 48.

which underlay westward expansion in the United States and the British Overseas Dominions.

For example, in the great trek into the interior of South Africa in the 1830s, the Boers were in a sense repeating the protest of their ancestors in Europe against the shackles on the freedom of the individual which characterised the governments of the eighteenth century, as they did also many of the policies of the government at the Cape which the Boers sought to escape. The movement was, of course, also based on economic motives and necessities. It was the first break into the interior to use the economic resources of Africa on a relatively extensive scale. Owing to the remoteness from world markets, it was not possible to do this as small-scale farmers. So the Boers became pastoralists, living the life of independence which, like so many of their age, they sought to obtain in the bosom of nature. Their subsequent suspicion – shared by the indigenous peoples – of immigrants from Europe was understandable: they foresaw that their own independent way of life in the bosom of the African garden could not continue if the garden was to become a commercial farm, a mine or a factory requiring techniques, industrial disciplines, and capital which the frontiersmen did not possess.

Thus originated the belief in the necessity of vast tracts of land, and the conviction (which they also shared with the Bantu) that it was necessary to bar others access to them. That conviction continued to affect land policy and industrial relations throughout Africa to the present day; the pastoralist and hunter, be he white or black, looks at life in terms of economic exclusiveness rather than mutual economic interdependence.

The later European immigrants attracted to south and central and east Africa also saw themselves as pioneers in a virgin continent. They too were casting off the shackles of Europe. But they were imbued by the belief in progress and by the conviction that they alone held in their hands the key to it on African soil. As ignorant of Africa as of the peoples – white and black – already there, many believed that with the tools and heritage of Europe they could repeat in Africa, as yeoman settlers, what Europeans had done and were doing in the virgin agricultural regions of the Americas, Canada and Australia. But the myth of repeating systems of yeoman independence, on any appreciable scale, foundered on the basic rocks of African reality. Africa might be suited to the plantation, the pastoralist, the miner or the capitalist farmer employing African labour, but, in general, it was not suited to the independent homesteader. The further north the European penetrated, the clearer became the

219

contrast between the myths born in Europe and African realities. For not only was Africa a continent where little could be done without the labour of black men – but it was a continent in which nothing could be done at all without tremendous capital investment to conquer distance and explore its real resources. That task even now continues to baffle modern man in tropical Africa. Thus we are brought to the great paradox: both age-old fears and customs and utopian hopes were steeped in exclusive and parochial attitudes to land, tribe and race. But in reality economic advance everywhere in Africa has come – where it has come at all – not from such exclusiveness, but from the more effective utilisation of resources for wider regional and world markets.

ECONOMIC GROWTH IN SOUTH AFRICA

Nothing illustrates the contrast between myth and reality more clearly than the remarkable industrial expansion in the Republic of South Africa, and the rapid urbanisation of its population. The transformation began during the First World War. It received official recognition and support in the 1930s with the inauguration of measures to solve the Poor White problem – the problem of what to do with the growing numbers of the landless white rural proletariat for whom a 'yeoman' independent existence had become impossible, owing to the use of native labour. The official 'industrialisation' of this white agrarian proletariat marked the first recognition in Africa that population increase was incompatible with isolation of men and women in the bosom of nature.

In consequence of a revolution in agricultural techniques (and vast sums spent thereon from Government revenues directly or indirectly obtained from the great expansion of mining), and also in consequence of the rapid growth of manufacturing industry in urban centres, advance has implied not the settlement of more people on the land, but moving workers away from it. It is of course to be expected that economic growth will be accompanied by a decline in the proportion of the occupied population on the land and in 'primary' production. But what is abnormal in South Africa is the racial distribution of employment. From 1911 to 1961 the number of Europeans employed in professional, commercial, mining and manufacturing activities multiplied about three-and-a-half times: it increased from about 285,000 to about 1,305,000. This was accompanied by an almost six-fold increase in non-whites employed in the same categories, from about 490,000 to 3,379,000. But these non-whites in industry are mainly confined to 'unskilled' work; they are and yet are not a part of the white economy; like Banquo's ghost, they are at the feast but not of it.

In 1908 the Transvaal Indigency Commission had expressed the fear that unless imported (native) labour was restricted – the white man *'would still remain a supervisor only. The pernicious theory that the line between White man's and Black man's work should coincide with the line between skilled and unskilled labour would continue to dominate the economic situation'* (Par. 60). *'. . . South Africa will at the best be numbered among the countries which are owned and governed but not peopled by the white races'* (Par. 95).

Sixty years later the situation, *as it might have been seen from the point of view of the eminent persons composing that Commission,* has grown worse. For in 1911 (three years after the Commission reported), the Census showed that the proportion of the total occupied *European* population in commerce and the professions was about 30 per cent. At the 1957 Census I estimated it to be more than 50 per cent, and by 1967 it would seem, from figures calculated by Steenkamp,[10] to have risen to 58 per cent, this being the proportion of *Europeans* in 'tertiary' employment as a percentage of all *Europeans* employed.

GROWTH OF MODERN ECONOMY

This is a convenient point for a reminder of the fact that no single country in sub-Saharan Africa has reached average *per capita* gross domestic product of the Republic of South Africa. The Republic (including for statistical purposes South West Africa, Lesotho, Botswana and Swaziland) in 1965 accounted for about 44 per cent of the G.D.P. of sub-Saharan Africa.[11]

In order to illustrate the growth of modern modes of production, it is useful to express the total number of African wage-earners as a percentage of total population. It is significant that this ratio was, in 1963, only about 4 per cent for Kenya, Madagascar, Malawi, Tanzania, Uganda and Zambia taken together – with Kenya 5·4 cent per and Zambia 6·4 per cent. The corresponding overall ratio of wage-earners in agriculture for all these territories was only 1·5 per cent compared with 2·6 per cent outside agriculture. In contrast to these low ratios, that of the Union of South Africa is about 30 per cent. The number of wage-earners in the Republic

[10] *Ibid.*, p. 105, Table 4. Steenkamp's figures are not strictly comparable with the author's. The latter are based on the analysis in 'Tyranny of Economic Paternalism', *ibid.*, p. 24.

[11] Economic Commission for Africa, *A Survey of Economic Conditions in Africa, 1967* (New York, United Nations, 1969), Table X, p. 10.

of South Africa in 1967 was about 5·2 million. Moreover, if we add the three other countries, Zambia, the Belgian Congo and Rhodesia, whose exports were predominantly based on mining (excluding oil production), it is probable that the number of Africans in wage employment in them, taken together, considerably exceeds the total in wage employment in the rest of sub-Saharan Africa.[12]

What is of special significance is that these four territories account for nearly 90 per cent of the mineral exports of all of sub-Saharan Africa. Mineral exports have been the magnet for most of the private, and indirectly also for the public capital investment from abroad. It is, for example, not just a quirk of history that the building of the Tanzania railway to the copper-belt in Zambia, on which the Chinese are currently engaged, should in a sense reflect motives of the President of Zambia not dissimilar to those which led President Kruger to negotiate with the Kaiser for the construction of the railway line from the Witwatersrand gold mines to the port of Lourenço Marques, before the First World War. The present international competition for access to the copper of Central Africa repeats the intense railway competition of the four provinces which eventually united to form the Union of South Africa – in no small part to overcome their uneconomic rivalries.

What enhances the role played by mining and mineral exploitation is that it is generally not so closely dependent on institutional changes as more specialised modern industrial and agricultural development. Capital and enterprise in mining have been brought together from all parts of the world and combined with available African labour resources, causing a rapid rise in incomes. Mining introduces the first stages of industrialisation without the need to await the growth of local markets in the rural areas for its products. It gives rise to associated manufacturing industries which are a valuable forcing ground for the acquisition (if permitted by law and custom) of industrial skills and disciplines which can then gradually spill over into the backward regions through the investment of higher private savings or public revenues.[13]

[12]U.N. Economic Survey of Africa, E/CN/14/370 and E/CN/14/401.

[13]Plantation enterprises have, of course, had similar effects in attracting capital from abroad and increasing exports. As in the case of mining, the communications and general infrastructure built up in connection with their development makes possible the expansion of cash crops by peasant producers, which provide very great scope, and are, indeed, essential, for further economic advance in tropical Africa. Peasant production of this kind is particularly valuable, because when basic rail or river communications have once been developed it is not dependent on further large investments from abroad.

OUTWORN BELIEFS AND PRACTICES

The advances which I have referred to have taken place in spite of, rather than as a consequence of, the beliefs which dominated this first century of modern economy in Africa. Even now, in the Republic of South Africa, the sterile debate continues unabated about land and occupational barriers between the races, and makes impossible the mature consideration of the real problems of the most advanced industrial economy in Africa.

Since the early years of this century restrictive trade-union practices, originally imported from Great Britain, have reinforced, in the industrial arena, the paternalism of the European landowner. In some cases collusive arrangements between European labour and the monopsonistic power of European capital have further weakened the bargaining power of the African worker. In any case, there was substituted for a free market for African labour, a complex system of regulations to control the African's movements and remuneration. Economic growth in the Republic of South Africa has not led to an amelioration of these restrictions. On the contrary, in the last twenty years there has actually been an intensification of the economic unfreedom of the African worker in the European economy. At any time, workers or dependents may no longer be 'required' by the authorities to reside in them and find themselves evicted to the undeveloped and overcrowded Bantu 'Homelands'. In whatever direction he turns, the African – whether he wishes to become a permanent property owner, a professional worker, or a secure tenant on the land – finds that law, custom and arbitrary decrees may, and do, bar his way. The result has been the growth of a vast migrant labour force – property-less and defenceless against any economic or political forces that may, as suddenly as the tropical storms of Africa, be unleashed against it.

It is forty-five years since I read a paper to Section F of the British Association for the Advancement of Science, which, in 1926, held its meeting in South Africa. The paper was entitled 'The Position of the Native as a Factor in the Economic Welfare of the European Population in South Africa'.[14] I pointed out that no serious attempt had until then been made to analyse the actual position which the native peoples occupy in the economic structure of the Union, or *the effect of their economic status on the white element of the community*. I tried to show that the welfare of the European and African peoples was interdependent, and that the inefficiencies and

[14]A shortened version was published in the *Journal of the Economic Society of South Africa*, Vol. XI, No. 1 (February 1928).

lack of productivity resulting from the barriers to opportunity for the African would in the long run undermine the position of the European. The meeting was presided over by Professor Edwin Cannan, who had been my teacher at the London School of Economics. When I had finished reading the paper he remarked: 'You are wasting your time, young man. They will never believe you because they do not want to.'

The formulation of highly-sophisticated models for economic growth is an easier process than the successful propagation of ideas. It is indeed significant that in 1971 one finds Professor W. F. J. Steenkamp still having to write:

'If it may be doubted that these legal colour bars served any purpose in the 'fifties and the 'sixties, the question arises whether there is any economic sense in maintaining them in the 'seventies. The answer, surely, must be in the negative. Far from facing serious cyclical or structural unemployment among its whites – as well as, be it noted, among its Coloureds and Indians – our economy has entered a decade of shortages in skills more acute than any it has experienced since the Second World War. If ever there was fear of a depression that would cause the Whites to lose their jobs to the non-Whites, there certainly is no reason for it in these 'seventies – unless, that is, we South African Whites fail to learn from the experience of past oligarchies, namely, that one way to undermine the stability of a society is to maintain excessive restrictions on the rights of other people for too long. . . . The time has come, we must conclude, to withdraw our discriminatory labour legislation. It no longer seems to serve a useful purpose. On the contrary, it is fast becoming a threat to progress in economic terms. The very least we need to do is to decide on a programme of withdrawal without further hesitation.'[15]

POLITICAL DANGERS

This first century of modern advance in Africa exhibits a dichotomy of beliefs. In some territories the rate of economic advance has been inhibited through policies designed to 'protect' the European – and in other parts of Africa it has been stultified, frequently, by similar 'paternalistic' colonial land and economic policies to 'protect' the indigenous institutions of the African.

The century began with the mythical belief that Africa could only be developed by the white man. It is ending with the belief that it should only be developed by the black man. Much of the current

[15]*Ibid.*, pp. 108–9.

revolt against the legacy of the past is a healthy sign of necessary economic change and social awakening. But in some quarters it is in danger of being perverted into a new myth – that of the limitless powers of African nationalism.

It is worth considering again for a moment the basic factors which enabled modern economy to develop at all in Africa. They were law and order, stable government, skilled administration, monetary stability sufficient to attract public and private capital, and guarantees against arbitrary confiscation of venture capital and its rewards. Throughout Africa, capital was required from abroad for developing export income – the sources for which are still as yet restricted mainly to minerals and mono-culture. Most of Africa still lacks the modern industrial and commercial expertise, the legal and governmental institutions, and even the communications for rapid economic expansion. Some of these can be imported, but they depend in the last resort on new institutional advances by the people of Africa themselves. As Henry Rosovsky has rightly stressed, decades of preparatory activity may be necessary before modern economic growth can begin, and much of this activity will have to be outside the range of what is usually termed 'economic'.[16]

Even the economic advance in South Africa is seen in a different dimension against the background of the undeveloped continent as a whole. A large part of South Africa's European, and nearly the whole of its African population, had within this century to be absorbed into modern forms of economic activity. It was a slow process. It should and could have been more rapid and free. But let us not delude ourselves – the process itself owed much to the accidents of history – not only to the diamond and gold discoveries but to the fortuitous development of contacts with the specialised financial markets of Britain and Europe.[17] Such relationships were, for example, not developed in Australia, and caused her mineral resources to remain relatively unexplored until quite recently.

WARNING FROM LATIN AMERICA

There are in my opinion some disquieting parallels between the

[16]Cf. 'Japan's Transition to Modern Economic Growth 1868–1885', in *Industrialisation in Two Systems* (John Wiley and Sons, London, 1966).

[17]On this the late Sir Theodore Gregory's book *Ernest Oppenheimer and the Economic Development of Southern Africa* (Oxford University Press, 1962), is a mine of information. See also S. Herbert Frankel *Investment and the Return to Equity Capital in the South African Gold Mining Industry 1882–1965: An International Comparison* (Basil Blackwell, 1967), and *Capital Investment in Africa* (reprinted in 1970 by Fertig, New York).

ECONOMIC DEVELOPMENT IN THE LONG RUN

problems which now challenge Africa's newly independent governments and those which faced the Spanish-Americans. As Professor R. A. Humphreys has reminded us, 150 years ago they also faced 'the problem of how to combine free government with effective government . . . of how, while making Spanish America safe for democracy, to make democracy safe for Spanish America'. To Bolivar – the Liberator – 'freedom meant more . . . than political independence; it meant freedom for the slaves; and it meant freedom from arbitrary government'. Bolivar's life was lived and lost in the battle for the principles of justice, liberty and political equality, and the sovereignty of the people as the sole legitimate authority of a nation.

But 'the fact remains that the peoples of Spanish-America were unprepared for self-government. They were the orphan children, not the adult heirs, of imperial Spain . . . ', as Bolivar put it, 'without practice in public affairs, still too little elevated from servitude to rise easily to the proper enjoyment of liberty.' Bolivar was soon to experience the difference between utopian hopes and the sharp facts of government, or more accurately speaking, the lack of it. The words he wrote in 1812, after the fall of the first federal republic of Venezuela, might well be inscribed on the walls of the ministerial offices of most African states today:

'The codes consulted by our law-givers [he wrote] were not such as could teach them the practical science of government, but rather the construction of certain well-meaning visionaries who, thinking in terms of ideal republics, sought to attain political perfection on the presupposition of the perfectibility of the human race. So we were given philosophers for leaders, philanthropy for legislation, dialectic for tactics and sophists for soldiers.'

Substitute the words 'economists and experts' for 'philosophers' and the quotation will fit present-day Africa even more perfectly. There is no need for me to re-tell Bolivar's tragic calvary. By 1826, as Professor Humphrey has shown, he was convinced that his America could only be ruled through an able despotism:

'It had come to that: the principle of authority. Had it not been the principle of Spanish rule? And Spanish rule he had destroyed. . . . The end was tragedy. All his hopes, all his plans, collapsed.The liberator became a dictator. . . . At the last he trod the road to exile, and on that road, in 1830, he died. He was forty-seven. Five weeks before his death he penned the famous sentence: "He who serves a revolution ploughs the sea".'

226

THE TASKS AHEAD

The fact is that African peoples have to fight on many fronts. At their back lie tribalism and subsistence economy. In front there are those who, deliberately or in ignorance, continue to permit the road of escape from the past to be blocked. But there is a third battle to be won: the battle for the extension of freedom and liberty within a framework of dependable law and order suited to the essential economic social and political intercourse between emergent African states and between them and the outside world. The task of the future is to continue the work of the remarkable century now closing, which by opening the continent to the peaceful commerce and enterprise of the world laid the first foundations for modern advance to replace the isolation of men's minds, work, and spirit. The danger is that a new isolationism, based on the whims of tyranny, will bring back the African bush, the erosion and the Malthusian checks. The bush reconquers quickly in Africa; but the numbers of those who know how to keep it at bay are as yet very limited. Should their work be interrupted, the disease, the outworn ways of thought, and the idolatries of the past may easily recur; and the hopes of the New Africa be shattered as the Free World withdraws from the continent, leaving it at the mercy of new conquerers from within or from without.

The economic task in Africa under the new political dispensations is really no different from the old: it is to find and create the most suitable institutional arrangements for utilising natural resources to yield new and additional net income to the inhabitants. In this search, generalised modern theories such as those of the 'take-off' or the 'big-push' have very little relevance – for the belief in the miracles to be wrought by capital investment *per se* is illusory.

The African states are entering upon a stage of world economic development in which the great technical and transport developments of our time are so rapidly reducing the barriers to communication of every kind, that almost any country or region which has something to contribute by way of labour or natural resources can, given even a modicum of reliability in the conduct of its affairs, attract to it those able to assist it to commence the development of potential assets. Probably at no previous time in history has there been available such an expanding network of private and public international agencies seeking to assist in the exploitation of the natural resources of the world, and experimenting in the problems of training and technique in order to do so.

227

In a technically shrinking world there is little room for absolute political or economic independence. If this is realised the problems of Africa will be seen as little different in kind from those elsewhere: as problems arising from the relative rates of change of economic and political institutions.

10

What are the 'Lessons' of Japanese Economic History?

Harvard University

I

To start with, a possibly controversial assertion: modern economic growth in Japan (i.e. the period encompassed by the past century) should be divided into two segments – the years before 1900 and the years after 1900. I will argue that the pre-1900 period is relatively devoid of 'lessons' for the less developed countries; and that the post-1900 economic history of Japan does contain some suggestive episodes for those seeking to further growth.[1] In other words, in interpreting the meaning of the Japanese experience for the present, two distinct styles of growth should be considered, and only one of these has current relevance.

Some may see this as a perverse interpretation. It is undoubtedly true that most of those attempting to derive lessons or policy implications based on the Japanese case have focused on the Meiji Era (1868–1912), because that is when 'things got started', and we are now interested in getting things started elsewhere. But my own view is that initial economic development in Japan had many idiosyncratic qualities, and this is likely to be the case in other countries. Early modern economic growth is strongly marked by a nation's institutional heritage: when development (or, more broadly speaking, modernisation) has been in effect for some time, both the economy and other institutions achieve a greater level of international comparability. At that time, the range of problems as well as their solutions have a more meaningful common denominator.

[1] Due to the outstanding performance of her post-World War II economy, one now frequently hears speculations concerning Japan as a model for rapid growth in mature economies. This very interesting proposition will not be considered here.

II

At first sight, the so-called Meiji or nineteenth-century pattern of economic development has enormous appeal. No one can say with any degree of certainty what Japanese G.N.P. *per capita* was before modernisation began in the 1860s, but it is clear that it was 'low' compared to European and North American levels at a similar time. Certainly it was below the standards achieved prior to the industrial revolution in the United Kingdom, France, the Low Countries, and the United States. What we can say with complete certainty is that between the early 1870s and the early 1900s there began a crucial transformation of the Japanese economy. Compared to the two hundred or more years of very slow growth and periodic stagnation which preceded the Restoration, there now occurred secular growth of G.N.P. at perhaps 3 per cent per year. Population, during the last third of the nineteenth century, was expanding at about 1 per cent per year, and thus significant *per capita* gains were registered as well.

Meiji indicators of economic performance are not unimpressive. Between the 1870s and the turn of the century, the output of factory manufacturing tripled; agricultural output increased at some 2 per cent per year; a most effective entrance was made into world markets through the export of silk and tea; important and entirely new import-substituting industries using Western techniques were introduced: cotton and wool textiles; the manufacture of glass, bricks, and cement; and the building of railroads. Finally, gross domestic capital formation as a proportion of G.N.P. must have exceeded 12 or 13 per cent.

Despite these early stirrings and real gains, one should not exaggerate the economic achievements of the Meiji Era. Japan was not – even by the standards of the time – a modern economy by 1900 or 1910. A brief glance at some of the aggregate evidence should make this very clear. For example, in 1905 manufacturing output was under 10 per cent of net national product; agricultural output constituted 40 per cent of the total; and the agricultural labour force was about 67 per cent of the entire labour force. Nevertheless, a very impressive start had been made.

There can be no mystery concerning the appeal of Meiji economic history to those attempting to further national development, because the Japanese succeeded in doing what many underdeveloped countries are attempting today: to exploit a traditional economy for the purpose of introducing and nurturing a growing modern economy.[2] The keystone in this process undoubtedly was the existence of a vigorous and growing peasant agriculture. During the Meiji years the following was evident:

1. Agriculture supplied the workers for a rising proportion of secondary production, while maintaining increases in output.
2. These increases in output were, to a considerable degree, the result of improved traditional methods of cultivation, often referred to as 'Meiji technology'. The main point is that this technology relied only minimally on know-how imported from Europe or America.
3. Agriculture also was the primary source of foreign exchange through its exports of silk and tea.
4. Funds for industrial development were also closely tied to agriculture. Public expenditures depended, in the main, on the proceeds of the land tax, and, in numerous cases, private capital was transferred by rural capitalists from primary or tertiary to secondary production.
5. Finally, the agricultural sector – absorbing as it did close to 80 per cent of the gainfully-employed labour force in the 1870s – was the largest and most important domestic market especially for the products of early and primitive industrialisation.

From the point of view of Japan, this was an 'economic' pattern of development. Advances in agriculture made relatively little use of the scarce factor of fixed capital, while making liberal use of the relatively plentiful factor of labour. The same was true of other areas of the economy in which traditional techniques continued to be useful. In residential and commercial construction, as well as in the broader category of social overhead investment, it was possible for Japan to expand capacity by labour-intensive methods which remained almost unchanged throughout the entire nineteenth century. The Meiji pattern was economic in two additional senses. First, the surpluses needed for development – whether they originated in agriculture, in industrial profits, or in a redistribution of income – came nearly entirely from domestic sources. Foreign capital and

[2]Although the terms 'modern' and 'traditional' are frequently used, my own meaning is quite specific. The traditional economy uses techniques and forms of organisation which were already in existence at the time of the Restoration (1868). Peasant agriculture is the best example, although many crafts could be cited as well. By contrast, the modern economy owes its techniques (e.g. power-driven machinery) and organisation (e.g. wage labourers working in factories) to the West. Sometimes a modern technique can be combined with a traditional form of organisation (or vice versa); for example, electric motors in small-scale industry used with unpaid family labour. This would be an instance of the hybrid economy.

enterprise played almost no part at this stage, thereby avoiding many of the tensions and frustrations seen so frequently in other parts of Asia. Secondly, both in the domestic and international spheres, Meiji industrialisation appears to have followed lines of comparative advantage. At home, especially after the 1880s, the government did not compete with the private sector, and engaged in direct production only when major bottlenecks appeared – as in the case of railroads and iron and steel. Abroad, the existence of unequal treaties which forbade protective tariffs, forced the Japanese to concentrate on those exports which could really be produced efficiently: silk, tea, and, eventually, cotton textiles.

I intend now to examine the proposition that the Meiji years provide little that is relevant to the underdeveloped world. This is so because I believe that the 'initial conditions' in Japan were peculiar – compared either to the early industrialisers of the West[3] or to the more backward countries of Asia, Africa, and South America.

In terms of the ordinary Kuznetsian indicators, late Tokugawa and early Meiji Japan show all the signs of economic backwardness: an overwhelming proportion of the working population engaged in agriculture, a relatively unchanging industrial structure dominated by primary production, and the absence of modern science and technology applied to industry. At the same time, Japan possessed some rather unusual non-economic attributes: a comparatively literate population, fertility control within marriage, an effective central and local government, an efficient system of roads and communications, large cities, excellent art, architecture, literature, etc.[4] This incongruity between the economic and non-economic state created a 'gap' – and the extent or comparative size of this gap constitutes the essence of Japan's peculiarity in the 1860s.

It would be most valuable to trace the forces which brought this gap into existence. Unfortunately I am able to do so only in a symptomatic manner. Its major source is clear: before the 1860s Japan was a progressive, advancing traditional society. Between 1603, when Ieyasu became the first shogun of the Tokugawa line,

[3]However, Reischauer, Hall, Nakamura and some others have suggested 'that Japan's pre-Meiji socio-economic system was more akin to those of feudal Europe than to those of traditional oriental societies in those important aspects which affect the aptitude to modernise'. See James Nakamura and Matao Miyamoto, 'Social Structure and Population Change: A Comparative Study of Japan and China' (mimeographed).

[4]Nakamura and Miyamoto, *op. cit.*, have very similar ideas, and talk of a pre-Meiji 'infrastructure' which included 'a relatively efficient bureaucracy, an educational plant, a flourishing publishing industry, a habit of experimentation by gifted farmers to raise productivity in agriculture, a national market, transportation and communications system, banking systems, and the like'.

and 1868, the quality of government and of civilisation in general had made significant advances. Because it was a traditional society – i.e. without the benefits of Western technology and consequently without the possibilities of generating rapid increases in productivity – the rate of economic progress was slow, and at times it may have been negligible on a *per capita* basis. But it was always there, and thus modernisation meant the move from one rate of progress to another, rather than the infinitely more difficult transition from stagnation or retrogression to modern economic growth which is so typical of most of the underdeveloped world. The very size of this (perhaps unmeasurable) gap also made economic development in Japan an easier task than in most countries. In effect, society was more advanced than the economy, and this permitted rapid and efficient internal change preparatory to the massive induction of Western technology and organisation in the twentieth century.[5]

These thoughts are rather general, and I would like to make them more specific by returning again to agriculture's contribution in enhancing initial modern economic growth.[6] What made these contributions possible?

[5]It is tempting to speculate about the causes which produced the vigorous traditional society of Tokugawa Japan. In my view, the Tokugawa policy of *sakoku* (the closed country) – in effect from the 1630s to the 1850s – played an important role. At a time when many countries in Asia were coming into colonial-type contact with the advanced nations of the West, Japan continued to develop at its own pace and according to its own talents. Two significant consequences follow. First, indigenous ways of doing things had attained high levels and were relatively uncorrupted when modern economic growth became a national goal in the 1870s. For example, in housing, food, style of clothing, etc. the Japanese remained content to stick to their own methods, and this was economically rational since the rapid adoption of imported methods would have been more expensive. Secondly, the Japanese did not bear the psychological burden of looking back towards a previous high-point of national achievement. Unlike nineteenth-century China, India, Korea, or Indonesia – each of these countries had done better at some earlier date – the Japan of *sakoku* continued on its measured path.

[6]In recent years there has been considerable controversy concerning the role of agriculture in Meiji economic development. The following items are representative of the various views: James I. Nakamura, *Agricultural Production and the Economic Development of Japan, 1873-1922* (Princeton: Princeton University Press, 1966); Henry Rosovsky, 'Rumbles in the Rice Fields', *Journal of Asian Studies*, Vol. XXVII, No. 2 (February 1968); Y. Hayami and S. Yamada, 'Technological Progress in Agriculture' in L. Klein and K. Ohkawa (eds), *Economic Growth: The Japanese Experience Since the Meiji Era* (New York: Richard D. Irwin, 1968); K. Ohkawa, 'Phases of Agricultural Development and Economic Growth' in K. Ohkawa, B. Johnston, and H. Kaneda (eds), *Agriculture and Economic Growth: Japan's Experience* (Princeton: Princeton University Press, 1970); Kee Il Choi, 'Technological Diffusion in Agriculture Under the Bakuhan System', *Journal of Asian Studies*, Vol. XXX, No. 4 (August 1971).

Let us begin with the increases in output.

1. Success depended on the availability of a high level and improving *indigenous* (Meiji) technology. At first the Japanese believed that Western techniques would prove useful in improving agricultural methods, and in 1871 the government actually sponsored a Western farm machinery exhibition at Tsukiji (Tokyo). Similar efforts were made on behalf of imported crops, livestock, and seedlings. By the middle of the 1880s, however, it was clear that this was not a fruitful path: Japanese factor supply conditions – i.e. land, labour, capital, and climate – made nearly all foreign techniques and many products uneconomical and impractical. At this early stage of development the Japanese had to revert to their own know-how.

2. Two elements were crucial in raising the level of Meiji agricultural practices. One was the ability to improve what is sometimes called 'productivity proper' through better (native) seed selection, larger applications of (organic) fertilisers, and the more widespread use of tools. The other element is referred to as 'the eastward movement of agricultural techniques' (*inasaku gijutsu no tōzeh*). It points to the fact that western Japan was ahead in nearly all economic aspects, and the transfer of its superior agricultural methods to the more backward east was a vital component in the higher growth of output which was achieved in the last third of the nineteenth century.

3. Increases in output also depended on the existence of improving landlords and peasants who were sufficiently flexible and/or educated to adopt new methods, and most of all on agriculturalists who were certain enough of institutional stability to believe that they could retain a proportion of the gains which rightfully belonged to them.

4. Of equal importance was the presence of a central and local government willing and able to formulate strong supportive measures: extension services, veteran farmers' groups, seed exchange societies, etc., etc.

My impression is that the capability to raise agricultural output depended heavily on unusually favourable initial conditions: an available technology susceptible to improvement, relatively advanced regions, flexible and secure peasants, and effective public policy. The *exploitation* of agriculture for purposes of growth depended even more on the social setting.

That the land tax accounted for approximately two-thirds of central government revenue during most of the Meiji Era has already been mentioned. Frequently it was an inadequate source of revenue, but sufficient substitute sources were not developed until shortly before World War I. What made it possible to collect the land tax?

1. One factor must have been a long-standing custom of regular and 'reasonable' taxation which antedates the Restoration. Tokugawa agricultural taxes were largely paid in kind and were assessed on the harvest rather than on the value of the land; sometimes the individual *han* set extremely steep rates and there were certainly instances of peasant tax rebellions. Nevertheless, the average picture was different: harvest taxes were collected regularly and assessed reasonably, and in this sense, the new land tax did not represent a sharp break with the past.[7]

2. A closely-related matter was the manifest willingness of the Japanese peasantry to market its surplus produce. The switch from taxes in kind to cash payments created little confusion. Peasants already marketed a certain share of their produce in Tokugawa days, and it appears that they were quite familiar with the uses of money.

3. One should also remember that pre-modern Japan was – to borrow a European term – a *Grundherrschaft* rather than a *Gutswirtschaft*. Japanese peasants were not serfs performing labour services on the estate of a lord. Rather, they cultivated their own soil – held by right of customary tenure – rarely saw the lord, who lived in Edo or the local castle town, and performed their servile duties almost exclusively through tax payments. Under these circumstances, land reform is a rather simple matter: it can be accomplished with the stroke of a pen by which customary tenure is transformed into full ownership (which, of course, includes the right of sale). And this avoids the incredible tensions and conflicts inherent in separating the lord from the peasants – an event which had occurred in Japan in the first half of the seventeenth century.

4. Equitable and efficient land taxes are closely linked with the availability of accurate cadastral surveys. Such surveys make considerable demands on pre-modern societies, since they require many administrators, surveyors, and people who can read and write; in addition, one also needs adequate records of ownership. Problems are especially severe when land morselisation prevails – as in Japan. The Meiji land tax was based on a cadastral survey which lasted nearly the

[7]There is some disagreement about the comparative burden of the Tokugawa harvest tax and the Meiji land tax. It had generally been believed that similar amounts were collected by the old and the new regimes. Some scholars now feel that the Meiji tax considerably lowered the peasant's burden. I doubt the validity of this revisionist hypothesis.

entire decade of the 1870s. The whole of the country was covered; and while it is undoubtedly true that mistakes and evasions took place, it was nevertheless a most impressive administrative performance for a pre-industrial country. To my knowledge, no foreign technical assistance was involved.

5. Finally, in considering reasons for the collectability of the land tax, one should also mention the speed and ease with which the Meiji government achieved 'legitimacy'. From the point of view of the rural tax-payer, the new (revolutionary?) government simply said: You have been paying taxes to the daimyo and shogun; we have taken their place and the payments must now be made to us. And they were – on the whole without major protest or disruption.

Some colleagues and friendly critics with whom I have discussed these ideas have tried to convince me that the Meiji economy does contain valuable lessons for underdeveloped countries. After all, if Japan's early and quite rapid success can be related to a 'gap' between the economic and non-economic state of affairs, then an implication of current interest would follow. Perhaps the emphasis in less-developed countries should be on the creation of this gap through a long-term programme of institution building. To put it another way, on the basis of the Japanese experience, one can preach patience and urge the creation of Meiji-type preconditions. But I find this to be impractical and harmful advice. In effect, this says to countries and policy-makers with urgent problems that a long period of time is necessary to prepare a society for modern economic growth. I prefer to take the position that this suggestion is irrelevant; if this is indeed the lesson of the past, then we must search for substitute patterns in the present.

III

Let us now shift to the twentieth century, in which the Japanese pattern of development becomes, in my opinion, more pertinent to today's L.D.C.s.[8] We will now be concerned with Japan's transformation from a state of initial modern economic growth to a level of semi-development, a process which seems more amenable to

[8]The separation of Meiji and post-Meiji growth patterns does not imply, of course, that Japan's success in the twentieth century was unrelated to previous policies and achievements. On the contrary, in bringing about the conditions that permitted modern economic growth to begin, Japan exploited 'traditional' sources of strength both in the economy and the society. The question is: can present-day underdeveloped countries do the same thing? Perhaps similar possibilities exist in China and India, and in a few other places. But I remain sceptical about the wider promise of this process.

orthodox economic analysis and perhaps also to the drawing of 'lessons'.[9]

One preliminary point needs to be settled. What basis is there for a division into two styles of development, one prevailing in nineteenth-century and the other in twentieth-century Japan? Although dating a change of style or pattern necessarily involves a degree of arbitrariness, there can be little doubt about the event itself. Three elements may be briefly considered: agriculture, investment, and institutions.

1. We have already commented on the important and well-researched role of agriculture in supporting Meiji growth. In the twentieth century, agriculture became increasingly less supportive, and eventually – certainly after World War I – this sector could be considered one of the few retarding factors in Japanese growth.[10] In contrast to the Meiji years, throughout this century the land tax declined in importance as a source of central and local government revenue; the structure of exports increasingly shifted towards manufactured products, and they became the principal earners of foreign exchange; and lastly, as the country became more urbanised, an ever-larger proportion of the growing non-agricultural labour force originated outside of agriculture.

2. A similar disparity is noticeable in the pattern of nineteenth-century and twentieth-century capital formation. In the Meiji era, investment was heavily 'traditional' and dominated by the public sector. By 'traditional', I mean to underline the fact that much, and frequently most, of the investment activities – including road and riparian work, residential and commercial construction – involved techniques that had been used in Japan for hundreds of years. These investments did not, therefore, embody a great deal of imported technological and organisational progress. This changed as modern industries gradually became weightier in the mix of new investments, and this is related to the declining relative share of public capital formation in post-Meiji Japan.

3. Finally, one can also draw a distinction from the institutional point of view. The Meiji years of initial modern economic growth

[9]Neither 'initial modern economic growth' nor 'semi-development' are intended to be used in a vague sense. That Japan, by 1900, had barely started to industrialise, has already been made clear. Even today, when Japan's G.N.P. is the second largest in the non-communist world, she ranks only fifteenth or sixteenth in G.N.P. *per capita*. The reason is, of course, that a dual economic structure has persisted to the present, and this is the meaning of semi-development.

[10]See Kazushi Ohkawa, 'Phases of Agricultural Development and Economic Growth' in K. Ohkawa, B. F. Johnston, and H. Kaneda (eds), *op. cit.*, Ch. I.

and initial modernisation were a most active *public* institution-building time. Even if the enumeration is confined to a rather narrowly-defined economic sphere, the list is impressive: a new currency and banking system; a new system of tax-collection; abolition of feudal barriers to mobility and employment; establishment of absolute private property in agriculture; creation of a central bank and adoption of the gold standard; and, perhaps most symbolic of all, the abolition of unequal treaties with the Western Powers, fully implemented in 1910. By the time the Meiji era ended, the pace of public institution building – economic and other – had slowed down considerably. The national societal parameters had been established and remained unaltered until after World War II.

Having drawn a distinction between the nineteenth- and twentieth-century patterns of growth, we can now concentrate on the latter period. In a variety of joint studies Professor K. Ohkawa and myself have pointed to three key features of the current era: a rapid trend rate of growth of aggregate output, trend acceleration, and periodic investment spurts.[11]

Between 1900 and the outbreak of World War II, Japan's real G.D.P. grew at an average annual real rate of approximately 4 per cent. Since World War II the annual real rate has been above 10 per cent. For the prewar years, long-term growth at 4 per cent is 'rapid' in the sense that very few other countries did as well at that time.[12] In the postwar era Japan's growth supremacy is a matter of record and requires no elaboration. Trend acceleration can also be observed with these figures by simply contrasting the pre- and postwar secular growth rates of G.D.P.[13]

While the growth of aggregate output was rather smooth, capital formation – and most especially private non-agricultural investment – expanded in great waves whose positive slopes may be called 'investment spurts'. The (private non-agricultural) quantitative dimensions were as follows:

[11]See especially K. Ohkawa and H. Rosovsky, 'Post war Japanese Growth in Historical Perspective: A Second Look' in P. L. Klein and K. Ohkawa (eds), *op. cit.*, Ch. I.

[12]Similar performances were achieved by the United States and Canada, and perhaps also by the U.S.S.R. and Sweden.

[13]This is undoubtedly the most unambiguous way of establishing trend acceleration. But we should make clear that this phenomenon affected the Japanese economy since about 1900. With the exception of the 1920s, when G.D.P expanded at the comparatively slow rate of 3·5 per cent, and the years of reconstruction and rehabilitation following World War II, each decade of the twentieth century averaged a higher rate of growth than its predecessor.

	G.D.P.	ΔI/I (%/yr; constant prices)
1901–17*	4·1	13
1917–31	3·5	2
1931–7*	4·9	23
1956–62*	10·6	19
1962–6	9·2	5

These investment spurt periods (marked *) display a number of systematic associations with the rest of the economy:

1. They coincide with the years of most rapid G.D.P. expansion.
2. They have driven up the aggregate investment proportion to very high levels: from about 12 per cent in 1900 to about 34 per cent in 1966.
3. They are generally associated with declining values of capital-output ratios in the most rapidly expanding industries.
4. Finally, each spurt brings to the forefront a new set of industries. The years from 1901 to 1917 saw the creation of the large integrated cotton-spinning and weaving mills. In the 1930s 'heavy' armament-related industries became prominent. The first postwar spurt was especially concentrated in machinery, electronics, and petro-chemicals. It is somewhat early to characterise the most recent spurt which began in 1966, but no doubt automobiles and computers are industries that will achieve full stature during its time-span.

My purpose in this brief essay is not to provide a technical treatment of investment spurts and their consequences. A number of questions can therefore remain unanswered. Why does investment grow in spurts? Why do the spurts begin and end when they do? Are they the cause or effect of rapid and accelerating growth? Instead of dealing with these issues, I will merely assume that investment spurts were a central feature of twentieth-century development because:

1. They were the vehicles which made possible the rapid absorption of technological and organisational progress.
2. They made for trend acceleration because of the gradual introduction of ever more advanced and more productive imported technology.
3. And this explains why – throughout this century – the 'residual' has been getting larger and growing at a more rapid rate.

This is only a very partial presentation of Japanese economic growth during the past seventy years, but I have chosen to emphasise those aspects which seem to me to contain the promise of 'lessons' for other countries. Let us therefore assume, for the moment, that my general interpretation is valid, and that no one will be too stern about the exact meaning of 'lessons'; let us treat it as a word which we all understand but do not wish to define.

IV

The notion that imported technology played a critical role in Japanese economic modernisation is not exactly revolutionary. It is an interesting finding *only* if the Japanese either overcame greater obstacles and/or did it better than other countries. I am tempted to answer 'yes' to both questions, and to base certain 'modest suggestions' on Japan's experience.[14]

Students of economic development have long been aware of the fact that technology is created in advanced countries, and that its developmental direction is responsive to the mix of factor proportions and skills existing in these countries. And it is equally well known that this creates an obstacle for L.D.C.s attempting rapidly to absorb sufficient quantities of imported technology. An especially serious obstacle exists because, if an underdeveloped country wishes to develop an export market, considerations of cost and quality may require the use of very up-to-date methods. Given this situation, it may be important to create specific institutions designed to raise a less-developed country's capability to import technological and organisational progress. Japanese economic history shows both the significance of the rapid absorption of imported technology via the repeated investment spurts, and also the development of specific institutions that facilitated the entire process.

Throughout this century a number of specific institutions come to mind that raised Japan's social capability to absorb technological and organisational progress of foreign origin. They share some common characteristics: a loose relationship with individual investment spurts, an additive dimension meaning that methods developed in one spurt continue beyond it and may assume even greater importance at a later time, and finally, close ties to the functionings of modern enterprise that set them apart from the earlier reforms of Meiji times.

Let us briefly reconsider each one of the investment spurts in this light. The first one produced two institutions of lasting significance: *zaibatsu* and permanent employment. It is true, of course, that the

[14]That the Japanese did it better than other countries is implicit in the rate of growth of national income and the residual.

most famous zaibatsu (Mitsui, Mitsubishi, Sumitomo, and Yasuda) originated in the Meiji era, but they reached their greatest power towards the end of the 1920s, and it was largely based on the rapid industrialisation which had occurred in the first two decades of this century. While it is difficult to generalise, perhaps one can say that in the nineteenth century commerce was the major activity of zaibatsu; around World War I it was industry with particular emphasis on coal mining, shipbuilding, engineering, and glass; and in the 1920s it became finance.

The zaibatsu were leaders in the development of technologically more sophisticated industries. They were major importers of Western technology and innovators. They provided a low-income Japan with the possibility of exploiting scale economies, and their diversification permitted what Lockwood has called 'combined investment' – i.e. the simultaneous development of complementary industries.[15] Zaibatsu also economised what must have been a scarce factor, i.e. individuals capable of running modern businesses; and through the operation of their affiliated banks they were most adept at mobilising scarce capital resources. Given that the issue of that day – as now – was growth rather than economic democracy, there developed in Japan a certain kind of 'bigness' which was unacceptable elsewhere[16] but quite suitable in this setting.

Permanent employment is another peculiarly Japanese invention which came into prominence between 1900 and 1920. It was very much out of keeping with the nineteenth-century industrial labour situation when piracy of workers was common and turnover rates were extremely high. Now, a growing number of workers – especially in large enterprises – were hired on a life-time basis, and more attention was devoted to non-cash benefits such as housing, stores, medical care, etc. Undoubtedly an immediate reason for the creation of this system was the desire of enterprises to undermine the powerful and troublesome regional labour recruiters, and the consequent 'Balkanisation' of labour markets was most convenient for the big producers.[17] But there must have been a more fundamental and long-run reason, because permanent employment gave the Japanese entrepreneur a labour force without incentives to oppose technological and organisational progress even of the labour-saving type.

[15]Cf. W. W. Lockwood, *The Economic Development of Japan* (Princeton: Princeton University Press, 1954), p. 227.

[16]It may be worth recalling that Louis D. Brandeis' attack on trusts and monopolies, *Other People's Money*, first appeared in 1913–14.

[17]See Koji Taira, 'Characteristics of Japanese Labour Markets', *Economic Development and Cultural Change* (January 1962).

It was also the type of labour force in which the enterprise had incentives to invest through, *inter alia*, on-the-job training. Of course, I am not speaking of the entire work force: this system was essentially confined to modern large-scale industry, and there were always temporary workers who could be and were laid off when business conditions deteriorated.

The 1930s were far less productive and interesting when it comes to the development or expansion of business institutions. Yet this decade does show the considerable resilience of Japanese enterprise, and some of its creations have had, in my opinion, a lasting influence. Three factors characterised the growth of industry. First, there was an increasing emphasis on military-related heavy industry, and by 1936 one can speak of *Junsenji keizai* or quasi-wartime economy. Secondly, the expansion of colonial economies – particularly in Manchukuo – became more important to Japanese business circles. Thirdly, there arose an intense conflict between the zaibatsu and both the military and the remaining representatives of the traditional economy. The military found the zaibatsu not sufficiently co-operative in their attempts to prepare the economy for war, and the peasants and small industrialists tended to blame the enormous combines for their suffering during the Great Depression. Amidst these events, two items merit particular attention: the rise of the *shinzaibatsu* (new zaibatsu) and the cartelisation movement.

Shinzaibatsu were new combines that came into being as a result of rising military requirements. They were especially closely involved in producing military equipment and in exploiting resources of the colonies; Nakajima and Nissah are excellent examples. I mention shinzaibatsu only to underscore the element of flexibility: when the established zaibatsu became somewhat recalcitrant and insisted on directing business in accordance with preferences of private gain, there appeared to be no difficulty in finding other entrepreneurs who were willing to make their plans fit the strategic plans of the military.

The cartelisation movement of the 1930s, especially strong between 1930 and 1932, was a direct outgrowth of the Depression. At a time when economic conditions were extremely precarious, government and business jointly attempted to govern 'excessive and unregulated competition' through schemes to control output and prices, and the allocation of markets and sales quotas. Some forty-five diverse industries were affected, including alloy iron, anthracite, steel plates, chemicals, coal, oil, and pig-iron. Although once again attempts of this type were not unknown before the 1930s, nothing on this scale had ever been attempted previously. The details of this episode are not significant[18] since the majority of cartels never operated as intended; there were always too many firms prepared to violate the agreements. What is most significant, I think, is that the cartelisation movement established the habit of 'administrative guidance' (*gyosei shido*) which has become a useful tool of Japan's postwar technology policy. This will be discussed below.

Turning now to postwar Japan and its magnificent economic achievements, one must recognise immediately that fortuitous events and good luck played some role. The war, and especially the defeat, pushed aside older leadership groups and opened the way for new men with new energies. In this atmosphere, talent became more important than pedigree. Sustaining the defeat presented two other opportunities. Physical destruction eliminated much antiquated capital equipment and eventually led to Japan possessing a rather young and up-to-date capital stock. Losing a war to the United States was an opportunity of another kind, bringing with it large amounts of aid and military protection at very low cost. And finally, the Korean War – and to a lesser extent the Vietnamese War – have provided windfall gains to the Japanese economy.

The years since World War II have also given birth to an institution which has, on balance, greatly increased Japan's capability to import foreign technology. And here I am referring to the 'notorious M.I.T.I.', or as it is known in official circles: the Ministry of International Trade and Industry.[19] It is a ministry dedicated to the interests of producers, especially those who operate on a large scale. It is notorious abroad because of its rather unfriendly attitude towards trade liberalisation and direct foreign investment. It is equally notorious in Japan because of its power in affecting the destiny of individual firms and industries.

Although M.I.T.I. is a direct descendent of the prewar Ministry of Commerce and Industry, its current activities are quite new in an age when technology has assumed supreme importance. The Ministry reviews the import of technology; it has to grant approval for licensing agreements and joint ventures; it allocates foreign exchange necessary for the importation of equipment or the purchase of knowhow. M.I.T.I. officials continually survey the foreign technology scene, encourage and discourage certain lines of advance, set priorities – in a word they have attempted to reach and implement a national and rational policy of technological change. The popularity

[18]For an excellent account of this period see G. C. Allen's Chapter XX in E. B. Schumpeter *et al.*, *The Industrialisation of Japan and Manchukuo, 1930–1940* (New York: Macmillan and Co., 1940).

[19]Another institution that might be mentioned here is the Japan Development Bank.

of this ministry is not great, even among certain industrialists, but in view of Japan's performance as a technology importer it would be hard to argue that private initiative has been stifled by excessive government interference.[20]

As Japanologists know, M.I.T.I. operates in mysterious ways, and methods of implementation are not easily described. A few rather sparse examples will have to suffice.

Earlier, I had mentioned 'administrative guidance' which came into being as a result of the postwar 'advice cartels' run by M.I.T.I. These were (and are) informal and sometimes unsuccessful cartel arrangements jointly set up by the industry and government. They have no statutory standing, but do not lack muscle in matters of output, capacity, or pricing policy. A Japanese minister once explained to me why he opposed wholly-owned direct foreign investment. Something like this was said: 'Assume that "administrative guidance" discussions are taking place in an industry, and that one of the firms is foreign. We decide that for the good of all, production will have to be reduced by 20 per cent in the next quarter. And what if the foreigner then asks: Mr M.I.T.I. bureaucrat, show me the law which authorises you to give this order? And once the question is asked, "administrative guidance" is dead.' Presumably no Japanese would dare ask such a question! What is the connection to improving the inflow of technology? Merely that through the industry-wide 'harmonisation of new investment' (a M.I.T.I. phrase) which takes place at sessions of this type, and in other ways, the flow can be shaped, controlled, and made more effective.

Japan must be the only capitalistic country in the world in which the government decides how many firms there should be in a given industry, and then sets about to arrange the desired number. Thus it is well-known today that in the opinion of the Government there are too many automobile and computer firms, and we can expect the requisite reductions to take place soon – a process which has already occurred in the paper, petro-chemical, synthetic fibre, cement, and steel industries. Spurred by the inevitability of trade liberalisation, M.I.T.I. has been, in the 1960s, especially concerned with arranging these mergers. Their purpose is clear: to control effectively the expansion of capacity and to form strong (large) and technologically up-to-date forms that can compete with the best foreign producers.

[20]Some may be surprised that the Economic Planning Agency is not taken up as a major new institution. However, compared to M.I.T.I. it is a midget. The powers of the E.P.A. are largely 'indicative', and it has been subject to strong political pressures. See Tsunehiko Watanabe, 'National Planning and Economic Development: A Critical Review of the Japanese Experience' (mimeographed).

Let me give a final example from the computer industry. Within the past year M.I.T.I. decided that Japanese producers of computers *must* in the future provide for software compatability - i.e. all software will have to be usable on any domestic machine. This is a major technological decision that imposes certain constraints on hardware architecture, but its economic advantages could be enormous in local and world markets. American experts remain sceptical concerning the possibility of achieving an 'impossible dream'; but too often we have underrated Japan's capacity in these matters.[21]

I would like now to deal with the matter of modest suggestions. Is there really anything of value in this account for underdeveloped countries? John Diebold has put the matter very well in a recent address:[22]

Again and again we encounter this phenomenon – innovations with great promise for important segments of our future, applied with enthusiasm by talented people, turning into business disasters! I have come to believe that this is not a series of chance mishaps, confined to education, or computers or other advanced technologies in isolation; rather it is a basic problem growing more common as, in the tasks we undertake, we encounter the realities of our age: rapid technological change acting as an agent for major social change, which in turn demands widespread *institutional* change for business success.

Diebold was talking about advanced countries, but his observation and conclusion apply equally to low income countries. For them, a major task is to bring in new technologies and forms of organisation, and this may require specific institutions designed to raise a country's capability to take advantage of the gap between itself and advanced countries.

This suggestion could easily be subject to misinterpretation. I am not recommending that L.D.C.s opt for zaibatsu, shinzaibatsu,

[21]Some will, no doubt, wonder why in this recital nothing has been said concerning improved education as a means of raising Japan's social capability to import technology. I have not dealt with it for two reasons. First, education is a matter of national policy, and therefore less specifically related to business. Secondly, and more important, Japan entered the Meiji Era with relatively respectable educational levels, and by the beginning of the twentieth century schooling was already widespread. In 1905, the country-wide attendance in primary schools was 95·62 per cent. See Japan National Commission for U.N.E.S.C.O., *The Role of Education in the Social and Economic Development of Japan* (Tokyo, 1966), p. 52.

[22]'New Rules and Opportunities for Business as We Enter the Post-Industrial Era', Keynote Address, Third Tri-Annual International Productivity Congress, Vienna, p. 13.

cartels, and M.I.T.I. – although their functions have to be performed. 'To each his own' is not a bad slogan, and I am fully aware of the evils associated with all Japanese institutions discussed above. (More of this later.) And yet, it would be a mistake to judge Japan by the standards of Western liberalism. In this connection, two issues should be kept in mind. First, Japan's 'establishment' has been growth-oriented for nearly a century.[23] It set a target of catching up with the West, and since increased welfare would have interfered with the rate at which the target was attainable, they were generally willing to postpone other problems. Japan is just now getting tired of 'growth at any cost', and her leaders are showing increasing concern for all aspects of the quality of life. Perhaps Japan has been too growth-oriented – who can really say? – but that is hardly the point. We should judge the institutions not in terms of our own political preferences, but in terms of their efficiency in furthering growth; that is the point.

The second issue is related to the common features of these institutions. In general, they are disliked by liberal economists because they imply trusts rather than anti-trust, state interference, monopoly or oligopoly power, etc. I would not presume to defend these monsters, but we should again retain a proper perspective. Usually there are two types of objections voiced: one on behalf of consumers and the other on behalf of innovation. As for the former, all one can say is that the Japanese consumer may have suffered, but it could have been short-run suffering for long-run gain, and in any event consumer sacrifice was a price willingly paid by those in charge. The matter of innovation is also not simple. Much of the literature tells us that monopolies and oligopolies have little incentive to innovate since they can exist comfortably on monopoly profits.[24] This may be a plausible position when a firm or an economy finds itself at the technological frontier. Then, in the absence of competition, there may be little urge to explore new ways of doing things. For a 'follower country', however, we should look at the situation differently. Now the issue is not to exercise inventiveness and to push into the unknown, but rather to adopt what is known and proved elsewhere. To be sure, there are risks and costs, but basically the opportunities for increased profits are much clearer. Furthermore, we must always remember the international dimension (and perhaps also that the U.S. attitude towards monopolies and cartels developed in a setting in which international markets were relatively unimportant). Most of Japan's

[23]Japan's first national development plan. *Kōgyō Iken*, was published in 1884.
[24]As is well known, J. A. Schumpeter did not share this view. See *Socialism, Capitalism, and Democracy*.

modern industries, by definition already using imported technology, were intent eventually on exporting their products. And this meant competing with the best foreign firms, frequently under difficult circumstances. Therefore the Japanese had great incentives to reduce costs by using the latest and best methods, and this is exactly what happened most prominently in textiles before the war and in nearly everything else after the war.

No doubt I am protesting too much, since surely no one will claim that Japan's combines or state intervention have led to technological conservatism. In any case, my modest suggestion to L.D.C.s is far less specific. I am merely saying that Japanese economic history demonstrates the need for specific institutions to improve technological import capabilities, and that some of the fears associated with certain forms of organisation have been – from this point of view – exaggerated.

V

There are a few more modest suggestions which I would like to mention. One of these might be called – somewhat awkwardly – the conscious development of factor proportion mitigation, and it has been dealt with elsewhere.[25] I am referring to the previously mentioned incongruity between advanced technology and the factor proportions of L.D.C.s and historical latecomers. The Japanese handled this problem in a number of imaginative ways, all of which are still relevant today. Modern industry encompasses a wide spectrum of techniques, and it is possible to concentrate on its more labour-intensive components. This is why Japan selected textiles in the early part of the century, and also why the light machinery industry has been so important in postwar Japan. One is particularly tempted to stress this in view of Asia's rather high-quality labour resources compared to those, say, in nineteenth-century Russia. Japan also demonstrates the possibility of fuller utilisation of scarce capital by the more intensive use of labour through the wide use of multi-shift production. It is also possible, even in modern enterprises, to substitute capital by labour through subcontracting. This has been a very economical way of tying small-scale industry into the modern production process.

All of the above is standard advice. There is, however, another sphere in which Japan has managed to squeeze more out of scarce capital, and this is in developing the art (should one say science?) of

[25]See Kazushi Ohkawa and Henry Rosovsky, 'Postwar Japanese Growth in Historical Perspective: A Second Look' in K. Ohkawa and L. Klein (eds) *op. cit.*, Ch. I.

247

'improvement engineering'. A review of Japanese economic modern-isation would quickly reveal that it has been a history virtually devoid of core inventions. The basic techniques have come from the United States and Europe, but not infrequently these have been systematically improved by the importers. By now this sort of activity has become a deeply engrained tradition among certain Japanese entrepreneurs, and many historical and current examples can be cited. In the Meiji Era, when the Japanese first began to build textile machinery, they discovered that it was possible to substitute wood for iron in the beams of the machines, so long as the joints were made of iron. A significant cost reduction was achieved. In the 1930s they pioneered in scientific cotton blending, i.e. turning out a desired quality of cloth based on using the cheapest possible varieties of raw cotton. (One has the feeling that the British, at least at that time, considered the method *infra dig.*!)

A most interesting set of examples comes from recent years. Japanese small- and medium-sized computers are available abroad with a four to five year warranty, while competitive U.S. and Euro-pean firms, until recently, offered nothing similar. The reasons for Japan's advantage are closely related to improvement engineering. All computers destined for export are subject to rigorous inspection, the costs of which are fully tax-deductible. (This has been a common practice for many Japanese products beginning with raw silk in the 1880s.) At the same time, two key production improvements are also involved. Both apply to the memory core – a weak link from the point of view of reliability and durability. In the core many wires cross and some touch, and these have a tendency to corrode at points of contact. Some time ago, Japanese manufacturers began to gold-plate cross-points. Furthermore, when a core is made, quantities of dirt enter into wiring, causing eventual failures. Japanese manu-facturers now wash cores before they are installed.

No major innovations were involved in any of these improvements, but their economic impact has, in all instances, been considerable. Improvement engineering reduces the real cost of imported techno-logy by making it more productive. At the margin, it will permit the adoption of some techniques that otherwise would not have been profitable to operate. If, by means of these efforts a technique is made more economical, it could also result in a greater domestic and foreign market, leading to otherwise unexploitable economies of scale. The very act of improvement engineering can also raise the quality of certain categories of workers. It is largely an activity of 'carefully taking apart and putting together a little better'; it is concrete and directly related to production, especially when compared to basic research. In contrast to the pursuit of core innovations, this type of activity is less risky and much cheaper: in effect, one is working in already proven directions. What is the message for underdeveloped countries? Simply this: Western technology need not be treated as a given; simple and small improvements suited to local conditions are frequently possible.

I am tempted to make a few additional modest suggestions, but since these are rather removed from the framework specified in Section III, they will have to be considered *obiter dicta*.

In considering the sweep of Japanese economic history, I am struck by the notion that government-business relations were, from the local point of view, well arranged. Japan retained some advantages of capitalism (i.e. efficient producers), while reaping certain benefits of socialism (i.e. considerable public control of the economic effort and direction). Harmony of this variety was undoubtedly not the result of explicit policy. One can, however, identify two basic and useful strands of long-run policy. In general, the Government – at least since the 1880s – stayed out of areas in which the private sector had comparative advantage. The Government engaged in very little production and did so only when national defence was involved, or where bottlenecks prevented private entry. For example, silk and cotton textiles were left pretty much alone, but in the early 1900s the Government did establish the Yahata steel works. Furthermore, public investment programmes were, by and large, concentrated in the non-spurt periods, and therefore did not compete too much with private investment.

We should also remember that it took Japan fully one hundred years to reach the fifteenth or sixteenth position in world *per capita* income. Patience would seem to be indicated. More to the point, the recurring investment spurts and rising levels of capital formation were primarily financed out of domestic and *personal* savings. Obviously the savings propensities of the population were a critical issue, and this brings forth a possibly harsh suggestion. Japan has been extremely deliberate in the development of all variety of social welfare programmes, and it is quite clear that keeping welfare a private responsibility has raised the savings propensities of the people.

VI

In any attempt to squeeze relevance out of a nation's historical experience, the temptation to 'accentuate the positive' is strong. One cannot, however, review certain aspects of Japan's long-term record without commenting also on its darker side. The obligation is particularly strong because my account has stressed the economic achievements of modern Japan. That is not the whole story, and countries having any interest in emulation should be made fully aware of the potential dangers.

Twentieth-century Japan enjoyed rapid economic growth, but by the 1930s this came to be combined with an aggressive, totalitarian military government, which eventually plunged the country into a disastrous war. It would be terribly simple-minded to draw a direct connection between economic growth on the one hand and military aggression on the other. Nevertheless, the question remains: was there something in Japan's economic structure as it developed in this century, which encouraged, fostered, and supported the political forces leading the country to war, and eventually to inevitable defeat at the hands of the United States and its allies?

A fundamental aspect of the problem must have been the unequal development of the Japanese economy from around 1900 until at least the middle of the 1960s. Frequently this has been referred to as an aspect of 'dual economy', while Ohkawa and I have preferred the term 'differential structure'. Whatever one chooses as label, there cannot be any doubt about what was happening. Throughout these years – cyclical fluctuations apart – the modern economy was progressing at a satisfactory pace. Using continually-improved techniques it could, by and large, provide better standards for capitalists and workers. By contrast, the traditional sectors – essentially agriculturalists, craftsmen, and small entrepreneurs – were not able to participate in this progress. The particular set of factor proportions under which they were forced to operate – little land, many workers, and expensive capital – effectively prevented the adoption of superior Western techniques. And gradually, a growing wedge came between the modern and traditional economies. In the modern sectors, productivity and wages rose rapidly; in the traditional sectors productivity and wages either stagnated or rose much more slowly. By 1931, for example, the ratio of output per worker in agriculture relative to manufacturing stood at 26 per cent; his wage was approximately 50 per cent of what industrial workers earned. (In the middle of the 1880s these figures were respectively 50 per cent and 70 per cent.) The impact of these differences is easy to imagine. With the coming of the 1920s and 1930s there is much discussion of an 'agricultural problem', and a 'small-scale industry' problem, and the meaning of 'problem' was clear. It simply meant that these sectors were depressed, that their incomes were low and frequently inadequate, and that they were a source of social discontent. E. O. Reischauer labelled the situation 'something new and as yet unique in the world – an industrialised nation supported by the toil of people living not far above the subsistence level'.[26] While this statement is exaggerated, and certainly not unique to Japan – what would one say about prewar Italy or the Soviet Union? – there can be no doubt about the identity of the toilers. They were not the large businessmen or landlords; they were not the male workers in the large zaibatsu plants; they were not the bureaucrats. Instead, one found them among the small owner-cultivators and tenants in the countryside, in small-scale industry, and in many traditional and in some modern services. And, let us remember, that these groups represented *well over 50 per cent* of the gainfully employed population.

As usual, the evolvement of this situation – or to put it in another way: the symptoms – appear most openly in agriculture. One has only to look at the frequently-cited statistics on the number of tenancy disputes: 85 in 1917, over 2,000 by 1927, and nearly 7,000 in 1936. The economic factors underlying these disputes were numerous: resentment against landlord absenteeism, demand for rent reduction during poor harvests, and the decline in farm prices especially since 1925, and foreign competition. (If the price of rice is taken as 100 in 1926, it stood at 57·5 in 1933; similarly, the price of silk was 44·9, and the price of all commodities was 75·9. Cash income of 'average farm families' during the period fell by about 60 per cent.) At the bottom of it all there were a set of most intractible given conditions: too many people, too little land, and the task of feeding a growing population. In the 1920s the 'tenant problem' was at the forefront. By the 1930s it had become the 'problem of the villages' and the 'problem of agriculture', focusing 'on the bigger conflict of interests between the peasants as a whole on the one hand, and "the towns", "the capitalists", and "the government" on the other'.[27] This is seeing the issues in broader and better perspective. One could, of course, put it in even broader terms by calling it the 'problem of the differential structure', and it was equally intractable.

What does all of this have to do with Japanese militarism and aggression? What are the possible links between the distress of the traditional sector – including agrarian distress as the main component element – 'and the rise of totalitarianism at home accompanied by expansion abroad'? Many links are plausible.[28] A powerful motive for expansion may have been to secure opportunities for emigration to relive domestic under-employment. Severe domestic

---

[26] *The United States and Japan* (1957), p. 62.
[27] R. P. Dore, *Land Reform in Japan* (London: Oxford University Press, 1959), p. 89.
[28] For an excellent analysis, see R. P. Dore, *op. cit.*, pp. 116–25.

dissatisfaction, especially on the part of those in less productive occupations, created dangers for the rulers of Japan, and members of these groups – army leaders, politicians, bureaucrats, industrialists – may have seen expansion as a means of diverting attention from distress at home, and as a way of healing rifts in the social structure by fostering a sense of national unity in the face of common danger. There was also a close relation between Young Officer rebels of the 1930s and the peasantry from which some of them came, and whose supposed 'traditional values' they widely admired.[29] They saw an increasing cleavage in Japanese society between the 'Westernised', 'individualistic', and 'mechanised' towns, and the depressed countryside which still preserved 'truly Japanese' techniques, values, and personal relations. Of course, to call the towns 'Westernised', 'mechanised', and 'individualistic' does not give an exact picture except in a symbolic sense. The economic and social problems were the same for large segments of the urban population, but it is undoubtedly also true that the Army was more directly concerned with and sympathetic to the peasantry. Peasants were, for the usual reasons, preferred as soldiers, and the general anti-capitalistic bias of the military also implied an admiration for the virtues of rural life. It was no accident that the doctrines of *nōhon-shugi* (a shinto-based ideology which emphasised agriculture as the foundation of the policy, and which by the late 1920s turned right-wing and anti-urban) appealed to some of the military extremists, and that there was no corresponding ideology which extolled the traditional occupations in the cities.

No simple connections between the structure of the economy, as it developed in the 1920s and 1930s, and Japanese aggression can be made here. Probably none exists. But the economic structure certainly did not help the deteriorating political atmosphere and must be seen as a major contributory factor in the demise of Japan's brief democracy at the end of the 1920s.

And what is there to learn from this sad episode? We know well enough that the differential structure phenomenon is extremely common; it exists today throughout Latin America and much of Asia. We also know that it is an unavoidable aspect of modern economic growth, because sectors applying Western technology

[29]One of the leaders of the abortive 1932 rebellion said at his trial: '. . . no person of feeling could be indifferent to the plight of the villages. . . . While the zaibatsu capitalists amass ever greater wealth and indulge every appetite, without giving a thought to the farmers, the tender school-children in the starving villages of the north-east go to school without their breakfasts; their families nibble at rotten potatoes. . . .' Cited by R. P. Dore, *op. cit.*, p. 94.

inevitably surpass traditional methods in the growth of productivity and wages. After all, that is one meaning of 'industrial revolution'. Finally, we can also assert that a differential structure is social dynamite, having contributed to explosions in Japan, Pakistan, much of Latin America, and in parts of the Middle East. The danger lies not so much in the absolute deterioration of conditions in traditional sectors – although this is common enough – as in their increasing relative deprivation.

These thoughts focus attention on the distributional and welfare aspects of growth. I have not had much to say about this topic because Japan contributed little that was either new or imaginative in these areas. In this sense the magnificent economic achievement of Japan remained flawed until recent times, and when one considers the last hundred years sitting in the comfortable armchair named 'hindsight', it is tempting to say that a few percentage points of the growth rate might well have been sacrificed for greater social welfare. I know that this is a far too simple conclusion; it does not even deserve to be called a modest suggestion. Nevertheless, when Japan is held up as an admired example, the blemishes of the 1920s and 1930s, as well as the immense suffering of the 1940s, should not be forgotten.

Index